About the Author

JAMES P. STERBA is professor of philosophy at the University of Notre Dame. He has written widely in the fields of ethics, and social and political philosophy for the *Journal of Philosophy, American Philosophical Quarterly, Philosophy and Public Affairs,* and *Ethics,* among others. His publications include *The Demands of Justice, Morality in Practice* (2nd ed.), and *The Ethics of War and Nuclear Deterrence.* Professor Sterba is President of the International Association for Philosophy of Law and Social Philosophy, American Section, and general editor of the Wadsworth Basic Issues in Philosophy Series.

D1251724

How to Make People Just

How to Make People Just

*A Practical Reconciliation of
Alternative Conceptions of Justice*

James P. Sterba

Rowman & Littlefield
PUBLISHERS

To all those who would be just

ROWMAN & LITTLEFIELD

Published in the United States of America in 1988
by Rowman & Littlefield, Publishers
(a division of Littlefield, Adams & Company)
81 Adams Drive, Totowa, New Jersey 07512

Library of Congress Cataloging-in-Publication Data

Sterba, James P.
  How to make people just: a practical reconciliation of
alternative conceptions of justice / James P. Sterba.

  Bibliography: p. 187
  Includes index.
  ISBN 0-8476-7583-1.   ISBN 0-8476-7584-X (pbk.)
  1. Justice.   2. Social justice.   3. Distributive justice.
I. Title.
JC578.S743   1988
320'.01'1—dc19   88-475
                                                         CIP

90 89 88
5   4   3   2   1

Printed in the United States of America

Contents

Preface

This book cuts against the grain of much of contemporary political philosophy. First, it aims to resolve controversy rather than create it. Second, it aims to provide practical results that are neither skeptical nor inconclusive. Basically, the book sets out five alternative conceptions of justice and then argues that, when correctly interpreted, each of these five conceptions supports the same practical recommendations. It also argues that a non-question-begging conception of rationality requires that we endorse one or another of these five conceptions of justice. Obviously, if my argument is sound, it could have a profound effect on the way political philosophy is done today as well as on the way that political philosophers are perceived by the educated public.

The argument of this book has expanded and matured through numerous presentations at various universities, conferences, and meetings over the last few years. As a result, many people have contributed to the book with their comments and criticisms on one or another aspect of the argument. In particular, I would like to thank Robert Audi, Kurt Baier, Michael Baylis, Tom Beauchamp, Hugo Bedau, John Boatright, David Braybrooke, Dan Brock, Norman Daniels, Richard DeGeorge, C. F. Delaney, Michael DePaul, Alan Donagan, Thomas Donaldson, James Doyle, David Duquette, Richard Feldman, James Fishkin, Mark Fowler, R. G. Frey, Marilyn Friedman, Alan Fuchs, Jorge Garcia, Alan Gewirth, Carol Gould, R. M. Hare, John Harris, Gilbert Harman, Virginia Held, Montey Holloway, Robert Holmes, John Hospers, Mark Lenssen, Tibor Machan, Larry May, William McBride, Diana Meyers, Jan Narveson, David O'Connor, Andrew Oldenquist, Susan Okin, Derek Parfit, Jeffrey Paul, Terry Pinkard, Betsy Postow, Philip Quinn, Douglas Rasmussen, John Rawls, Joseph Raz, Tom Regan, Michael Sandel, George Schedler, Robert Simon, David Solomon, Peter Tapke, Laurence Thomas, Rosemarie Tong, Karen Warren, Carl Wellman, and Iris Young. I would also like to thank the editors of *Social Theory and Practice, Syntheses,* and *American Philosophical Quarterly* for permission to draw on previously published work, and the University of Notre Dame, the

University of Rochester, and the Earhart Foundation for financial assistance. Special thanks as usual go to my wife and colleague, Janet Kourany, who was always a helpful critic, and now appears to accept the argument of this book, as I do, without liking its (redistributive) conclusions. For their assistance and encouragement in putting the manuscript in its final form, I also want to thank Janet Johnston and Mary D. Simmons of Rowman & Littlefield.

1 / *Introduction*

It is generally recognized that in today's society, academic philosophers have little impact on moral and political decision-making. In contrast to members of other disciplines, philosophers have rarely been called upon to serve as advisors to governors, labor leaders, presidents, prime ministers, or even dictators. To some extent, this is because philosophers have not, until recently, directed their attention to the practical issues that concern our moral and political leaders. But just as important, it is because philosophers have done so little to resolve the fundamental conflicts between the opposing moral and political ideals of our times.

In this book I propose to go some way toward resolving the conflicts between contemporary moral and political ideals, at least at the practical level. More specifically, I will set out five alternative conceptions of justice and then argue that, when correctly interpreted, all five conceptions actually support the same practical requirements. To further strengthen the case for practical reconciliation, I will also show that a non-question-begging conception of rationality requires that we endorse one or another of these five conceptions of justice. Since most people already accept one or another of these conceptions of justice, to make people just, it should suffice to show them that these different conceptions of justice, as well as the non-question-begging conception of rationality which underlies them, actually support the same practical requirements.

Of course, people who are already sincerely committed to any one of the five conceptions of justice are most likely already acting "from justice" in the sense that they are already acting from the motive of abiding by their particular conception of justice. But if I am right that these five conceptions of justice support the same practical requirements, many people who are acting "from justice" will not be acting "in accord with justice," since they will not be acting in accord with the same practical requirements.

It is the aim of this book to make people just in this second sense, that is, to make people act in accord with justice. My hope is that by showing that the conceptions of justice to which people are in fact committed have the same practical requirements, and by showing them further that a non-question-begging conception of rationality requires commitment to some such conception of justice, people will be led by the force of argument to act in accord with justice. Of course, people suffering from weakness of will cannot be moved effectively by the force of argument alone to act in accord with even their deepest commitments, and I don't propose to show how this affliction can be overcome. The argument of my book is simply directed to those people who can be counted upon to act upon their deepest commitments once it becomes clear to them what these commitments practically require. These are the people I hope to make just by the force of the argument that follows.

In discussing each of these five conceptions of justice, I will focus on two questions: (a) Do the poor have a right to welfare, or should the rich be free to help the poor only as they see fit? (b) Do women and certain minorities have a right to affirmative action with respect to educational and job opportunities, or should affirmative action be rejected as unfair to men and non-minorities? (Welfare, I am assuming, is given only to those who are unable to work or for the support of dependent children. Affirmative action, I am assuming, is given only when there has been a denial of basic educational or job opportunities in the past.)[1]

As one would expect, conceptions of justice tell us whether programs like welfare or affirmative action can be justified. Further, we all have an interest in whether they can be justified, for as long as such programs exist in our society, each of us will stand to benefit from them or will have to pay for them. Either way, each of us has an interest in whether such programs can be justified.

It seems to me that five conceptions of justice relate to the justification of programs like welfare and affirmative action. First is a Libertarian Conception of Justice. In recent elections, libertarian party candidates have not done very well. But Ronald Reagan and Margaret Thatcher, whose views on economic issues are close to a Libertarian Conception of Justice, have been successful politically and have refashioned the economies of their respective nations. According to this conception of justice, liberty is the ultimate political ideal. Thus all assignments of rights and duties are ultimately to be justified in terms of an ideal of liberty.

Second is a Socialist Conception of Justice. In the United States there has never been a viable socialist presidential candidate, but elsewhere there have been many successful socialist candidates. For example, the late Olof Palme led the Social Democrats back to power in Sweden; François Mitterrand, a socialist, was elected president of

France; and Andreas Papandreou's Socialist Movement gained control of Greece's parliament. According to a Socialist Conception of Justice, equality is the ultimate political ideal. Thus all assignments of rights and duties are ultimately to be justified in terms of an ideal of equality.

Third is a Welfare Liberal Conception of Justice. This is the conception of justice endorsed, for example, by the left wing of the Democratic party in the United States, whose leaders have been George McGovern, Ted Kennedy, and Jesse Jackson. According to this conception of justice, the ultimate political ideal is a blend of liberty and equality, and this blend, as we shall see, can be characterized as fairness, or more specifically, as contractual fairness. Thus all assignments of rights and duties are ultimately to be justified in terms of an ideal of contractual fairness.

Fourth is a Feminist Conception of Justice. This is the conception endorsed by the National Organization of Women (NOW) and by numerous other women's organizations in the United States and elsewhere. According to a Feminist Conception of Justice, the ultimate political ideal is androgyny. Thus all assignments of rights and duties are ultimately to be justified in terms of an ideal of androgyny.

Last is a Communitarian Conception of Justice. This conception is somewhat difficult to associate with any particular political group, but it does seem to be reflected in a wide range of Supreme Court decisions in the United States today, and has its roots in the republicanism of Madison and Jefferson.[2] According to this Communitarian Conception of Justice, the common good is proclaimed to be the ultimate political ideal, and this ideal is said to support a virtue-based conception of human flourishing.

So we have five conceptions of justice: a Libertarian Conception that takes liberty to be the ultimate political ideal; a Socialist Conception that takes equality to be the ultimate political ideal; a Welfare Liberal Conception that takes a blend of liberty and equality, which can be characterized as contractual fairness, to be the ultimate political ideal; a Feminist Conception that takes androgyny to be the ultimate political ideal; and a Communitarian Conception that takes the common good to be the ultimate political ideal. Each of these conceptions is a conception of justice, I claim, because it provides a way of assigning purportedly morally defensible rights and duties in the basic institutions of society.[3] And it seems to me that while there are other contemporary conceptions of justice, all of them can be subsumed under one or another of these five conceptions.

However, some might object that conceptions of justice grounded ultimately on the commands of God cannot be subsumed under any of the above ideals. The traditional problem with grounding justice or morality on the commands of God has been that it leads to the objectionable conclusion that just anything could be made morally right by the commands of God.[4] Recent work in "modified divine command theory" has sought to avoid this conclusion while showing that some elements of morality can be grounded simply on the commands of God; for example, that God's commands could make something that was morally permissible in itself be morally required for believers.[5] Nevertheless, to avoid the objectionable conclusion that just anything could be made right by the commands of God, it is necessary to admit that when the basic requirements of morality are at issue, what is needed is correspondence with some evaluative standard or ideal that is independent of the commands of God.[6] Moreover, when such standards or ideals are fully set out, they turn out to be quite similar to the ideals upon which our five conceptions of justice are grounded.

Of course, there may be contemporary conceptions of justice that cannot be subsumed under one or another of these five conceptions of justice. I am not convinced that there are any, but I have no a priori argument against their possibility. Accordingly, if faced with a nonsubsumable conception of justice, I would simply attempt to show that, when it was correctly interpreted, it too could be practically reconciled with the requirements of the other five contemporary conceptions of justice.

Before we consider these five conceptions of justice in detail, we should note what they all have in common. First, each of these conceptions regards its requirements as belonging to the domain of obligation rather than to the domain of charity; the conceptions simply disagree about where to draw the line between these two domains. Second, each of these conceptions is concerned to give people what they deserve; the conceptions simply disagree as to what it is that people deserve.

While some might object to this identification of justice and desert, there is a fairly neutral notion of desert upon which defenders of all these conceptions of justice can agree. It can be captured by the following analysis:

X deserves Y if and only if

There is a fact about X

1. that is a reason for X's being suitably related to Y (for example, if I deserve an increase of salary, there must be a reason for giving me an increase);
2. that does not describe the consequences of X's being suitably related to Y (for instance, a child cannot deserve a bicycle simply because it is certain to make her happy);
3. that generally does not characterize all those who along with X

could conceivably be similarly appraised (e.g., if I deserve blame for the way I treat my child, then *generally* other parents would not be treating their children in exactly the same way);
4. that indicates what grade properly belongs to the feature or behavior of X that is being appraised in some specific manner (for instance, if you deserve the Employee of the Year Award at your workplace, then the basis for your deserving this award must indicate what [high] grade properly belongs to the work you perform).

Condition (1) simply indicates that there must be some basis for X's deserving Y. Condition (2) expresses the idea that the immediate basis for X's deserving Y must be nonconsequentualist, but it leaves open the possibility that the ultimate grounds for X's deserving Y might still be consequentualist. Condition (3) serves to distinguish the grounds for desert from claims of general entitlement, like the claim that all human beings have a right to life, which holds for all those in the relevant comparison class. Finally, condition (4) distinguishes the grounds for desert from claims of special entitlement (such as the claim that you have a contractual right to a certain income) because claims of special entitlement do not indicate what grade properly belongs to the X concerning whom the claim is made.[7]

It should be evident that the conditions of this analysis can be satisfied by each of the five conceptions of justice, although the basis for desert surely tends to be different for each conception of justice. In fact, even to claim that all people deserve to have their basic needs met is not logically ruled out by condition (3), provided that the relevant comparison class is taken to be broader than the class of all human beings.

I should also point out that my goal of achieving a practical reconciliation of apparently conflicting moral and political ideals is very similar to the goal that John Rawls has endorsed for political philosophy. As Rawls puts it:

> We must now ask: how might political philosophy find a shared basis for settling such a fundamental question as that of the most appropriate institutional forms for liberty and equality?

> Thus, the aim of justice as fairness as a political conception is practical, and not metaphysical or epistemological. That is, it presents itself not as a conception of justice that is true, but one that can serve as a basis of informed and willing political agreement between citizens viewed as free and equal persons.[8]

Clearly, both Rawls and I hope to build a practical consensus in political philosophy. We differ in that Rawls hopes to build this practical consensus by uniting the ideas of a well-ordered society, a conception of the person, and a veil of ignorance into a social contract theory of justice. In contrast, I think that a practical consensus can be built only by taking Rawls's social contract theory as an interpretation of just one conception of justice, which then must be practically reconciled with other competing conceptions, some of which most certainly reject the idea of a veil of ignorance.

Nevertheless, someone might object that the degree of conflict between opposing moral and political ideals is more serious than either Rawls or I seem to allow. For example, recent discussion of moral dilemmas might suggest that there are opposing contemporary moral and political ideals that cannot be practically reconciled.[9] Unfortunately, most of this discussion of moral dilemmas has proceeded at a very abstract level, and nowhere in this discussion have the practical implications of the relevant contemporary moral and political ideals (that I will consider) been carefully worked out. When these practical implications are worked through, as I will do in this book, an argument for practical reconciliation can be constructed that, I claim, is strong enough to make people just.

In Part I (Chapters 2–6) I devote a chapter to each of the five conceptions of justice, setting out each conception as it is typically understood and defended. In Part I, I spend more time setting out and defending the Welfare Liberal Conception of Justice than I do setting out and defending the other four conceptions. This is because in Part II there is no separate discussion of the Welfare Liberal Conception of Justice. Instead, in Part II (Chapters 7–10) I attempt to show that each of the other four conceptions of justice can be reconciled with the practical requirements usually associated with a Welfare Liberal Conception of Justice. Accordingly, the Welfare Liberal Conception of Justice is discussed in Part II only insofar as it relates to this practical reconciliation of the other four conceptions of justice.

In Part III (Chapter 11) I make my practical reconciliation argument even more compelling by showing that a conception of rationality that is acceptable to a rational egoist leads, at least, to a Libertarian Conception of Justice. In this way, I will show that in virtue of my argument for practical reconciliation, even the egoist should accept the practical requirements of a Welfare Liberal Conception of Justice. Finally, in a concluding chapter, I review the entire argument of the book, consider some final objections, and make some overall observations.

Notes

1. My reason for focusing on these two questions is not to deny that other questions, such as those pertaining to civil and political rights, might not also

be relevant. Rather, it is that the five conceptions of justice I will be considering have been thought to disagree most radically with respect to their answers to these two questions.

2. See Cass R. Sunstein, "Interest Groups in American Public Law," *Stanford Law Review* 38 (1985): 29–87.

3. Compare with John Rawls, (1971: 4–5).

4. Plato, *The Euthyphro,* in *The Dialogues of Plato,* Vol. 1, trans. B. Jowett (New York, 1937).

5. See Robert Merrihew Adams, "A Modified Divine Command Theory of Ethical Wrongness," in Paul Helm, ed., *Divine Commands and Morality* (Oxford, Oxford University Press 1981), pp. 83–108; Edward Wierenga, "A Defensible Divine Command Theory," *Nous* 17 (1983): 387–407. For the positive result, see R. G. Swinburne, "Duty and the Will of God," in Helm, *Divine Commands and Morality,* pp. 120–34; and Germain Geisez, "Practical Reason and Faith," *Proceedings of the American Catholic Philosophical Association* 57 (1984), pp. 2–14.

6. See John Chandler, "Divine Command Theories and the Appeal to Love," *American Philosophical Quarterly* 22 (1985): 231–39.

7. For a detailed discussion of these conditions, see Sterba "Justice and the Concept of Desert," *The Personalist 57 (1976):* 188–97.

8. John Rawls (1985: 228, 230). *See also* Rawls (1987: 1–25).

9. See Bernard Williams, "Ethical Consistency," in *Problems of the Self* (Cambridge, Cambridge University Press 1973); and Ruth Marcus, "Moral Dilemmas and Consistency," *The Journal of Philosophy* 77 (1980), 121–37.

PART I

Ideals

2 / *Libertarian Justice*

Libertarians like to think of themselves as defenders of liberty. For example, according to Murray Rothbard (1978:320), libertarians "are the only genuine heirs of Jefferson, Paine, Jackson and the abolitionists." Similarly, John Hospers believes that libertarianism is "a philosophy of personal liberty—the liberty of each person to live according to his own choices, provided that he does not attempt to coerce others and thus prevent them from living according to their choices" (1971:5). And Robert Nozick claims (1974:ix) that if a conception of justice goes beyond libertarians side-constraints, it cannot avoid the prospect of continually interfering with people's lives.

Libertarians have defended their ideal of liberty in basically two different ways.[1] Some libertarians, following Herbert Spencer, have (a) taken a right to liberty as basic and (b) derived all other rights from this right to liberty. Other libertarians, following John Locke, have (a) taken a set of rights, typically including a right to life and a right to property, as basic and (b) defined liberty as the absence constraints in the exercise of these rights. Both groups of libertarians regard liberty as the ultimate political ideal, but they do so for different reasons. For Spencerian libertarians, liberty is the ultimate political ideal because all other rights are derived from a right to liberty. For Lockean libertarians, liberty is the ultimate political ideal because liberty just is the absence of constraints in the exercise of people's fundamental rights.[2]

Spencerian Libertarians

Let us begin by considering the view of those libertarians who take a right to liberty to be basic and define all other rights in terms of this right to liberty. According to this view, liberty is usually interpreted as follows:

The Want Interpretation of Liberty: Liberty is being unconstrained by other persons from doing what one wants.

This interpretation limits the scope of liberty in two ways. First, not all constraints, whatever their source, count as a restriction of liberty;

11

the constraints must come from other persons. For example, people who are constrained by natural forces from reaching the top of Mount Everest do not lack liberty in this regard. Second, the constraints must run counter to people's wants. Thus, for people who do not want to hear Beethoven's Fifth Symphony, the fact that others have proscribed its performance does not restrict their liberty, even though the proscription does in fact constrain what they are able to do.

Of course, libertarians may wish to argue that even such constraints can be seen to restrict a person's liberty, once we take into account the fact that a person normally prefers to be unconstrained by others. But other philosophers have thought that the possibility of such constraints points to a serious defect in this conception of liberty,[3] which can be remedied only by adopting the following broader interpretation of liberty:

> *The Ability Interpretation of Liberty:* Liberty is being unconstrained by other persons from doing what one is able to do.

The advantage of this broader interpretation is that when applying it to the above example, we find that people's liberty to hear Beethoven's Fifth Symphony would be restricted even if they did not want to hear it (and even if, perchance, they did not want to be unconstrained by others), since other people would still be constraining them from doing what they are able to do.

Notice, however, that being unconstrained from doing what one is *unable* to do does not constitute a liberty. For if it did, it would follow that one could also lack the liberty to do, or be constrained from doing, what one is unable to do, which is absurd.

One reason why some philosophers hold that people can have the liberty to do what they are unable to do is that they believe that something of value is lost even when such a "liberty" is taken away.[4] F. A. Hayek suggests, for example, that penniless vagabonds who live precariously by their own wits have more liberty than conscripted soldiers with all their security and relative comfort, despite the fact that the vagabonds lack the ability to derive much benefit from their liberty (Hayek 1960:18). But while it is true that the vagabonds lack the ability to derive much benefit from their liberty, it is also true that they have the ability to exercise that liberty, however unsuccessfully, and it is this ability that is presupposed by the possession of any liberty whatsoever. Thus, in general, although it is possible to confuse having a liberty with having certain sorts of abilities (for instance, having the liberty to run a four-minute mile with the ability to succeed in doing so), at the same time, it should be recognized that having a liberty does presupposes the ability to exercise that liberty in some fashion, however unsuccessfully. As a consequence, all liberties determined by the Want Interpretation of Liberty will turn out to be liberties according to the Ability Interpretation, as well.

By contrast, there are numerous liberties determined by the Ability Interpretation that are not liberties according to the Want Interpretation. For example, highly talented students may not want to pursue careers in philosophy, even though no one constrains them from doing so. Accordingly, the Ability Interpretation but not the Want Interpretation would view them as possessing a liberty. And even though such liberties are generally not as valuable as those liberties that are common to both interpretations, they still are of some value, even when the manipulation of people's wants is not at issue.

Even if we accept all the liberties specified by the Ability Interpretation, we still need to decide what is to count as a constraint. On the one hand, libertarians would like to limit constraints to positive acts (that is, acts of commission) that prevent people from doing what they are otherwise able to do. On the other hand, welfare liberals and socialists interpret constraints to include, in addition, negative acts (acts of omission) that prevent people from doing what they are otherwise able to do. In fact, this is one way to understand the debate between defenders of "negative liberty" and defenders of "positive liberty." This is because defenders of negative liberty interpret constraints to include only positive acts of others that prevent people from doing what they otherwise are able to do, while defenders of positive liberty interpret constraints to include both positive and negative acts of others that prevent people from doing what they are otherwise able to do.[5]

Suppose we interpret constraints in the manner favored by libertarians to include only positive acts by others that prevent people from doing what they are otherwise able to do, and let us consider a typical conflict situation between the rich and the poor.

In this conflict situation, the rich, of course, have more than enough resources to satisfy their basic needs. By contrast, the poor lack the resources to meet their most basic needs, even though they have exhausted all the available means that libertarians regard as legitimate for acquiring such resources. Under circumstances like these, libertarians usually maintain that the rich should have the liberty to use their resources to satisfy their luxury needs if they so wish. Libertarians recognize that this liberty might well be enjoyed at the expense of the satisfaction of the most basic needs of the poor. Libertarians just think that a right to liberty always has priority over other political ideals; and since they assume that the liberty of the poor is not at stake in such conflict situations, they readily conclude that the rich should not be required to sacrifice their liberty so that the basic needs of the poor may be met.

From a consideration of the liberties involved, libertarians claim to derive a number of more specific requirements, in particular, a right to life, a right to freedom of speech, press, and assembly, and a right to property. Here it is important to observe that the libertarian's right to life is not a right to receive from others the goods and resources necessary for preserving one's life; it is simply a right not to be killed unjustly. Correspondingly, the libertarian's right to property is not a right to receive from others the goods and resources necessary for one's welfare, but rather a right to acquire goods and resources either by initial acquisitions or by voluntary agreements.

Rights such as these, libertarians claim, can at best support only a limited role for government. That role is simply to prevent and punish initial acts of coercion—the only wrongful actions for libertarians. And, as we shall see, libertarians are deeply divided over whether a government with even such a limited role (a night watchman state) can be morally justified.

Of course, libertarians allow that it would be nice of the rich to share their surplus resources with the poor. Nevertheless, according to libertarians, such acts of charity should not be coercively required. For this reason, libertarians are opposed to coercively supported welfare programs.

For a similar reason, libertarians are opposed to coercively supported affirmative action programs. This is because the educational and job opportunities one has under a Libertarian Conception of Justice are primarily a function of the property one controls; and since unequal property distributions are taken to be justified under a Libertarian Conception of Justice, unequal educational and job opportunities are also regarded as justified. But then there could not be any right to affirmative action, since affirmative action is designed to correct for failure to provide equal educational and job opportunities in the past.

Lockean Libertarians

The same results with respect to welfare and affirmative action obtain for those libertarians who take a set of rights, typically including a right to life and a right to property, as basic and then interpret liberty as follows:

The Rights Interpretation of Liberty: Liberty is being unconstrained by other persons from doing what one has a right to do.

According to this view, a right to life is simply a right not to be killed unjustly; it is not a right to receive the goods and resources necessary for preserving one's life. Correspondingly, a right to property is a right to acquire property either by initial acquisitions or by voluntary transactions; it is not a right to receive from others whatever goods and resources one needs to maintain oneself. Understanding a right to life and a right to property in this way, libertarians reject both coercively supported welfare and affirmative action programs as violations of liberty.

A Partial Defense

Let us now turn to a few examples advanced by defenders of a Libertarian Conception of Justice to justify it. The first two are taken from Milton Friedman (1962: 161–72), the last from Robert Nozick (1974: 160–64).

In the first example, you and three friends are walking along the street and you happen to find a $100 bill on the payment. A rich fellow had been throwing away $100 bills, and you have been lucky enough to find one. According to Friedman, it would be nice if you shared your good fortune with your friends, but they have no right that you do so and, hence, they would not be justified in forcing you to share the $100 with them. Similarly, Friedman would have us believe that it would be nice of us to provide welfare to the less fortunate members of our society; nevertheless, the less fortunate members have no right to welfare and, hence, would not be justified in forcing us to provide it.

The second example, which Friedman regards as analogous to the first, involves four Robinson Crusoes marooned on four uninhabited islands in the same neighborhood. One Robinson Crusoe happens to land on a large and fruitful island, which enables him to live easily and well. The others have landed on tiny and barren islands from which they can barely scratch a living. Suppose one day they discover each other's existence. According to Friedman, it would be nice of the fortunate Robinson Crusoe to share the resources of his island with the other three Crusoes, but the other three have no right that he share those resources, and it would be wrong for them to force him to do so. Correspondingly, Friedman thinks it would be nice of us to provide the less fortunate in our society with welfare, but the less fortunate have no right that we do so, and it would be wrong for them to force us to do so.

In the third example, Robert Nozick asks us to imagine a society that has distributed income according to some ideal pattern, possibly a pattern of equality. In this society Wilt Chamberlain (or Larry Bird, if we wish to update the example) offers to play basketball provided that he receives a quarter from every home game ticket sold. Suppose we agree to these terms and a million people attend the home games to see Wilt Chamberlain (or Larry Bird) play, thereby securing him an income of $250,000. Since such an income would surely upset the initial pattern of income distribution, whatever that happened to be, Nozick contends that this illustrates how an ideal of liberty upsets the patterns required by other conceptions of justice, and hence calls for their rejection.

The Minimal State

As we have seen, libertarians are strongly united in their rejection of a right to welfare or affirmative action. At the same time, however, libertarians are deeply divided over whether their ideal supports a minimal or a night watchman state. Recent debate on this issue has focused on Robert Nozick's attempt to show that a minimal state would emerge from the legitimate exercise of basic Lockean rights. Nozick argues that market forces and the advantages of monopoly with respect to providing protection for people's rights would first lead to the emergence of a dominant protection agency. Then, Nozick claims, by providing adequate compensations, such an agency could legitimately prohibit independents from employing certain risky procedures.[6]

Nozick contends that the risky procedures that could be legitimately prohibited are those that cause general fear and either violate the procedural rights of the members of a dominant protection agency to have their guilt fairly determined or are an illegitimate exercise by independents of their basic Lockean rights. According to Nozick, it is by passing on the risky procedures used by independents and prohibiting with compensation the use of some such procedures that a dominant protection agency legitimately comes to possess the two essential characteristics of a minimal state: it maintains a de facto monopoly on the use of force, and it protects the rights of everyone in a given territory.

Challenges to Nozick's Argument

Other defenders of libertarian justice have raised two different challenges to Nozick's argument for the legitimate emergence of a minimal state. Some contend that his argument fails to justify a minimal state, while others contend that, if sound, his argument justifies more than a minimal state.

In support of the first view, Robert Holmes and Jeffrey Paul have offered the following dilemma:

1. Either the use of certain risky procedures is rights-violating, or it is not.
2. If rights-violating, its prohibition does not require compensation.

3. If not rights-violating, its prohibition is not morally justified.
4. So either the prohibition of the use of certain risky procedures does not require compensation, or that prohibition is not morally justified.[7]

Nevertheless, it is possible to disarm this dilemma by grasping its second horn. Nozick could admit that the use of certain risky procdures is rights-violating, but then claim that the prohibition of those procedures would also be rights-violating, *unless* adequate compensation is paid. And provided adequate compensation is paid, Nozick could argue, no one's rights are being violated by a dominant protection agency, all things considered. From which it would follow that, all things considered, a dominant protection agency would be acting in a morally justified manner.[8]

Yet even assuming that a dominant protection agency would be acting in a morally justified manner when prohibiting the use of certain risky procedures, Murray Rothbard and Eric Mack have argued that this would not suffice to constitute a minimal state. As Rothbard and Mack point out, if independents adopt the approved procedures of a dominant protection agency, the agency could not legitimately interfere with them on the grounds that they were employing unreliable procedures. And in the absence of such interference, Rothbard and Mack contend, a minimal state could not legitimately arise.[9]

But Nozick could question whether independents could gain any competitive advantage by adopting the approved procedures of an efficiently run dominant protection agency. Surely such an agency must at some cost to itself develop and maintain a set of reliable procedures for dealing with possible rights violations. Yet, at the same time, it normally could charge enough for checking the procedures used by independents to keep them from benefiting from their non-membership. Nor would good behavior on the part of independents undercut the claims to statehood of a dominant protection agency any more than good behavior on the part of would-be criminals in existing societies would undercut the claim to statehood of existing political agencies. For whether an agency is a state depends solely on the powers it possesses and, in the case envisioned, the dominant protection agency would posses sufficient powers to constitute a minimal state.

But does Nozick's argument for the minimal state justify more than a minimal state? Eric Mack thinks it does.[10] According to Mack, Nozick's argument justifying prohibition with compensation turns on a distinction between productive and unproductive exchanges. On Nozick's account, a wide range of economic activities, such as boycotts or refusing to sell at one's lowest acceptable price, turn out to be unproductive and, Mack contends, thus, capable of being prohibited provided adequate compensation is paid.[11] But it is obvious that prohibition of such a wide range of economic activities would lead far beyond the minimal state.

Yet while Nozick's productive/unproductive distinction is ill conceived for exactly the reasons Mack and others have indicated,[12] the presence of an unproductive exchange for Nozick does not suffice to justify prohibitions with compensation. There must also be some prima facie rights violation to require compensation.[13] Nor is the presence of an unproductive exchange necessary even for determining the compensation required, because that is determined by the degree to which independents have been disadvantaged by the rights violation. Accordingly, the productive/unproductive distinction is not really central to Nozick's account and, consequently, it cannot be employed to undercut his argument for the minimal state.

Like Mack, Gerald J. Postema has attempted to show that Nozick's argument for the minimal state, if sound, would justify much more than a minimal state. Postema contends (1980: 311–37) that the compensation that Nozick justifies in his argument for the minimal state does not correct for any rights violations, and that consequently it should also be possible to justify compensation in other contexts where rights violations are not at issue. In particular, Postema suggests, it should be possible to show that compensation is due to those who have been disadvantaged in the marketplace by prohibitions supporting Lockean property rights. In this way, Postema contends, Nozick's argument for the minimal state can be extended to support the activities of a welfare state.

But, as we have seen, there are good reasons to reject this interpretation of Nozick's argument for the minimal state. For while the prohibitions with compensation that Nozick justifies do not violate anyone's rights, all things considered, they do constitute prima facie rights violations. By contrast, the disadvantages incurred by prohibitions supporting the exercise of Lockean property rights, according to the standard libertarian view, do not result from rights violations at all. Consequently, unless it can be shown that such violations obtain, Nozick's argument for the emergence of a minimal state cannot be extended to support the kind of compensation that is characteristic of a welfare state.

Libertarians, we have seen, are strongly united in their opposition to a right to welfare or affirmative action, but deeply divided over whether their ideal of liberty supports a minimal state. I have argued that the disagreement among libertarians can be resolved in favor of the minimal state view because Nozick's argument for the emergence of the minimal state can be defended against the challenges that have been raised against it. In Part II we shall see that grounds can also be found within the libertarian view for reaching a practical reconciliation with defenders of other conceptions of justice. But first we need to set out those other conceptions of justice. In the next chapter, we will consider the conception of justice that initially appears to be most opposed to the libertarian view: the Socialist Conception of Justice.

Notes

1. Quite a few years ago Jeffrey Paul suggested to me this way of approaching libertarianism. More recently, Tibor Machan has recommended a more multifaceted approach that classifies libertarians as Austrian economic, contractarian, evolutionary, Lockean, Stirnerite, or objectivist. But as far as I can tell, all the morally relevant issues are captured by the way I have interpreted Paul's approach.

2. Each of these approaches faces certain difficulties. The principal difficulty with the first approach is that unless one arbitrarily restricts what is to count as an interference, conflicting liberties will abound, particularly in all areas of social life. The principal difficulty with the second approach is that as long as a person's rights have not been violated, her liberty would not have been restricted either, even if she were kept in prison for the rest of her days. Now I don't propose to try to decide between these two approaches here. In Part II, however, I argue that on either approach, libertarian justice can be practically reconciled with the other four conceptions of justice.

3. Isaiah Berlin, *Four Essays on Liberty* (New York, Oxford University Press, 1969), pp. 38–40.

4. See John Gray (1980).

5. On this point, see Maurice Cranston, *Freedom* (New York, 1953), pp. 52–53; C. B. Macpherson (1973b: 95); and Joel Feinberg, *Rights, Justice and the Bounds of Liberty* (Princeton, Princeton University Press, 1980), chapter 1.

6. Nozick (1974), Part I. According to Nozick, the compensation provided by the dominant protection agency is said to consist in supplying independents with protective services and is limited to compensation only for any disadvantages incurred by the prohibition.

7. See Robert Holmes (1977: 247–56); and Jeffrey Paul (1980).

8. Admitted, Nozick's own argument here is not very clear on this point, but it does seem possible to interpret the "border-crossings" he rejects to be all-things-considered rights violations.

9. Murray Rothbard (1977): 45–88); and Eric Mack (1978: 43–62).

10. Eric Mack (1981: 206–31). It is a bit surprising to find Mack arguing both that (a) Nozick's argument (although proceeding from sound premises) fails to justify a minimal state and (b) that if Nozick's argument were sound, it would justify more than a minimal state. One way to preserve consistency, assuming that Mack has not changed his mind about Nozick's argument, is to interpret (a) as preceding from the legitimate (that is, the libertarian) part of Nozick's argument and (b) as proceeding from the illegitimate part of that argument. Personal conversation with Mack has confirmed this interpretation.

11. Unproductive exchanges being those with respect to which purchasers would have been better off if sellers had had nothing whatever to do with them of if they had never existed at all.

12. See Jeffrey Murphy (1980: 156–71).

13. Joshua T. Rabinowitz ignores this requirement in his critique of Nozick. Rather than view Nozick's theory of compensation as a theory that presupposes what basic rights people have and then show how prima facie violations of those rights can be morally justified, Rabinowitz views the theory as one that establishes what basic rights people have. See his "Emergent Problems and Optimal Solutions" (1977), especially pp. 85–86; and see Nozick (1974: 67n).

3 / *Socialist Justice*

Contemporary defenders of socialist justice occupy a contestable place within the socialist tradition. The controversy has its origins in Karl Marx's vehement rejection of conceptions of justice. At issue is whether the socialist ideal requires the rejection of all or only of some conceptions of justice. Put another way, does the socialist ideal by postulating a harmony of interests go beyond justice altogether, or does it simply mandate a different conception of justice?[1] Contemporary defenders of socialist justice endorse the latter view.

A Characterization of the Ideal

For contemporary defenders of socialist justice, equality is the ultimate political ideal. More precisely, as Karl Marx expressed the ideal more than a century ago, distribution is to proceed according to the principle "from each according to his or her ability; to each according to his or her needs."[2]

At first hearing, this conception might sound ridiculous to someone brought up in a capitalist society. The obvious objection is, how can you get persons to contribute according to their ability if income is distributed on the basis of their needs and not on the basis of their contributions?

The answer, according to a Socialist Conception of Justice, is to make the work that must be done in a society as much as possible enjoyable in itself. As a result, people will want to do the work they are capable of doing because they find it intrinsically rewarding. For a start, socialists might try to get people to accept presently existing, intrinsically rewarding jobs at lower salaries—top executives, for example, to work for $400,000, rather than $800,000, a year. Yet ultimately socialists hope to make all jobs as intrinsically rewarding as possible, so that after people are no longer working primarily for external rewards, when making their best contributions to society, distribution can proceed on the basis of need.

Socialists propose to implement their conception of justice, in part, by giving workers democratic control over the workplace.[3] The key idea here is that if workers have more to say about how they do their work, their work itself will be more intrinsically rewarding. As a consequence, they will be more motivated to work, since their work itself will be meeting their needs. Under democratic control, workers would also vote directly on major issues, including principal management positions and major policy changes, and indirectly through their representatives on the day-to-day business of management. In this way the hierarchical structure with its sharp distinction between workers and managers that presently characterizes capitalist firms would be radically transformed as workers gain more and more control over the workplace.

Yet even with democratic control of the workplace, some jobs, such as garbage collecting or changing bedpans, probably can never be made intrinsically rewarding. Socialists propose to divide up such jobs in some equitable manner.[4] For example, some people might collect garbage one day a week and work at intrinsically rewarding jobs the rest of the workweek. Others would change bedpans or do some other slop job one day a week and work at intrinsically rewarding jobs the other days of the workweek.

So socialists would want to make jobs as intrinsically rewarding as possible, in part through democratic control of the workplace and an equitable assignment of unrewarding tasks. But how would socialists deal with people who not only want an intrinsically rewarding job but also want the rewards that come from a good income? Without providing income differentials, how would socialists motivate such people to contribute according to their ability?

Surely socialists grant that some income differentials are necessary to motivate people to make their best contributions. But socialists strive to keep such differentials to a minimum by making the more talented members of society keenly aware of the social costs of having greater income differentials. Accordingly, socialists want to make it very clear that having greater income differentials would be at the cost of failing to satisfy the needs of people who are doing all in their power legitimately to satisfy their own needs. The knowledge that this is the case should provide the more talented members of a society with the moral incentive to oppose greater income differentials, so socialists argue. And if some people failed to respond to this moral incentive, socialists contend that they would be justified in forcefully requiring them to make whatever contribution is necessary so that the needs of everyone can be met.

By combining moral and self-interested reasons in this fashion, socialists hope to be able to motivate people to make their best contribution to society. In their appeal to moral incentives, however, socialists are no different from libertarians or welfare liberals, since they all recognize enforceable moral constraints on the pursuit of self-interest. Their disagreement concerns not the existence of such constraints, but rather the nature of the constraints and how they should be enforced.

Socialists also contend that only by socializing the means of production can people be brought to contribute according to their abilities while distributing proceeds according to need. In advanced capitalist societies, democratic control has already been extended to national defense, police and fire protection, income redistribution, and environmental protection. Socialists simply propose to extend this process of democratic control to include control of the means of production, on the grounds that the very same arguments that support democratic control in these recognized areas also support democratic control of the means of production. In addition, socialists contend that without such control, the means of production will eventually become concentrated in the hands of a few, who will use those means to benefit themselves at the expense of the needs of others.

So much for a characterization of a Socialist Conception of Justice. Let us now consider how such a conception relates to the issues of welfare and affirmative action. Would a Socialist Conception of Justice support a right to welfare? Obviously it would. Socialists would surely want to distribute welfare checks. But socialists would also want to claim that such a right does not go far enough and so provide for persons' nonbasic needs as well as for their basic needs. Likewise, a Socialist Conception of Justice would justify a right to affirmative action when persons are now presumed to be less qualified, because they were denied equal basic educational opportunities in the past. Hence, socialists would also want to distribute affirmative action acceptance letters. But again socialists would want to claim that such a right does not go far enough, since it stops short of requiring a program for restructuring jobs and socializing the means of production.[5]

It is also important to note that a Socialist Conception of Justice does not accord with what exists in countries like Russia or Albania. Judging the acceptability of a Socialist Conception of Justice by what takes place in countries like Russia or Albania, where national planning is pursued without worker control, would be just as unfair as judging the acceptability of a Libertarian Conception of Justice by what takes place in countries like Chile or South Africa where, as we know, citizens are arrested and imprisoned without cause. By analogy, it would be like judging the merits of college football by the way Vanderbilt's or Northwestern's team plays, rather than by the way Penn State's team plays or the way Notre Dame's team plays. Actually, a fairer comparison would be to judge a Socialist Conception of Justice by what takes place in countries like Sweden or Yugoslavia, and to judge a Libertarian Conception of Justice by what takes place in the United States. But even these comparisons are not quite appropriate, since none of these countries fully conforms with these conceptions of justice.

Defenses of the Ideal

From Marx to the present, defenders of a Socialist Conception of Justice have frequently supported their view by attacking nonsocialist conceptions of justice that most closely resemble it. The favored strategy has been to show that those conceptions of justice are inadequate in ways their defenders should have been able to recognize. Utilizing this approach, C. B. Macpherson argues that the right to self-development endorsed by both welfare liberals and socialists is compatible only with a Socialist Conception of Justice. According to Macpherson (1973b), capitalism encourages people to acquire the power to extract benefit from others, and this extractive power is usually acquired at the expense of the self-development of those over whom the power is exercised. Thus, under capitalism the extractive power of some is said to be increased at the expense of the developmental power of others; and while those whose extractive power is increased usually do experience an increase in developmental power as well, Macpherson claims, a net loss of developmental power still obtains overall.

Nor is it enough for the defender of a Welfare Liberal Conception of Justice to show that the transfer of power under capitalism allows for greater self-development than was possible under previous politico-economic systems. For the relevant goal is maximal self-development, and only with the elimination of all extractive power under a Socialist Conception of Justice, Macpherson claims, can that goal be reached.

More recently, Macpherson has attempted to defend socialist justice by a broader construal of a right to property (1985, chaps. 6 and 7). Under Libertarian and Welfare Liberal Conceptions of Justice, a right to property is narrowly construed as a right to exclude others from the use or benefit of some things. Yet, as the examples of common property and state property indicate, the right to property can be broadened to include a right not to be excluded by others from the use or benefit of some things. Macpherson thinks that a right to self-development requiring socialism can be shown to follow from this broader conception of a right to property. Macpherson also thinks that if we construe a right to life as a right to the material means of a fully human life, a right to self-development requiring socialism can similarly be derived (1985: chap.2).

The major difficulty with Macpherson's defense of socialist justice is that he does not consider sufficiently whether the right to self-development endorsed by socialists might not itself be justifiably limited by a right to liberty. In his discussion of alternative conceptions of liberty, Macpherson does criticize various formulations of negative liberty, but in the main he simply endorses a conception of positive liberty that entails a right to self-development. Macpherson never tries to meet the defenders of negative liberty on their own terms and show that even given a reasonable construal of their own ideal, a right to liberty would naturally lead to a right to self-development.

As one might expect, other attempts to defend socialist justice appeal more directly to an ideal of liberty. Carol C. Gould (1978) regards socialist justice as rooted in a conception of positive liberty understood as "the fullest self-realization of social individuals." According to Gould, socialist justice "refers to social relations in which no agents deprive any others of the conditions of their positive freedom." Since every individual has a capacity for self-realization simply in virtue of being human, Gould argues, no individual has more of a right to the conditions needed for the fulfillment of this capacity than any other. Thus an equal right to positive liberty or freedom is said to be at the heart of a Socialist Conception of Justice. Such a right, Gould argues, requires, among other things, an equal access to the means of production and, hence, is incompatible with capitalism.

Christian Bay (1981) adopts a similar approach to defending socialist justice. For Bay, socialist justice requires an equal right to positive liberty or freedom. Bay divides this freedom into psychological freedom (the degree of harmony between basic motives and overt behavior), social freedom (freedom in relations between people and between people and groups or organizations), and cultural freedom (freedom to outgrow culturally prescribed, conventional, or ideological restraints), and he suggests specific strategies for achieving each of these types of positive freedom in contemporary societies.

Unfortunately, neither Gould nor Bay sufficiently takes into account the challenge to socialist justice from defenders of negative freedom. Both seem content to point out that defenders of negative freedom usually ignore or misrepresent the ideal of positive freedom. Yet neither gives any compelling reason why defenders of negative freedom should recognize the requirements of socialist justice.

Still another defense of socialist justice has been developed by Kai Nielson. Taking a right to equal self-respect as basic, Nielson argues (1985) for the following principles:

1. Each person is to have an equal right to the most extensive total system of equal basic liberties and opportunities compatible with similar treatment for all.

2. After provisions are made for common social values, for capital overhead to preserve the society's productive capacity; after allowances are made for differing unmanipulated needs and preferences and due weight is given to the just entitlements of individuals; income and wealth are to be so divided that each person will have a right to an equal share. The necessary burdens requisite to enhance human well-being are also to be shared equally, subject, of course, to limitations by differing abilities and differing situations.

Nielson's principles obviously point toward a statusless, if not a classless, society in which there is an equality of political and economic power.

But why should equality of political and economic power be necessary for equal respect? If "to respect a person" is understood as "to regard the person as powerful," then equal respect surely would require equal power. But if "to respect a person" is understood as "to regard the person as a moral agent with certain basic rights," then equal respect need not require equal power unless every moral agent has a basic right to equal power. Even if "to respect a person" is understood as "to regard the person as excelling in some fashion," it would still not follow that equal respect required equal power, since it is possible for people to excel equally without possessing equal power. Unfortunately, Nielson neglects to consider these other interpretations of respect for persons, and in fact he relies on John Rawls's discussion of respect in *A Theory of Justice* where these interpretations are not clearly distinguished.

Appealing more directly to Rawls's work, other defenders of socialist justice have attempted to support their ideal by showing that a correct application of Rawls's welfare liberal conception of justice to current conditions would lead to the practical requirements of socialist justice. The favored strategy has been to argue from the principles of justice Rawls claims to have derived from the original position. For example, according to Macpherson (1973a: 341–47), "It is not difficult to show . . . that a socialist system can meet the requirements of [Rawls's] principles of justice. But it can do so not as a 'modification' of the capitalist market system, but by its rejection of exploitative property institutions."

Similarly, David Schweickart (1980) and Gerald Doppelt (1981) view Rawls's practical recommendations as inconsistent with his principles of justice. According to Doppelt, "If Rawls had taken up his own problem of how the 'worst-off' can be raised up, in terms of 'power and prerogatives of authority' as well as income, he would immediately have confronted the problem of capitalism—or socialism—in different terms" (1981: 270). Jeffrey Reiman has even proposed a "labor theory" of Rawls's principles of justice which, he claims, requires socialism "when historical conditions are such that incentives are no longer necessary to maximize the share of the worst off" (1984: 159).

The basic problem with these defenses of socialist justice is that they rely on the correctness of Rawls's derivation of his principles of justice from the original position, and this is generally recognized to be the weakest link in Rawls's theory. For, as I and others have argued, principles of justice requiring the highest possible social minimum would not invariably emerge from the original position.[6] Unfortunately, it is just the "maximin" character of Rawls's principles that critics have appealed to when arguing that his principles would lead to socialism.

Probably the most novel of recent defenses of socialist justice is that set forth by Michael Walzer. According to Walzer (1983: 6), the socialist ideal of equality requires the absence of domination, which in turn requires that different social goods be distributed "for different reasons in accordance with different procedures by different agents and that all these differences derive from different understandings of the social goods." Walzer claims that our understanding of social goods, such as money, education, political power, welfare, and honor, requires a plurality of principles of distribution constituting autonomous "spheres of justice." In particular, Walzer argues that welfare and security should be distributed according to a shared understanding of people's needs, which vary over time and between societies (1983: chap. 3). He also argues (291–303) that the sphere of democratic control extends not only to cities and towns but also to firms and factories, because any reason that can be given for claiming that cities and towns should be subject to democratic control (rather than ownership) is also a reason for claiming that firms and factories should be subject to democratic control (rather than ownership). Walzer contends that as long as the spheres of justice are kept distinct so that no particular social good dominates over other social goods, inequalities with respect to particular social goods, like money or honor, will not give rise to injustices. In this way, Walzer claims to have shown that while the socialist ideal of equality requires industrial democracy and distribution according to need, it is not opposed to certain forms of inequality.

Human Nature As a Social Product

One issue that has continued to divide defenders of socialist justice is the degree to which their ideal assumes that human nature is a social product. For example, Bay relies minimally on this assumption. He grounds his defense of socialist justice on what he takes to be three broad classes of universal basic human needs: (a) physical needs, which include subsistence needs and the need to be protected against violence; (b) community needs, such as the need for self-esteem, dignity, and social recognition; and (c) subjectivity needs, the needs we have to develop ourselves to the limits fixed by the material conditions and capacity of the time. According to Bay, physical needs have priority over community needs, which in turn have priority over subjectivity needs; yet, when possible, socialist justice requires the satisfaction of all three classes of basic needs.

By contrast, Milton Fisk (1980) maintains that human nature is a social product, since he recognizes only a narrower category of universal basic needs: food, sex, support, and deliberation. Further, Fisk claims that these universal basic needs have no priority over those needs that are socially produced because of the groups to which one belongs. It follows that for Fisk, principles of justice cannot arbitrate many of the conflicts that exist, such as between workers and owners, because such conflicts cannot be resolved without curtailing the realization of the socially produced needs of one or the other group.

A basic difficulty with Fisk's view is that it would seem possible for people's socially produced needs to require the exploited to submit to their exploiters. To rule out this possibility, Fisk assumes that the group morality of the exploited will always require them to reject any "imposed needs" whose satisfaction would lead to such submission. Nonetheless, this would occur only if human beings had a universal need to avoid all forms of domination, and this is just what Fisk denies.

The reason why Fisk is reluctant to ground his socialist conception of justice on universal basic needs is that he thinks that principles of justice must be action-guiding in a very strong sense. Thus, for there to be a conception of justice grounded on universal basic needs, Fisk thinks that there must be some expectation that all rational agents will act on that conception. Since normally all that we can expect is that rational agents will tend to abide by conventional norms serving the needs of the particular group to which they belong, Fisk concludes that there is no universally binding conception of justice.

Yet by limiting applicable moral standards to those that are action-guiding in this very strong sense, Fisk's view deprives the exploited of an important tool for changing their society, namely, the possibility of morally condemning their exploiters. For even if such condemnation does not produce a change of heart in the exploiters, it still may inspire the exploited and their allies to press for needed reforms. So here again it seems that an ethics without a universally binding conception of justice can work against the interests of the exploited.

Yet it is obvious that many defenders of socialist justice share the view that there is no universally binding conception of justice.[7] According to this view, socialist justice is not an appropriate ideal for all times and places. Rather it becomes appropriate only when social conditions have developed sufficiently to make the ideal of equality of need fulfillment a feasible ideal. The greatest achievement of capitalism, socialists argue, is that it has created just those social conditions in which it is now appropriate to apply a Socialist Conception of Justice. For the expansion of productive forces under capitalism has now, for the first time, made it possible to fulfill the socialist ideal of equality of need fulfillment.

It should be noted, however, that those who claim that there is a universally binding conception of justice tend to agree that its practical requirements are different in different social conditions. They claim that social conditions are relevant in two ways to the determination of the particular requirements of justice. First, social conditions are said to determine what sort of opportunities are available for fulfilling the particular requirements of justice. Second, social conditions are said to significantly determine the knowledge and beliefs that agents bring to the opportunities available to them. For example, given the ignorance and false beliefs pervading our understanding of sexist practices in today's society, it is quite difficult for some people to appreciate the opportunities available for ridding society of such practices. And unless agents have access to the appropriate knowledge and beliefs along with the appropriate opportunities, it will be incorrect to say that justice demands that they behave in some specific manner, or that under such conditions they are blameworthy for failing to behave as justice demands. So it would seem that those who endorse a universally binding conception of justice might well grant that the application of such a conception is relative to particular social conditions in much the same way as socialists claim.

Of course, there remains the question of to what degree human nature is a social product. Yet, if I am right that socialist justice can be practically reconciled with the other four contemporary conceptions of justice under consideration, then whatever is the correct answer to this question will surely lack the practical significance it is usually assumed to have.

Notes

1. For a sample of the debate, see Marshall Cohen, Thomas Nagel, and Thomas Scanlon (1980); and Tom Campbell (1983).

2. Karl Marx, *Critique of the Gotha Program,* ed. C. P. Dutt (New York: International Publishers, 1966).

3. For a discussion of worker control, see David Schweickart (1980); Branko Horwat, *The Political Economy of Socialism* (Armonk, 1982); and Carole Pateman, *Participation and Democratic Theory* (New York, Cambridge University Press, 1970).

4. See Edward Nell and Onora O'Neill (1980).

5. For reasons why a social program that guarantees a right to welfare and a right to affirmative action does not appear to go far enough, see John H. Schaar, "Equality of Opportunity and Beyond," in *Equality,* ed. J. Roland Pennock and John W. Chapman (New York, Atherton Press, 1967).

6. See Chapter 4.

7. In addition to Fisk's work, see Steven Lukes, *Essays in Social Theory,* Parts 2 and 3 (New York, Columbia University Press, 1977); and William Ash (1977).

4 / *Welfare Liberal Justice*

Finding merit in both the libertarian's ideal of liberty and the socialist's ideal of equality, welfare liberals take the ultimate political ideal to be a blend of liberty and equality, which can be characterized as fairness, or better, as contractual fairness.[1] More precisely, welfare liberals can be understood as maintaining that the fundamental rights and duties in a society are those that people would agree to under fair conditions. Welfare liberals do not claim that the fundamental rights and duties in a society are those to which people actually do agree, for the rights and duties to which people actually do agree might not be fair at all. For example, people might agree to a certain system of fundamental rights and duties only because they have been forced to do so or because their only alternative was starving to death. So actual agreement is not sufficient, nor is it even necessary, for determining a Welfare Liberal Conception of Justice; what is necessary and sufficient is that people would agree to such rights and duties under fair conditions.

Fair Conditions for Agreement

But what are fair conditions for agreement? According to John Rawls, the most prominent contemporary defender of this conception of justice, specifying fair conditions for agreement requires an account of (a) a well-ordered society with respect to which agreement is made, (b) the persons making the agreement, and (c) an original position in which the agreement is made.[2]

A Well-Ordered Society

Rawls characterizes a well-ordered society with respect to which a fair agreement is made in the following manner. First, it is a society that is effectively regulated by a public conception of justice such that everyone accepts, and knows that others likewise accept, the same principles of justice. In addition, the basic institutions of the society satisfy, and are believed by all to satisfy, the same public conception

31

of justice. Moreover, this public conception of justice must be founded upon reasonable beliefs as established by the society's generally accepted methods of inquiry, and the same holds for the application of this conception to the basic institutions of the society.

Second, it is a society whose members are, and so regard themselves, as free and equal moral persons. They are moral in that, once they have reached the age of reason, each has, and views the others as having, an effective sense of justice. They are equal in that they regard each other as having a right to determine, upon due reflection, the principles of justice by which the basic institutions of their society are to be governed. Last, they are free in that they think of themselves (a) as entitled to make claims on the design of their common institutions in the name of their fundamental aims and interests, and (b) as not inevitably tied to the pursuit of the particular final ends they have at any given time, but rather as capable of revising and changing those ends on reasonable and rational grounds.

Third, it is a society that is stable with respect to its conception of justice in that its basic institutions generate an effective sense of justice. In such a society, coercive sanctions are rarely, if ever, applied, since offenses are infrequent.

Fourth, it is a society that exists under the circumstances of justice. Objectively, this means that conditions of moderate scarcity obtain. Subjectively, this means that persons and groups within the society have a diversity of fundamental interests and ends and a variety of opposing and incompatible basic beliefs, which seem likely to persist in the absence of a sustained and coercive use of power that aims to enforce the requisite unanimity.

Fifth, it is a society all of whose members are capable of being fully cooperative members of that society over the course of a complete life.

Last, it is a society in which the primary subject of justice is the basic institutions of the society, because those institutions are the ones that fundamentally mold people and determine their options.

A Conception of the Person

The persons making a fair agreement are conceived by Rawls as having two powers: the capacity for a sense of justice and the capacity for a conception of the good. The capacity for a sense of justice is the capacity to understand, to apply, and normally to be moved by an effective desire to act from (and not merely in accordance with) the principles of justice as the fair terms of social cooperation. The capacity for a conception of the good is the capacity to form, to revise, and rationally to pursue such a conception, that is, a conception of what we regard as a worthwhile human life. Such a conception normally consists of a determinate scheme of self-regarding and other-regarding ends and desires. Persons so conceived are also said to have highest-order interests in promoting the full exercise of these two powers and a subordinate interest in advancing their conceptions of the good, whatever they may be, as best they can.

The Original Position

The original position from which fair agreements are said to emerge is essentially characterized by a veil of ignorance. This veil deprives persons so situated of the knowledge of their natural and social assets. It also deprives them of the knowledge of their conception of the good and their particular psychological dispositions and propensities.

We all know that judges sometimes ask jurors to discount certain information they have heard so that they can reach fair decisions. The veil of ignorance simply generalizes this practice, maintaining that if we are to have fair conditions for determining principles of justice, we too must discount or imagine ourselves to be ignorant of certain information about ourselves when reaching agreement concerning principles of justice. The veil of ignorance is also said to reflect the judgment that persons do not deserve their starting places in society or their natural abilities. Because these assets are not deserved, Rawls thinks, it is appropriate to discount or imagine ourselves to be ignorant of them when reaching agreement concerning principles of justice.

In addition, the veil of ignorance is assumed to be as thick as possible. This means that persons in the original position are not privy to any information unless that information is absolutely necessary for reaching a rational agreement. Furthermore, persons in the original position are not required to apply, or to be guided by, any prior or antecedent principles of right or justice, but only to be guided by what they think is in their interest as far as the limits on information allow them to determine. Yet since persons in the original position have highest-order interests in advancing their moral powers, their motivation is not purely self-interested either.

Following from their highest-order interests in advancing their moral powers, persons in the original position are said to have a preference for "primary goods." These are goods that are generally necessary as social conditions and all-purpose means to enable human beings to realize and exercise their moral powers and to pursue their final ends. More specifically, these goods are of five types: (a) basic liberties, such as freedom of thought, liberty of conscience, and freedom of association; (b) freedom of movement and free choice of occupation and roles against a background of diverse opportunities; (c) powers and prerogatives of offices and positions of responsibility; (d) income and wealth; and (e) the social bases of self-respect. In the original position, deliberation proceeds in terms of these primary goods, and certain priorities are established among them.

According to Rawls, the conceptions of the well-ordered society and the person are fundamental and operate as constraints upon the conception of the original position. But actually the relationship is closer than that, since the three conceptions are not logically distinct. First, Rawls's conception of the person is already contained in his characterization of persons in the well-ordered society. To be a "free and equal moral person" in a well-ordered society is to possess and effectively exercise the two powers attributed to persons by Rawls's conception of the person. Second, the conceptions of the well-ordered society and the person can be seen to entail, and not merely constrain, Rawls's conception of the original position, because Rawls argues that without the veil of ignorance, "the original position would represent the parties not solely as *free and equal moral persons,* but instead as persons also affected by social fortune and natural accidents."[3] It seems best, therefore, to regard Rawls's three conceptions as alternative ways of specifying his account of fair conditions for agreement.

But what would be agreed to under such conditions? Rawls has argued that maximin principles of justice, which maximize benefit to the least advantaged members of a society, would be chosen in the original position.[4] Others, most notably John Harsanyi, have argued the utilitarian principles of justice, which maximize average expected utility, would be chosen; and still others have argued that compromise principles, which strike a compromise between the more advantaged and the less advantaged members of a society, would be chosen.[5] Let us consider each in turn.

Maximin Principles

According to Rawls, the original position is a situation where the maximin rule for choice under uncertainty applies and, as a result, persons in the original position would choose principles of justice that guarantee the highest possible social minimum. Since the maximin rule assumes that the best one can do is maximize the payoff to the least advantaged position, the principles that would be chosen by persons in the original position are considered to be the same as those a rational person would choose for the design of a society in which her enemy would determine her position, which, of course, would be the least advantaged position. This is not to say that persons in the original position believe that their place in society is so determined, because then their reasoning would be based on false premises, and that would be unacceptable. Still, the principles that persons would select in both situations would be the same, according to Rawls, because both situations are such that the maximin rule for choice under uncertainty applies.

Rawls argues that the original position possesses, to a striking degree, the three features that make a choice situation appropriate for applying the maximin strategy. The person choosing has:

1. a reason to discount the probabilities that are arrived at in the choice situation;
2. a conception of the good such that she cares little, if at all, for what she might gain above the minimin she can in fact be sure of gaining by following the maximin strategy;
3. alternative strategies with unacceptable outcomes.

According to Rawls, the first feature is characteristic of the original position because persons in the original position would not have any objective grounds for assigning probabilities to their turning up in different positions in society, and it would not be reasonable for persons so situated to rely on an probability assignments in the absence of such grounds. In addition, Rawls argues, since persons in the original position would want their choice of principles to seem reasonable to others, particularly their descendants, they would have still another reason for not relying on probability assignments that would be made in the absence of objective grounds.

In discussing the second feature, Rawls begins by arguing that his principles of justice would guarantee a satisfactory minimum. He then goes on to claim that if basic liberties could be shown to have priority in the original position, persons so situated would have no desire to sacrifice basic liberties for greater shares of other primary goods and would be content with the minimum provided by the maximin strategy.

To show that the original position possesses the third feature characterizing situations where the maximin strategy is said to apply, Rawls simply claims that utilitarian principles of justice, under certain conditions, might lead to serious infractions of liberty, which would be unacceptable to persons in the original position.

Utilitarian Principles

Challenging Rawls's derivation of principles of justice in the original position, John Harsanyi and others have argued that persons so situated would favor principles of justice that maximize average expected utility. Harsanyi claims that persons in the original position would first assign an equal probability to their occupying each particular position in society and then select the alternative with the highest average expected utility. To determine utility assignments, persons in the original position are said to compare what it would be like to have particular distributive shares in society while possessing the subjective tastes of persons who have those shares. Harsanyi further assumes that with the knowledge of the appropriate psychological laws and factual information, persons in the original position would arrive at the same comparative utility judgments form which it would then be possible to determine which alternative maximizes their average expected utility.

For example, consider a society with just the three members, X, Y and Z, facing the following alternatives:

	Alternative A	Alternative C
X	60	30
Y	10	20
Z	10	20
	80	70

Given these alternatives, Harsanyi thinks that persons in the original position would assume that it was equally probable that they would be either X, Y, or Z, and therefore would select Alternative A as having the higher average expected utility, even though Alternative C provided the higher social minimin. If the utility values for two alternatives were the following:

	Alternative B	Alternative C
X	50	30
Y	10	20
Z	10	20
	70	70

Harsanyi thinks that persons in the original position would be indifferent between the alternatives, despite the fact that Alternative C again provides the higher social minimum.

According to Harsanyi, any risk aversion that persons in the original position might have in evaluating alternatives would be reflected in a declining marginal utility for money and other social goods. Thus, in our example, we could imagine that a yearly income of $250,000 may be required to provide a utility of 60, while a yearly income of only $10,000 may be needed for a utility of 10. Similarly, a $80,000 yearly income may be required for a utility of 30, but only a $30,000 yearly income for a utility of 20. Harsanyi thinks that persons in the original position would not be risk averse to inequalities of distribution per se, but only insofar as such inequalities resulted in a lower average expected utility in a society.

Compromise Principles

Others, like myself, have disagreed with both Rawls and Harsanyi concerning choice in the original position. Against Rawls, I have argued that persons in the original position would choose principles of justice that guarantee a high social minimum but not the highest *possible* social minimum. The main reason for this preference, I claim, is that persons so situated would consider the possibility that they might be among the more advantaged members as well as among the less advantaged members of their society, and this would lead them to compromise the interests of both groups by favoring a high social minimum, but not the highest possible social minimum.

Rawls might object that to adopt principles of justice that do anything less than maximally favor the least advantaged members of a society is "to favor the more fortunate twice over" (1975a: 98–99). But to be favored in the distribution of natural advantages, and not in the distribution of social advantages, is hardly to be favored at all. So it is odd to talk about two distributions of advantages in this case—one natural and one social—as though one could benefit a great deal from the first, but hardly at all from the second. Rather the issue seems to be best put as follows: To what degree should people be allowed to benefit from the use of their natural and social assets? And here the answer of the compromise view is; as much as possible provided that a high social minimum is guaranteed.

In support of the compromise view against Harsanyi, I have argued that even if we assume that persons in the original position were making judgments in terms of utilities and that declining marginal utility of social goods has been taken into account, persons so situated would still have grounds for preferring Alternative C to both Alternatives A and B in the above examples.[6] This is because persons would take two factors into account in reaching decisions in the original position. One factor is the average utility payoff, and this factor would favor Alternative A. The other factor, however, is the distribution of utility payoffs, and this factor would clearly favor Alternative C. Moreover, given this set of alternatives, the second factor would be decisive for persons in the original position who are seeking to compromise the interests of the more advantaged and the less advantaged members of a society.

Of course, as Kenneth Arrow has pointed out, it is still possible to view the preferences of persons in the original position as maximizing average expected utility, provided that the distribution factor is incorporated into the calculation of utilities.[7] Thus, for example, the distribution factor (DF) might be incorporated into the calculation of utilities in the previous examples as follows:

	Alternative A	Alternative B	Alternative C
X	60	50	30
Y	10	10	20
Z	10	10	20
DF	−10	−10	+5
	70	60	75

Since the standard Von Neumann–Morganstern procedure for assigning utilities in situations of uncertainty can incorporate such a distribution factor into the calculation of utilities, we can view the preferences of persons in the original position for Alternative C over Alternatives A and B as one that maximizes average expected utility.[8]

Interpreting the preferences of persons in the original position in this way, however, does nothing to establish the moral adequacy of utilitarianism as traditionally conceived. For to introduce a distribution factor into the calculation of utilities over and above the individual utility payoffs is to abandon utilitarianism as traditionally conceived in favor of a form of ideal utilitarianism. In this particular form of ideal utilitarianism, the standard conflict between justice as a distribution factor and utility as average individual utility payoff is transformed into a conflict between two types of utility. Yet the moral adequacy of utilitarianism as traditionally conceived is not established by the possibility of such a transformation, because virtually any moral conflict can be represented as a conflict of utilities. Rather, the adequacy of utilitarianism as traditionally conceived depends on showing that when the utilities of the above form of ideal utilitarianism conflict, the utility of the average individual payoff always has priority over the utility of the distribution factor. But since persons in the original position would reject such a priority by preferring Alternative C to Alternatives A and B, this clearly raises a serious challenge to the adequacy of utilitarianism as traditionally conceived.[9]

These reasons for favoring the requirements of the compromise view over those of the maximin and utilitarian views, however, presuppose that sufficient resources are available for securing a variety of possible social minimums to all legitimate claimants. What we need to determine, therefore, is whether this presupposition still holds once the moral problem of distant peoples and future generations is taken into account.

Of course, some might think that at this stage of working out a conception of justice, it is premature to consider the moral problem of distant peoples and future generations. Rawls, for example, has argued that it would be more reasonable to abstract from such problems and first attempt to work out a conception of justice for a well-ordered society viewed as a closed and self-sufficient system of cooperation

(Rawls 1980: 524). For instance, we know that in physics it can be illuminating to consider the movements of bodies in certain idealized conditions before complicating the account by introducing considera-tins of friction, air pressure, etc. Likewise in political philosophy, a defender of this approach might argue, it can be illuminating to consider first what principles of justice would be chosen in the original position to govern a closed and self-sufficient society before complicat-ing the account by introducing questions of international justice, pop-ulation policy, etc.

Yet for this analogy to justify the proposed approach, it would have to be the case that focusing on the idealized problem of justice illuminates more than distorts our understanding of real-life problems of justice. But, as we have just noted, the reasons for favoring the requirements of the compromise view over those of the maximin and utilitarian views rest upon the presupposition that there *are* sufficient resources for securing a variety of possible social minimums to all legitimate claimants. If that presupposition fails to hold once the moral problem of distant peoples and future generations is taken into ac-count, then focusing on the idealized problem of justice is sure to distort, more than it illuminates, our understanding of real-life prob-lems of justice. Accordingly, there is no way that we can put off addressing the moral problem of distant people and future generations.

Distant Peoples and Future Generations

It is unfortunate that professional philosophers have only recently begun to discuss the moral problem of distant peoples and future generations. There are many reasons for this neglect, not all of them complimentary to the philosophical profession. Suffice it to say that once the possibility of using modern technology to benefit or harm distant peoples and future generations became widely recognized, philosophers could no longer ignore the importance of this moral problem.

Nevertheless, a generally acceptable way of even setting out the problem has yet to develop. Some philosophers have even attempted to "solve" the problem, or at least part of it, by arguing that talk about "the rights of future generations" is conceptually incoherent and thus analogous to talk about "square circles." Accordingly, the key ques-tion that must be answered first is: Can we meaningfully speak of distant peoples and future generations as having rights against us or of our having obligations to them?

Answering this question with respect to distant peoples is clearly much easier than answering it with respect to future generations. Very few philosophers have thought that the mere fact that people are at a distance from us precludes our having any obligations to them or their having any rights against us. Some philosophers, however, have argued that our ignorance of the specific membership of the class of distant peoples does rule out these moral relationships. Yet this cannot be right, given that in other contexts we recognize obligations to indeterminate classes of people, such as a police officer's obligation to come to the aid of persons in distress or the obligation of food processors not to harm the consumers of their products.

Yet others have argued that while there may be valid moral claims respecting the welfare of distant peoples, such claims cannot be rights because they fail to hold against determinate individuals and groups.[10] But in what sense do such claims fail to hold against determinate individuals and groups? Surely all would agree that existing laws rarely specify the determinate individuals and groups against whom such claims hold. But morality is frequently determinate where existing laws are not. And at least there seems to be no conceptual impossibility to claiming that distant peoples have rights against us and that we have obligations to them.

Of course, before distant peoples can be said to have rights against us, we must be capable of acting across the distance that separates us. As long as this condition is met—as it typically is for those living in most technologically advanced societies—it would certainly seem possible for distant peoples to have rights against us and we obligations to them.

By contrast, answering the above question with respect to future generations is much more difficult and has been the subject of considerable debate among contemporary philosophers. One issue concerns the referent of the term *future generations*. Most philosophers seem to agree that the class of future generations is not "the class of all persons who simply could come into existence." But there is some disagreement concerning whether we should refer to the class of future generations as "the class of persons who will definitely come into existence, assuming that there are such," or as "the class of persons we can reasonably expect to come into existence." The first approach is more "metaphysical," specifying the class of future generations in terms of what will exist; the second approach is more "epistemological," specifying the class of future generations in terms of our knowledge. Fortunately, there appears to be no practical moral significance to the choice of either approach.

Another issue relevant to whether we can meaningfully speak of future generations as having rights against us or we obligations to them concerns whether it is logically coherent to speak of future generations as having rights *now*. Of course, no one who finds talk about rights to be generally meaningful should question whether we can coherently claim that future generations *will* have rights at some point in the future (specifically, when they come into existence and are no *longer* future generations). But what is questioned, since it is of considerable practical significance, is whether we can coherently claim that future generations have rights *now* when they don't yet exist.

Let us suppose, for example, that we continue to use up the earth's resources at present or even greater rates, and as a result the most pessimistic forecasts for the 22nd century are realized.[11] Future generations will face widespread famine, depleted resources, insufficient new techology to handle the crisis, and a drastic decline in the quality of life for nearly everyone. If this were to happen, could persons living in the 22nd century legitimately claim that we in the 20th century violated their rights by not restraining our consumption of the world's resources? Surely it would be odd to say that we violated their rights more than a hundred years before they existed. But what exactly is the oddness?

Is it that future generations generally have no way of claiming their rights against existing generations? While this does make the recognition and enforcement of rights much more difficult (future generations would need strong advocates in the existing generations), it does not make it impossible for there to be such rights. Or is it that we don't believe that rights can legitimately exercise their influence over long durations of time? But if we can foresee and control at least some of the effects our actions will have on future generations, why should we not be responsible for those same effects? And if we are responsible for them, why should not future generations have a right that we take them into account?

Perhaps what troubles us is that future generations don't exist when their rights are said to demand action. But how else can persons have a right to benefit from the effects our actions will have in the distant future if they do not exist just when those effects will be felt? Our contemporaries cannot legitimately make the same demand, for they will not be around to experience those effects. Only future generations can have a right that the effects our actions will have in the distant future contribute to their well-being. Nor need we assume that for persons to have rights, they must exist when their rights demand action. Thus, to say that future generations have rights against existing generations we can simply mean that there are enforceable requirements upon existing generations that would benefit or prevent harm to future generations.[12]

Most likely what really bothers us is that we cannot know for sure what effects our actions will have on future generations. For example, we may at some cost to ourselves conserve resources, yet the same resources may perhaps be valueless to future generations who may develop different technologies. Or we may now be destroying or depleting resources that future generations might find to be essential to their well-being. Nevertheless, we should not allow such possibilities to blind us to the necessity for a social policy in this regard, for whatever we do will have its effect on future generations. The best approach is to use our present knowledge and to assume that future generations will also require the same basic resources we now find valuable. If future generations instead require different resources to meet their basic needs, at least we will not be blamable for acting on the basis of the knowledge we have.[13]

A final issue that is relevant to whether we can meaningfully speak of future generations as having rights and our having obligations to them concerns whether in a given case the actions of the existing generations that affect future generations can actually benefit or harm those generations. For some philosophers would surely hold that only in cases where future generations can be benefited or harmed by our actions can there be a question of future generations having rights against us or our having obligations to them.

Of course, no one doubts that certain of our actions that affect future generations actually do benefit or harm them. An artist who creates a great work of art that will survive will surely benefit future generations. Just as surely, harm will be done to future generations by the careless manner in which many governments and private corporations today dispose of nuclear wastes and other toxic substances.

But suppose some of our actions affect future generations by affecting the membership of future generations. That is, suppose our actions cause different people to be born than otherwise would have been born had we acted differently. For example, a woman who is taking a particular medication will give birth to a defective child if she conceives now. But if she stops taking her medication and waits three months before becoming pregnant, she will almost certainly have a normal child. If the woman decides not to wait and gives birth to a defective child, has she harmed that child? If the mother had waited three months, the child she would have then given birth to would certainly have been a different child.[14] So it does not seem that she has harmed the child to which she did give birth, provided that the child's life is worth living. Some people, however, would surely think that the mother was wrong not to wait and give birth to a normal child. But how can such a judgment be supported?

At the level of social choice we can also imagine a similar situation. Consider a developing country choosing between a laissez-faire population policy and one that restricts population growth. If the restrictive policy is followed, capital accumulation will produce general prosperity within a generation or two. But if the laissez-faire policy is followed, low wages and high unemployment will continue indefinitely. Since either choice will, over time, produce different populations, those born subsequently under the laissez-faire policy could hardly claim that they were harmed by the choice of that policy, since, if the restricted policy had been adopted, they would not have been born. Still, some people would surely want to claim that it was wrong for the country to pursue a laissez-faire policy. But how could such a claim be supported if no one in subsequent generations is harmed by the choice of that policy?

Contemporary philosophers have sought to deal in basically two ways with the question of whether we can wrong future generations without harming them. The first is simply to recommend that we "bite the bullet" and claim that if no one is harmed then no wrong is done. This approach is not very satisfactory since it flies in the face of our strong intuitions about examples of the above sort. The second and more promising approach is to claim that wrong can be done not only by harming but also by failing to benefit others, provided that bringing people into existence counts as a way of benefiting them. On this approach, the woman who neglected to bring into existence a normal child did wrong by failing to benefit that child, and the country which neglected to adopt a restrictive population policy did wrong by failing to bring into existence a more prosperous population. This second approach is also more suitable to a Welfare Liberal Conception of Justice, which recognizes an obligation to benefit others as well as an obligation not to harm others, than it is to a Libertarian Conception of Justice, which recognizes only an obligation not to harm others.[15]

Suppose we attempt to apply the original position decision procedure to the problem of distant peoples and future generations to determine what practical requirements would result. To deal with the problem of future generations, Rawls has suggested (1971: 284–93) that it would suffice if persons in the original position, while knowing that they are contemporaries, simply did not know to which generation they belong. So characterized, Rawls thinks persons in the original position would choose something like the following principle:

The Principle of Saving: The rate of saving for each generation should represent its fair contribution toward realizing and maintaining a society in which all the members can fully enjoy the benefit of its just institutions.

Unfortunately, given Rawls's characterization of the original position, it would be reasonable for persons so situated to favor their own generation by refusing to accept the Principle of Saving and the sacrifices it entails. Previous generations have either saved or they have not, and by agreeing in the present to the Principle of Saving, persons in the original position can in no way affect how they were treated by previous generations. Persons in the original position may have self-interested and self-glorifying reasons for providing the next generation with a certain supply of capital and natural resources, but such reasons clearly would not suffice to motivate them to choose the Principle of Saving.

To handle this problem Rawls has postulated that persons in the original position are interested in the welfare of at least the next generation. Yet, since Rawls does not specify how interested persons in the original position are in the welfare of the next generation, it is unclear whether they would come to any unanimous agreement on an acceptable rate of saving. In any case, they would not have sufficient reason to make the sacrifices required by the Principle of Saving, because they are only (to an unspecified degree) benevolently interested in the next generation. Later generations are beyond the concern of persons in the original position, except insofar as the welfare of subsequent generations would contribute to the welfare of the immediate descendents of those in the original position. This would not provide sufficient grounds to motivate the accumulation of social and economic resources and the preservation of natural resources required by the Principle of Saving.

To remedy this problem I have proposed to extend the veil of ignorance so that persons in the original position do not know whether they are contemporaries or whether they belong to some unspecified future generation (Sterba 1980b: 58–61). If the veil of ignorance is drawn in this fashion, it would be in the self-interest of persons in the original position to choose the Principle of Saving. They may well turn out to belong to a future generation, hence it is in their interest to secure a reasonable rate of saving and guard against a reckless use of natural resources.

More recently, Rawls has chosen a different remedy. He has dropped the assumption that persons in the original position are at least interested in the welfare of the next generation, and assumed instead that persons so situated want all *previous* generations to follow whatever principle of saving they would choose. According to Rawls (1978: 58–59), the advantage of this new assumption is that it does not require that we modify the initial characterization of persons in the original position.

Nevertheless, while this new assumption has the advantage that it leads to the Principle of Saving, it does so, contrary to what Rawls claims, only by introducing an additional moral motivation into the characterization of persons in the original position. (How else do we account for why persons in the original position would want all previous generations to follow the Principle of Saving?)[16] Thus it seems preferable to secure the choice of the Principle of Saving, in the way I proposed, so as not to require such a significant alteration in the initial motivation assumption governing persons in the original position.

But given this characterization of the original position, exactly what principles of justice would be chosen? The Principle of Saving requires a fair contribution from each generation. But what would persons in the original position understand a fair contribution to be?

It seems clear that once choice in the original position is modified to apply to the problem of distant peoples and future generations, then both distant peoples and future generations would be recognized as having a legitimate claim to some type of a social minimum. Persons in the original position, thinking that they might be in the position of distant peoples or future generations, would surely want to extend the guarantee of a social minimum to them. As a consequence, the presupposition underlying the reasons for favoring the requirements of the compromise view (over those of the maximin and utilitarian views) would fail to hold. There simply would not be sufficient resources available for securing a variety of possible social minimums to all legitimate claimants.[17]

Since both the maximin and the compromise views would want to require a minimum that could be guaranteed to all legitimate claimants, both views would favor a minimum that is lower than the one they would otherwise favor for the members of an affluent, technologically advanced society. As we shall see, this lower minimum can be specified in terms of the satisfaction of a person's basic needs. The utilitarian view would also favor the same sort of minimum, but it would do so for reasons of declining marginal utility. Providing such a minimum would simply be the best way of maximizing average expected utility among so many claimants. Moreover, the inequalities that the utilitarian view could theoretically justify would not in fact be justified, since most resources would have to go to simply providing this minimum to all legitimate claimants. Hence, once choice in the original position is modified to be applicable to the moral problem of distant peoples and future generations, persons in the original position would recognize and endorse the social minimum that is favored by all three views.

A Basic Needs Minimum

The social minimum recognized and endorsed by persons in the original position, as was noted, can be specified in terms of the satisfaction of a person's basic needs. A person's basic needs are those that must be satisfied in order not to seriously endanger a person's mental or physical well-being. Needs in general, if not satisfied, lead to lacks and deficiencies with respect to various standards. Basic needs, if not satisfied, lead to significant lacks and deficiencies with respect to a standard of mental and physical well-being. Thus, a person's needs for food, shelter, medical care, protection, companionship, and self-development are, at least in part, needs of this sort. From the perspective of the original position, it is to satisfy basic needs that primary goods are typically sought.[18]

Societies vary in their ability to satisfy a person's basic needs, but the needs themselves would be subject to variation only to the degree that there is a corresponding variation in what constitutes health and sanity in different societies. Consequently, to require the satisfaction of a person's basic needs is a fairly determinate way of specifying the minimum of goods and resources each person has a right to receive.

Actually, specifying a minimum of this sort seems to be the goal of the poverty index used in the United States since 1964.[19] This poverty index is based on the U.S. Department of Agriculture's Economy Food Plan (for an adequate diet) and on evidence showing that low-income families spend about one-third of their income on food. The index is then adjusted from time to time to take changing prices into account. To accord with the goal of satisfying basic needs, the poverty index would have to be further adjusted to take into account (a) that the Economy Food Plan was developed for "temporary or emergency use" and is inadequate for a permanent diet, and (b) that recent evidence shows that low-income families spend one-fourth rather than one-third of their income of food.[20]

Of course, one might think that a minimum should be specified in terms of a purely conventional standard of living that varies over time and between societies. Benn and Peters, following this approach, have suggested specifying a minimum in terms of the income received by the most numerous group in a society.[21] For example, in the United States today the greatest number of households fall within the $25,000 to $34,999 income bracket (in 1984 dollars).[22] Specifying a minimum in this way, however, leads to certain difficulties. Suppose that the most numerous group of households in a society with the wealth of the United States fell within a $1000–$1499 income bracket. Certainly, it would not thereby follow that a guarantee of $1500 per household would constitute an acceptable minimum for such a society. Or suppose that the income of the most numerous group of households fell within the $95,000–$99,999 income bracket. Certainly, a minimum of $100,000 per household would not thereby be required. Moreover, there seem to be similar difficulties with any attempt to specify an acceptable minimum in a purely conventional manner.

Nevertheless, it still seems that an acceptable minimum should vary over time and between societies, at least to some degree. For example, it could be argued that today a car is almost a necessity in the typical

North American household, a fact not true fifty years ago nor true today in most other areas of the world. Happily, a basic needs approach to specifying an acceptable minimum can account for such variation without introducing any variation into the definition of the basic needs themselves. Instead, variation enters into the cost of satisfying these needs at different times and in different societies.[23] For in the same society at different times and in different societies at the same time, the normal costs of satisfying a person's basic needs can and do vary considerably. These variations are due in large part to the different ways in which the most readily available means for satisfying basic needs are produced. For example, in more affluent societies, the most readily available means for satisfying a person's basic needs are usually processed so as to satisfy nonbasic needs at the same time as they satisfy basic needs. This processing is carried out to make the means more attractive to persons in higher income brackets who can easily afford the extra cost. As a result, the most readily available means for satisfying basic needs are much more costly in more affluent societies than in less affluent societies. This occurs most obviously with respect to the most readily available means for satisfying basic needs for food, shelter, and transportation, but it also occurs with respect to the most readily available means for satisfying basic needs for companionship, self-esteem, and self-development. For a person in more affluent societies cannot normally satisfy even these latter needs without participating in at least some relatively costly educational and social development practices. Accordingly, there will be considerable variation in the normal costs of satisfying a person's basic needs as a society becomes more affluent over time, and considerable variation at the same time in societies at different levels of affluence. There will even be variation between individuals in the same society at the same time. For example, the normal costs of meeting the basic self-development and health care needs of those who are disabled or have special health problems will be greater than those of the average member of the society.

Difficult cases will arise, however, in which it will not be possible to satisfy everyone's basic needs. For example, given the developments in modern medicine, meeting the basic needs of all those with special health care problems can conflict with the satisfaction of the basic needs of others. To resolve such conflicts, it is necessary to return to the moral framework used to justify the basic needs approach in the first place—in this case, the original position. Thus, from the perspective of the original position, persons for whom the normal costs of meeting their basic needs are less would have priority over those for whom the normal costs of meeting their basic needs are more. This means that, in the above example, meeting the basic needs of those without costly special health care problems would have priority over meeting the basic needs of those with such costly problems.

Some people have thought that the variation entering into the normal costs of satisfying people's basic needs shows the criterion of needs to be a purely conventional standard that is ill-suited to be incorporated into a conception of justice. According to this view, while basic needs may be conceived abstractly, what really counts is the conventional determination of what is needed. As William Leiss has said, "It is trivial to calculate the need for food in terms of minimum nutritional requirements. The real issues are: What kinds of foods? In what forms? With what qualities?" (Leiss 1976: 62).[24] But while conventions are certainly required to specify what is needed at the practical level, this specification is still governed by a person's basic needs, abstractly conceived. For we can always ask whether the existing conventions have been successful in meeting people's basic needs and to what degree they have been successful. Consequently, abstractness is no objection to a standard of basic needs, provided that standard can be practically applied in a determinate fashion.

It also should be pointed out that at least some of the goods required for the satisfaction of people's basic needs are participatory in nature. These goods relate primarily to the satisfaction of people's basic needs for companionship and self-development. It also seems to be the case that a high level of participation in the institutions that control the distribution of goods in society is required to ensure that people's basic needs will be met.[25]

We have seen, therefore, that a basic needs approach to specifying an acceptable minimum would guarantee people the goods and resources necessary to meet the normal costs of satisfying their basic needs in the society in which they live. Thus, once the original position is modified to apply to the problem of distant peoples and future generations, persons so situated would choose to have just such a minimum guaranteed to all legitimate claimants as required by the maximin, compromise, and utilitarian views.

Basic Needs and World Hunger

At present the worldwide supply of goods and resources is probably sufficient to meet the normal costs of satisfying the basic nutritional needs of all existing persons in the societies in which they live. According to former U.S. Secretary of Agriculture Bob Bergland, "For the past 20 years, if the available food supply had been evenly divided and distributed, each person would have received more than the minimum number of calories.[26] Other authorities have made similar assessments of the available world food supply.[27] In fact, one has stated that if all arable land were optimally utilized, a population of between 38 and 48 billion people could be supported.[28]

Needless to say, the adoption of a policy of meeting the basic nutritional needs of all existing persons would necessitate significant changes, especially in developed societies. For example, a large percentage of the U.S. population would have to alter their eating habits substantially. In particular, they would have to reduce their consumption of beef and pork to make more grain available for direct human consumption. (Presently the amount of grain fed to American livestock equals the amount that all the people of China and India eat in a year.) Thus, the satisfaction of at least some of the nonbasic needs of the more advantaged in developed societies would have to be foregone to meet the basic nutritional needs of all existing persons in developing and underdeveloped societies.

Such changes, however, may still have little effect on the relative costs of satisfying people's basic needs in different societies. Even after the basic nutritional needs of all existing persons have been met, the normal costs of satisfying basic needs would still tend to be greater in developed societies than in developing and underdeveloped societies. This is because the most readily available means for satisfying basic needs in developed societies would still tend to be more processed to satisfy nonbasic needs along with basic needs. Nevertheless, once the basic nutritional needs of future generations are also taken into account, the satisfaction of the nonbasic needs of the more advantaged in developed societies would have to be restricted further to preserve the fertility of cropland and other food-related natural resources for the use of future generations.[29] And once basic needs other than nutritional needs are also taken into account, still further restrictions would be required. For example, it has been estimated that a North American uses fifty times more resources than an Indian. This means that in terms of resource consumption the North American continent's population is the equivalent of 12.5 billion Indians.[30] Obviously, this consumption would have to be altered radically if the basic needs of distant peoples and future generations are to be met. And eventually the practice of utilizing more and more efficient means of satisfying people's basic needs in developed societies would have the effect of equalizing the normal costs of meeting people's basic needs across societies.[31]

While the particular requirements that persons in the original position would place upon those in developed affluent societies are obviously quite severe, they are not unconditional. For those in developing and underdeveloped societies are under a corresponding obligation to do what they can to meet their own basic needs, such as to bring all arable land under optimal cultivation and to control population growth.

Yet we should not be unreasonable in judging what particular developing and underdeveloping societies have managed to accomplish in this
regard. In the final analysis, such societies should be judged on the
basis of what they have managed to accomplish, *given the options
available to them*. For example, developing and underdeveloped societies today lack many of the options, such as exporting their excess
population to sparcely populated and resource-rich continents, that
Western European societies utilized in the course of their economic
and social development. Consequently, in judging what developing and
underdeveloped societies have managed to accomplish, we must take
into account their particular circumstances. In practice this will mean,
for example, that it is not reasonable to expect such societies to reduce
their population growth as fast as ideally would be desirable. Nevertheless, from the perspective of the original position, it should be reasonable to expect that at some time all existing persons accept a population policy according to which the membership of future generations
would never be allowed to increase beyond the ability of existing
generations to make the necessary provision for the basic needs of
future generations.[32] In the meantime, it may be necessary (to meet
the basic needs of at least a temporarily growing world population) to
utilize renewable resources beyond what would secure their maximal
sustainable yield. (At present, certain renewable resources, such as
fishing resources, are being so utilized for far less justifiable ends.)
This, of course, would have the effect of reducing the size of succeeding generations that, according to the proposed population policy,
could justifiably be brought into existence. But while such an effect is
not ideally desirable, it seems less morally preferable to allow existing
persons to starve to death in order to increase the size of succeeding
generations that could justifiably be brought into existence.[33]

Affirmative Action

As we have seen, once the moral relevance of distant peoples and
future generations is taken into account, the maximin, utilitarian, and
compromise views all favor a right to welfare specified in terms of the
satisfaction of the basic needs of each legitimate claimant.[34] But would
these three views also favor the same right to affirmative action? If we
were to abstract from the moral problem of distant peoples and future
generations, it seems clear that the three views would favor conflicting
requirements. The maximin view would favor the highest possible level
of opportunity for the least advantaged members of a society and a
corresponding right of affirmative action when such opportunity has
been denied. The utilitarian view would favor a lower level of opportunity and a lesser right of affirmative action as required to maximize

average expected utility. And the compromise view would favor a level of opportunity and a right to affirmative action that falls between the requirments of these other two views.

But just as in the case of specifying a right to welfare, and for much the same reasons, once the moral problem of distant peoples and future generations is taken into account, all three views would agree to the same level of opportunity, specified (as was the social minimum) in terms of what is required for the satisfaction of the basic needs of each legitimate claimant. The maximin and compromise views would re-quire this level of opportunity because it can be guaranteed to all legitimate claimants. The utilitarian view would require the same level of opportunity for reasons of declining marginal utility. Accordingly, persons in the original position would have no choice but to endorse the provision of that same level of opportunity favored by all three views to each and every legitimate claimant, thereby endorsing a right to equal opportunity, as well as a corresponding right of affirmative action should this equal opportunity be denied to any legitimate claimant.

Someone might object that what goes by the name of affirmative action in society are programs that are typically directed not at persons who have been denied their rightful level of opportunity in the past, but rather at the progency of such persons.[35] And even when affirma-tive action programs are directed at those who have been wrongfully denied opportunities in the past, they typically benefit those who have been discriminated against the least.[36] This is because affirmative action programs benefit the most-qualified among those who have been discriminated against, and the most-qualified, so it is claimed, are likely to be those who have been the least discriminated against.

In response, it seems clear that in most societies affirmative action programs exist side-by-side with institutions and practices that con-tinue to deny people equal opportunity. Thus, it would be rare for anyone who benefits from an affirmative action program not to have been wrongfully denied equal opportunity in the past. Even if we were to assume that all public discrimination has ceased in a society, the effects of past discrimination upon family life would continue to deny rightful opportunities ot the children of those who have been discrimi-nated against unless the situation is corrected for, by remedial educa-tional or job-training programs or by some form of affirmative action.

Nor is it clear that the most qualified who benefit from affirmative action are the least deserving because they are the least discriminated against. The most qualified who benefit from affirmative action may not have been subjected to less discrimination; they may simply have resisted discrimination more vigorously. Even supposing the most qualified are those who have been least discriminated against in the past, why isn't affirmative action the correct response to the degree of discrimination incurred?[37] Surely, if we assume that affirmative action is provided only to those who have the capacity in conjunction with an affirmative action program of becoming, in short order, at least as qualified as those over whom they would be preferred, then affirmative action does seem to be the appropriate reason to this form of past discrimination. Other forms of discrimination whose effects upon a person's qualification and potential are even more detrimental would require other responses, such as remedial educational and job-training programs.

Important Challenges to Contractual Fairness

So far I have argued that rights to welfare and affirmative action specified in terms of the satisfaction of a person's basic needs would emerge from the original position once the problem of distant peoples and future generations is taken into account. But there are a number of important challenges to grounding a Welfare Liberal Conception of Justice on an ideal of contractual fairness that must be considered. Some of these challenges are directed at the very idea of the original position; others are directed at one or more of the conditions imposed on the original position.

The Very Idea of the Original Position

In an early challenge to the very idea of the original position, Ronald Dworkin (1973) argues that hypothetical agreements do not (unlike actual agreements) provide independent arguments for the fairness of those agreements. For example, suppose because I did not know the value of a painting I owned, if you had offered me $100 for it yesterday, I would have accepted your offer. Such hypothetical acceptance, Dworkin argues, in no way shows that it would be fair to force me to sell the painting to you today for $100 now that I have discovered it to be more valuable. Accordingly, Dworkin holds that the fact that a person would agree to do something in the original position does not provide an independent argument for abiding by that agreement in everyday life.

But while it seems correct to argue that hypothetical agreement in the painting case does not support a demand that I presently sell you the painting for $100, it is not clear how this undermines the normal relevance of the hyothetical agreement that emerges from the original position. For surely a defender of the original position is not committed to the view that all hypothetical agreements are morally binding. Nor could Dworkin reasonably argue that his example supports the conclusion that no hypothetical agreements are morally binding. For by parity of reasoning from the fact tht some actual agreements are not binding (such as an agreement to commit murder), it would follow that *no* actual agreements are morally binding, which is absurd. Consequently, further argument is required to show that the specific agreement that would result from the original position is not morally binding.

Another challenge to the very idea of the original position, developed by G. B. Thomas and Marcus G. Singer, is that principles of justice cannot be the object of choice.[38] According to Thomas and Singer, principles of justice, unlike laws and rules of a game, cannot be enacted or chosen. But this view seems too uncompromising. For while it is true that principles of justice cannot be grounded in choices or enactments that are not sufficiently morally constrained, it doesn't follow that such principles cannot be grounded in choices or enactments that are so constrained. And since actual choice situations frequently do not incorporate sufficient moral constraints, it does seem appropriate to look to adequately designed hypothetical choice situations to ground principles of justice.

Still another challenge to the very idea of the original position is that it requires us to view persons as stripped of their rightful natural and social assets. The original position is explicitly designed, of course, to reflect the judgment that persons do not deserve their natural assets or initial social assets. Yet this judgment, when correctly interpreted, does not imply that a person's natural assets or initial social assets are undeserved, but only that the notion of desert does not apply to them. Nor does the judgment presuppose that the grounds of desert must themselves be deserved, but it does imply that natural assets and initial social assets should be regarded, in effect, as common assets. Persons in the original position might even choose, for example, to require people to donate their surplus kidneys to those in need. For this reason, Robert Nozick and Michael J. Sandel, echoing Rawls's own complaint against utilitarianism, have claimed that the ideal of contractual fairness does not take seriously the distinction between persons.[39]

Nevertheless, it is possible to interpret the ideal of contractual fairness here as simply addressing a question every moral philosopher must address: What constraints, if any, should apply to people's use of their natural and social assets in the pursuit of their own welfare? For example, should people be able to use such assets in pursuit of their own welfare, regardless of the consequences to others? Ethical egoists, of course, would say that they should, but most moral philosophers would disagree. Even libertarians, like Nozick, would object to such unconstrained use of people's natural and social assets. For Nozick, people's use of their natural and social assets is constrained by the moral requirement that they not interfere with or harm other people, or at least that they do not do so without paying compensation.

For others, particularly welfare liberals, the use of people's natural and social assets sould be constrained not only when it interferes with or harms other people, but also when such use fails to benefit others in fundamental ways, for example, by not providing them with an adequate social minimum.

So the charge that the ideal of contractual fairness does not take seriously the distinction between persons ultimately comes down to the claim that although some constraints are morally justified, the ideal of contractual fairness puts too many constraints on the use of a person's natural and social assets. But to make this charge stick, critics of this ideal need to provide an argument that only a more limited number of constraints on the use of natural and social assets are morally justified, and this they have failed to do.

A related objection to the ideal of contractual fairness is developed by Robert Paul Wolff.[40] Wolff argues that the knowledge conditions imposed on the original position are impossible, because it is impossible for persons in the original position to be ignorant of particular facts about themselves and their society while possessing the general knowledge that Rawls attributes to them. For example, Wolff claims, persons in the original position cannot know the ideological character of the classical economic theory without knowing that they have advanced beyond the stages of hunting and gathering and primitive agriculture. But while Wolff is undoubtedly correct in claiming that a certain amount of particular information is contained in our general knowledge of social reality, this particular information does not appear to undermine the fairness of choice in the original position. It might also help in this regard to view persons in the original position not as persons who would be making choices from behind a veil of ignorance, but rather as persons who would be discounting, or not reasoning from, the knowledge of certain particular facts about themselves and their society in making their choices.

Another challenge to the very idea of the original position put forth by Milton Fisk (1975) is directed at Rawls's characterization of the parties in the original position as mutually disinterested persons. How can an adequate conception of justice, Fisk asks, be founded on mutual disinterest?

Actually this characterization of the motivation of persons in the original position no longer seems appropriate, given Rawls's more recent account of contractual fairness.[41] In that account, persons in the original position are said to have a highest-order interest in developing their capacity for a sense of justice, a capacity that incorporates a concern for the rights of others. Thus, although the motivation of persons in the original position is not linked to any particular conception of justice, it is not strictly mutually disinterested either.

In still another challenge to the very idea of the original position, Richard Miller argues that if the original position is specified to include the knowledge of the general facts of class conflict (especially the knowledge of the fundamental conflict between the proletariat and capitalist classes), then no agreement would be reached and, hence, no conception of justice would be chosen. Miller claims (1975) that if persons in the original position are aware of the facts of class conflict, they will know that members of different classes have diametrically opposed interests and needs, with the consequence that social arrangements that are acceptable to members of one class, say the capitalist class, would be quite unacceptable to members of an opposing (proletariat) class. For this reason, Miller claims that if persons know that conflicts between opposing classes cannot be resolved without leaving members of one or the other group extremely dissatisfied with the result, they will not be able to derive principles of justice in the original position.

Attempting to defend the original position from Miller's critique, Allen Buchanan argues (1982) that the knowledge of the general facts of class conflict should be excluded from the original position, even when the question of what should be done under unjust circumstances is at issue, because to include such knowledge would involve taking into account the actual needs and attitudes of persons occupying various social positions. But what Buchanan fails to see is that the effect that the inclusion of such knowledge would have on choice in the original position is crucial to determining whether people in class-divided societies have the capacity for a sense of justice. Thus, if Miller is correct that no conception of justice would emerge from the original position once the knowledge of the general facts of class conflict are included, then people in class-divided societies would lack the capacity for a sense of justice that is required by an ideal of contractual fairness.

To understand the force of Miller's critique, it is necessary to understand the various ways in which persons' needs and interests can be related in a society. One possibility is that the needs and interests of different members of a society are in fact perfectly complementary. If that were the case, there would be little difficulty in designing a social arrangement that was acceptable to every member. Nor would the original position be needed to design a fair solution. In such a society, no conflicts would arise as long as each person acted in her overall self-interest.

A second possibility is that the needs and interests of different members of a society are in moderate conflict. In deriving his principles of justice, Rawls actually limits himself to a consideration of social conditions where only moderate conflict obtains. For such conditions it seems clear that the original position could be usefully employed to design a fair social arrangement. In such a society the more talented members would be motivated to contribute sufficiently to support a social minimum, and the less talented would also be motivated to contribute sufficiently to reduce the burden on the more talented members. Consequently, persons in the original position would know that the members of such a society when aided by a minimal enforcement system would be able to abide by the principles that would be chosen.

A third possibility is that the needs and interests of the different members of a society are in extreme conflict, and that the conflict has the form of what Marx calls "class conflict." Let us consider the case in which the opposing classes are the capitalist class and the proletariat class. No doubt persons in the original position would know that in such a society compliance with almost any principles of conflict resolution could be achieved only by means of a stringent enforcement system. But why should that fact keep them from choosing any prinicples of social cooperation whatsoever? Surely persons in the original position would still have reason to provide for the basic needs of the members of the proletariat class, and thus would be inclined to favor an adequate social minimum. However, would they not also have reason to temper the sacrifice to be imposed on the members of the capitalist class in the transition to a society that accords with the principles they would favor, knowing, as they do, how much less prosperous and satisfied the members of that class would be under such principles? Yet if considerations of this latter sort could serve as reasons for persons in the original position, then it could be argued that any principles of social cooperation that would be derived would not constitute a morally adequate conception of justice for morally adequate conception of justice,would simply not provide grounds for tempering the sacrifice to be imposed on the members of the capitalist class in the transition to a just society.

Fortunately for an ideal of contractual fairness, this modified version of Miller's critique can be avoided. For it can be shown that considerations favoring tempering the sacrifice to be imposed on the members of the capitalist class in the transition to a just society would not serve as reasons for persons in the original position. This is because persons in the original position, imagining themselves to be ignorant of whether they belong to the capitalist or the proletariat class, would have grounds to discount such considerations in deciding upon principles of social cooperation. They would realize that members of the capitalist class would have a status analogous to that of criminals who have taken goods that rightfully belong to others. For the members of the capitalist class are not "compelled" to pursue their interest by depriving the members of the proletariat class of an acceptable minimum of social goods. They act as they do, depriving others of an adequate social minimum, simply to acquire more social goods for themselves. Unlike members of the proletariat class, the members of the capitalist class could be reasonably expected to act otherwise. Persons in the original position, therefore, to have no more reason to temper the sacrifice to be imposed on the members of the capitalist class than they would have to temper the sacrifice to be imposed on criminals who have grown accustomed to the benefits provided by their ill-gotten goods.

Someone might object to the analogy between criminals and capitalists on the grounds that while the actions of criminals are usually condemned by the conventional standards of their society, the actions of capitalists usually find approval from those same standards. How can we blame capitalists for acting in accord with the conventional standards of their society?

Despite the fact that capitalist exploitation differs from criminal activity in that it is supported by conventional standards, capitalists who engage in such exploitation still cannot escape blame for acting unjustly for two basic reasons. First, capitalists have alternatives to pursuing their own advantage to the limit allowed by conventional standards. For while some capitalists are pursuing their own advantage, others are attempting to restrict at least some of the rights enjoyed by capitalists under those standards, and still others are trying to effect a drastic reform, even a revolutionary change, of those rights. Second, although supported by conventional standards, capitalist exploitation is contrary to the moral presuppositions of capitalist society, in the same manner that "separate but equal education," although supported by state and local laws, was contrary to the supreme law of the land contained in the equal protection clause of the Fourteenth Amendment. This is because the moral presuppositions of capitalist society as standardly expressed by a Libertarian Conception of Justice or a Welfare Liberal Conception of Justice can be shown to be contrary to capitalist exploitation. For these reasons, capitalists cannot escape blame for acting unjustly if they deny people their rights required by these conceptions of justice, despite the existence of supportive conventional standards.

Nevertheless, while the disanalogies between capitalists and criminals would not lead persons in the original position to temper the sacrifice to be imposed on the members of the capitalist class, it would lead them to place some limits on the demands for restitution that can legitimately be made against capitalists. Thus, for example, they would not require of capitalists, as they typically would of criminals, that they not derive any net benefit from their past injustice.[42] Rather, they would simply require that the transition to a just society proceed with all due speed and without any special allowances for the special needs that capitalists have acquired in unjust societies.

Of course, it goes without saying that many capitalists will be reluctant to accept the practical requirements of their own conceptions of justice. Many would be strongly tempted to endorse uncritically the justification for their favored status provided by the conventional standards of their society. But this is exactly what they cannot do if they are to avoid blame for acting unjustly. For all of us when faced with choices that have social impact are required to evaluate critically the alternatives open to us in light of our conceptions of justice; and the greater the social impact our choices will have, the greater is our responsibility for performing this critical evaluation well. Since even a cursory examination of the alternatives open to capitalists in our times gives rise to serious doubts about the justice of the conventional standards supporting capitalist exploitation, capitalists who continue to engage in such exploitation surely will not be able to escape blame. Consequently, persons in the original position would have no reason to temper the sacrifice to be imposed on the members of the capitalist class in the transition to a just society.

Yet it is important to note that even though the assumption of class conflict would not lead persons in the original position to temper the sacrifice to be imposed on the members of the capitalist class, the assumption of moderate conflict would lead to somewhat different results. Under the assumption of class conflict, persons in the original position would tend to justify drastic measures, even violent revolution, to bring into existence a just society, together with a stringent enforcement system to preserve such a society by preventing capitalists from lapsing back into exploitative ways. On the other hand, under the assumption of moderate conflict persons in the original position would tend to justify only less drastic means both with regard to bringing into existence and preserving a just society. Accordingly, the question of which type of conflict characterizes a particular society is of considerable practical moral significance. But whichever obtains, persons in the original position would still be able to use the information to arrive at morally acceptable results.

The Conditions Imposed on the Original Position

Unlike critics who challenge the very idea of the original position, Thomas Nagel limits his criticism to the particular conditions imposed on that choice situation. Nagel argues (1973) that these conditions are not neutral between opposing conceptions of the good, but in fact favor a liberal, individualistic conception of justice over other conceptions.

In response Rawls has claimed that although the original position is not neutral in the sense that it permits all conceptions of the good, it is neutral in the sense that it is fair to all parties in the original position (1975b:539–40). But whether the original position is fair in this sense depends upon one's notion of fairness. Libertarians, for example, would surely regard the original position as an unfair choice situation. It seems best, therefore, to forego any defense of the original position on grounds of fairness. Rather I contend that welfare liberals should acknowledge that the original position embodies a substantive conception of the good and then attempt to show how this conception can at least be practically reconciled with the basic requirements of other conceptions of the good.

R. M. Hare has also challenged the conditions imposed on the original position. According to Hare, (1977b) all that is needed to secure impartiality is "an economical veil" of ignorance that deprives persons in the original position only of the knowledge of each persons' particular nature and circumstances (including the knowledge of whether they are contemporaries) while giving them complete knowledge of the course of history and the present conditions of society, as well as unlimited general information. Confident that this economic veil is sufficient for impartiality, Hare sees no justification for Rawls's thicker veil of ignorance, which also deprives persons in the original position of the knowledge of the course of history and the present conditions of society.

But actually there would be no practical difference between the thicker and thinner veils of ignorance once choice in the original position is modified to apply to the moral problem of distant peoples and future generations. The reason for this is that once the moral relevance of distant peoples and future generations is taken into account, the additional information that the thinner veil of ignorance permits cannot be used to support inequalities on the grounds of maximizing utility, because meeting the basic needs of the now-expanded class of legitimate claimants would be seen to have greater utility. Only when we abstract from the moral problem of distant peoples and future generations do the two veils produce different practical results, but then the thinner veil would be morally objectionable because of the inequalities it would support on utilitarian grounds.

In conclusion, none of these challenges to grounding a Welfare Liberal Conception of Justice on an ideal of contractual fairness has been shown to be successful. Rather, what has been shown is that the ideal of contractual fairness supports a right to welfare and a right to affirmative action specified in terms of the satisfaction of a person's basic needs. In the next chapter we will consider a Feminist Conception of Justice that at first glance appears to take us beyond the requirements of a Welfare Liberal Conception.

Notes

1. Notice that I am claiming only that a welfare liberal ideal can be characterized as contractual fairness, not that it *must* be so characterized. Nevertheless, welfare liberals like Bruce Ackerman and Ronald Dworkin who have attempted to characterize the welfare liberal ideal differently have, it turns but, not departed radically from a contractual fairness formulation. See Ackerman (1980); and Dworkin (1981: 185–246, 283–345). See also Sterba (1986: 8–10).

2. In what follows I shall piece together an account drawing mainly on the articles Rawls has published since *A Theory of Justice*. In particular, see his (1974b); (1975a), (1975b), (1980), and (1982b). Of course, there other contemporary social contract theories, but these views are not offered as a proper blend of the libertarian's ideal of liberty and the socialist's ideal of equality. For example, in his most recent book, *Morality by Agreement* (1986), David Gauthier attempts to ground his social contract theory in rational self-interest; and James Buchanan and Gordon Tullock, in their co-authored *Calculus of Consent* (1962) and later works, seem to be trying to ground their social contract theory in the libertarian's ideal of liberty alone. For a discussion of Gauthier's book, see Chapter 11.

3. Rawls, "Kantian Constructivism in Moral Theory," p. 523 (my emphasis).

4. See Rawls (1971), pp. 150–61. See also his (1974a) and (1975a).

5. For the utilitarian view, see John C. Harsanyi (1976: chaps 4 and 5); Harsanyi, "Morality and the Theory of Rational Behavior," *Social Research* (1977); and Mueller, Tollison, and Willett (1974). For the compromise view, see Sterba (1974); (1980b: chap. 2); and (1981b). See also David Gauthier (1974); and Michael Gardiner (1975).

6. For the plausibility of interpreting primary goods in terms of utility, see Jan Narveson (1982: 139–40).

7. Kenneth Arrow, "Some Ordinalist—Utilitarian Notes on Rawls's Theory of Justice," *The Journal of Philosophy* 70 (1973): 245–63.

8. There will, however, be a need to revise somewhat the standard axioms of utility theory. See Amos Tversky, "A Critique of Expected Utility Theory: Descriptive and Normative Considerations," *Erkenntnis* (1975): 163–73.

9. For an earlier discussion of this point, see Sterba (1978b: 293–303).

10. See Rex Martin (1985: chap. 2).

11. Donella H. Meadows, Dennis L. Meadows, Jorgen Randers, and William W. Behrens, III, *The Limits to Growth*, 2nd ed. (New York, 1974), chaps. 3 and 4.

12. Indeed, right claims need not presuppose that there are any rightholders either in the present or in the future, as in the case of a right not to be born and a right to be born. On this point, see Chapter 8.

13. For a somewhat opposing view, see M. P. Golding, "Obligations to Future Generations," *The Monist* 56 (1972): 85–99.

14. The example is from Derek Parfit, who has drawn attention to the

underlying problem. See his "Rights, Interests and Possible Persons," in *Moral Problems in Medicine,* ed. Samuel Gorovitz et al. (Englewood Cliffs: Prentice-Hall, 1976).

15. By an argument combining elements of the ones employed against the libertarian in Chapters 7 and 8, I believe that it is possible to bring the libertarian and the welfare liberal views together on this point.

16. See also Sterba (1980b: 60*n*).

17. Bernard Williams has objected that when contractual ethical theory is applied widely to questions of distant peoples and future generations, it generates at most a nonagression treaty. (See his *Ethics and the Limits of Philosophy,* (Cambridge, Cambridge University Press, 1985) pp. 99–104). But if we can reasonably ascertain that certain goods and resources are required for the satisfaction of the basic needs of distant peoples and future generations, why should only a nonagression treaty emerge? And even if that were all that would emerge, our discussion of a Libertarian Conception of Justice in Chapter 7 would still show that such a treaty has welfare liberal implications.

18. My account shares much in common with David Braybrooke's extremely valuable study *Meeting Needs* (1987). Yet it is surprising that to determine a list of basic needs and what should be the level of provision, Braybrooke in this study appeals to what is acceptable to the person who "has the least rich List and the lowest Minimal Standards of Provisions" (p. 64). Braybrooke allows that such a list "may call for very low levels of provision— a monotonous diet, one companion; one brief period of recreation per week" (p. 231). Unlike appeals to the original position or even to the "ought" implies "can" principle that I use in Chapter 7, the standard that Braybrooke employs here seems to have little to morally recommend it.

19. See Old Age Insurance submitted to the Joint Economic Committee of the Congress of the United States in December 1967, p. 186; and *Statistical Abstracts of the United States for 1986,* p. 429.

20. See Sar Levitan, *Programs in Aid of the Poor,* 5th ed. (Baltimore, 1985), pp. 1–5; David Gordon, "Trends in Poverty," in *Problems in Political Economy: An Urban Perspective,* ed. David Gordon (Lexington, Mass., 1971), pp. 297–98; Arthur Simon, *Bread for the World* (New York, 1975), chap. 8.

21. S. Benn and R. S. Peters, *The Principles of Political Thought* (New York, Free Press, 1959), p. 167.

22. *Statistical Abstracts for 1986,* p. 445.

23. See Bernard Gendron, *Technology and the Human Condition* (New York, 1977), pp. 222–27.

24. Also see Bob Bergland, "Attacking the Problem of World Hunger," *The National Forum* 69, no. 2 (1979): 4.

25. Iris Young, "Self-Determination as a Principle of Justice," *The Philosophical Forum* (1979): 30–46; Amy Gutman (1980: 178–83).

26. Bergland, "Attacking the Problem of World Hunger," p. 4.

27. Diana Manning, *Society and Food* (Sevenoaks, Ky., 1977), p. 12; Simon, *Bread for the World,* p. 14.

28. Roger Revelle, "Food and Population," *Scientific American* 231 (September 1974): 168.

29. Lester Brown, "Population, Cropland and Food Prices," *The National Forum* 69, no. 2 (1979): 11–16.

30. Janet Besecker and Phil Elder, "Lifeboat Ethics: A Reply to Hardin," in *Readings in Ecology, Energy and Human Society: Contemporary Perspectives,* ed. William R. Burch, Jr. (New York, 1977), p. 229.

31. There definitely are numerous possibilities for utilizing more and more efficient means of satisfying people's basic needs in developed societies. For example, the American food industry manufactured, for the U.S. Agriculture Department, CSM, a product made of corn, soy and dried milk, which supplied all the necessary nutrients and 70 percent of the minimum calorie requirement for children. Impoverished children throughout the world, but not in the United States, received half a million pounds of this product in 1967—at a cost of two cents per day per child. See Nick Kotz, *Let Them Eat Promises* (Englewood Cliffs, N.J., Prentice-Hall, 1969), p. 125.

32. This point is developed in Chapter 8.

33. The rejected option seems to be the one preferred by Garrett Hardin. See his "Lifeboat Ethics: The Case Against Helping the Poor," in *World Hunger and Moral Obligations,* ed. William Aiken and Hugh La Follette (Englewood Cliffs, N.J., Prentice-Hall, 1977), pp. 12–21.

34. It is worth noting that this represents a significant departure from my earlier attempts to work out a Welfare Liberal Conception of Justice. In those attempts, I endorsed what I now call the compromise view over the maximin and utilitarian views. But then I identified the requirements of this view with a basic needs minimum, failing to see both that this minimum only becomes appropriate once the moral problem of distant peoples and future generations is taken into account, and that once this moral problem is taken into account, the three views coincide in their practical requirements.

35. Christopher Morris, "Existential Limits to the Rectification of Past Wrongs," *American Philosophical Quarterly* 21 (1984); George Sher, "Ancient Wrongs and Modern Rights," *Philosophy and Public Affairs* 9 (1980).

36. Alan Goldman, *Justice and Reverse Discrimination* (Princeton: Princeton University Press, 1979); Barry Gross, *Discrimination in Reverse: Is Turnabout Fair Play?* (New York, Prometheus, 1978).

37. See Bernard Boxill, "The Morality of Preferential Hiring," *Philosophy and Public Affairs* 7 (1978).

38. G. B. Thomas, "On Choosing a Morality," *Canadian Journal of Philosophy* 5 (1975); Marcus Singer (1976).

39. Robert Nozick (1974); and Michael Sandel (1982). For further discussion of this objection, see Chapters 6 and 10.

40. Robert Paul Wolff, *Understanding Rawls* (Princeton: Princeton University Press, 1977).

41. Nevertheless, Rawls persists in using this characterization; see (1980: 527).

42. For why this would be required of criminals, see Sterba, "Is There a Rationale for Punishment?" *American Journal of Jurisprudence* (1984).

5 / *Feminist Justice*

Contemporary feminists almost by definition seek to put an end to male domination and to secure women's liberation. To achieve these goals, many feminists support the political ideal of androgyny.[1] According to these feminists, all assignments of rights and duties are ultimately to be justified in terms of the ideal androgyny.[2]

The Ideal of Androgyny

How is the ideal of androgyny to be interpreted? In a well-known article, Joyce Trebilcot distinguishes two forms of androgyny (1977: 70–78). According to the first form, which postulates the same ideal for everyone, the ideal person "combines characteristics usually attributed to men with characteristics usually attributed to women." Thus, we should expect both nurturance and mastery, openness and objectivity, compassion and competitiveness from each and every person who has the capacities for these traits.

By contrast, the second form of androgyny does not advocate the same ideal for everyone, but rather a variety of options from "pure" femininity to "pure" masculinity. As Trebilcot points out, this form of androgyny shares with the first the view that biological sex should not be the basis for determining the appropriateness of gender characterization. It differs in that it holds that "all alternatives with respect to gender should be equally available to and equally approved for everyone, regardless of sex." (1977: 72)

It would be a mistake, however, to distinguish sharply between these two forms of androgyny. Properly understood, they are simply two different facets of a single ideal. For, as Mary Anne Warren has argued (1982: 178–79), the second form of androgyny is appropriate *only* "with respect to feminine and masculine traits which are largely matters of personal style and preference and which have little direct moral significance." When we consider so-called feminine and masculine *virtues,* however, the first form of androgyny is the one required because, other things being equal, the same virtues are appropriate for everyone.

63

We can formulate the ideal of androgyny even more abstractly so that it is no longer specified in terms of so-called feminine and masculine traits. For example, we can specify the ideal as requiring no more than that the traits that are truly desirable in society be available equally to both women and men, or in the case of virtues, inculcated equally in both women and men.

There is a problem, of course, in determining which traits of character are virtues and which traits are largely matters of personal style and preference. To make this determination, Trebilcot has suggested that we seek to bring about the second form of androgyny, where people have the option of acquiring the full range of so-called feminine and masculine traits (1977: 74–77). But surely when we already have good grounds for thinking that certain traits are virtues, such as courage and compassion, fairness and openness, there is no reason to adopt such a laissez-faire approach to moral education. Although, as Trebilcot rightly points out, proscribing certain options will involve a loss of freedom, nevertheless we should be able to determine at least with respect to some character traits when a gain in virtue is worth the loss of freedom. It may even be the case that the loss of freedom suffered by an individual now will be compensated for by a future gain of freedom to that same individual once the relevant virtue or virtues have been acquired.

So understood, the class of virtues will turn out to be those desirable traits that can be justifiably inculcated in both women and men. Admittedly, this is a restrictive use of the term *virtue*. In normal usage, "virtue" is almost synonymous with "desirable trait."[3] But there is good reason to focus on those desirable traits that can be justifiably enculcated in both women and men, so for the present purposes I will refer to this class of desirable traits as virtues.

Unfortunately, many of the challenges to the ideal of androgyny fail to appreciate how the ideal can be interpreted to combine a required set of virtues with equal choice from among other desirable traits. For example, some challenges interpret the ideal as attempting to achieve "a proper balance of moderation" among opposing feminine and masculine traits, and then question whether traits like feminine gullibility or masculine brutality could ever be combined with opposing gender traits to achieve such a balance.[4] Other challenges interpret the ideal as permitting unrestricted choice of personal traits and then regard the possibility of Total Women and Hells Angels androgynes as a *reductio ad absurdum* of the ideal.[5] But once it is recognized that the ideal of androgyny can be interpreted not only to require of everyone the same set of virtues, which need not be interpreted as means between opposing extreme traits, but also to limit everyone's choice simply to desirable traits, then such challenges to the ideal clearly lose their force.

Of course, anti-feminists might still challenge the ideal of androgyny on the grounds that the sex-based differences that the ideal seeks to eliminate are essential for sexual attraction or desire. Thus, anti-feminists might view the sex drive as totally passive, waiting to be triggered by gender traits different from those of the agent. So understood, different sex roles would be needed to provide guidance for a person's sex drive. Without such guidance, anti-feminists might claim, sexuality could be expected to diminish or even to atrophy.

In response to this challenge, it should be noted, first, that androgyny is compatible with considerable diversity in personal traits. Even if a wide variety of virtues were required of everyone, there would still be many desirable traits that people could adopt or not adopt as they see fit. In no sense would the adoption of the ideal of androgyny make us all the same. There would certainly be considerable diversity in personal traits for others to find sexually attractive.

Second and more important, as Robert Pielke has noted (1982: 187–96), to understand the impact of androgyny on sex attraction, we need to consider not whether stereotypical women and men would be sexually attracted to androgynes, but whether androgynes would be attracted to androgynes. And there seems to be no reason to think that persons who have renounced or never adopted stereotypical sexual roles would be sexually attracted to other persons who have also renounced or never adopted such roles.

Assuming then that sexual desire will persist among androgynes, the really important question is how reproduction and childcare would be affected by the adoption of the ideal. It seems clear that if the same virtues are to be expected of everyone and if the opportunities to acquire other desirable traits are to be equally available to everyone, then the burdens associated with reproduction and childcare must, as far as possible, be equally shared by everyone. Moreover, by requiring people to have the same virtues and by providing them with the same relevant opportunities, the ideal of androgyny would dramatically increase the possibilities for friendship because, as Aristotle says, friendship is most perfect among equals.

Actually, the main challenge raised by feminists to the ideal of androgyny is that the ideal is self-defeating in that it seeks to eliminate sexual stereotyping of human beings at the same time that it is formulated in terms of the very same stereotypical concepts it seeks to eliminate.[6] Or as Warren has put it, "Is it not at least mildly paradoxical to urge people to cultivate both 'feminine' and 'masculine' virtues, while at the same time holding that virtues ought not to be sexually stereotyped?"

In response one can argue that to build a better society we must begin where we are now, and people now speak of feminine and masculine character traits. Consequently, if we want to refer to such traits and formulate an ideal with respect to how they should be distributed in society, it is plausible to refer to them as they are now referred to, as feminine or masculine traits.

Alternatively, to avoid misunderstanding altogether, the ideal could be formulated in the more abstract way I suggested earlier so that it no longer specifically refers to so-called feminine or masculine traits. So formulated, the ideal requires that the truly desirable traits in society be equally available to both women and men, or in the case of virtues, equally inculcated in both women and men. So formulated the ideal would, in effect, require that men (*andros*) and women (*gyne*) have in the fullest sense an equal right to self-development. This is because if certain virtues are not equally inculcated in both women and men, or if other desirable traits are not equally available to both women and men, then everyone would not have an equal right to self-development.

So characterized the ideal of androgyny represents neither a revolt against so-called feminine virtues and traits nor their exhaltation over so-called masculine virtues and traits.[7] Accordingly, the ideal of androgyny does not view women's liberation as *simply* the freeing of women from the confines of traditional roles, thus making it possible for them to develop in ways heretofore reserved for men. Nor does the idea view women's liberation as *simply* the revaluation and glorification of so-called feminine activities, like housekeeping or mothering, or so-called feminine modes of thinking, as reflected in an ethic of caring. The first perspective ignores or devalues genuine virtues and desirable traits traditionally associated with women, while the second ignores or devalues genuine virtues and desirable traits traditionally associated with men. By contrast, the ideal of androgyny seeks a broader-based ideal for both women and men that combines virtues and desirable traits traditionally associated with women with virtues and desirable traits traditionally associated with men. Nevertheless, the ideal of androgyny will reject any so-called virtues or desirable traits tradition- ally associated with either gender that have supported discrimination or oppression against either gender.

When one relates this ideal of androgyny to the issues of welfare and affirmative action, it is clear that the ideal would require a right to welfare and a right to affirmative action. Contemporary feminists would surely want to distribute welfare checks to those who through no fault of their own could not meet their basic needs, and affirmation action acceptance letters to those who are presumed to be less qualified now because they were denied equal opportunity in the past. But at least some contemporary feminists would also want to claim that these rights do not go far enough to secure for everyone an equal right to self-development as required by the ideal of androgyny.

Defenses of Androgyny

There are various contemporary defenses of the ideal of androgyny. Some feminists have attempted to derive the ideal from a Welfare Liberal Conception of Justice; others have attempted to derive the ideal from a Socialist Conception of Justice. And still others, in the face of challenges to these two defenses, have attempted to provide a still more radical defense of the ideal. Let us briefly consider each of these defenses.

In attempting to derive the ideal of androgyny from a Welfare Liberal Conception of Justice, feminists have tended to focus on the right to equal opportunity that is a central requirement of a Welfare Liberal Conception of Justice.[8] Equal opportunity could be interpreted minimally as providing people only with the same legal rights of access to all advantaged positions in society for which they are qualified. But this is not the interpretation given by welfare liberals. In a Welfare Liberal Conception of Justice, equal opportunity is interpreted to require *in addition* the same prospects for success for all those who are relevantly similar. Where relevant similarity involves more than simply present qualifications. For example, Rawls claims (1971:73) that persons in his original position would favor a right to "fair equality of opportunity," which means that persons who have the same natural assets and the same willingness to use them would have the necessary resources to achieve similar life prospects.

The point feminists have been making is simply that failure to achieve the ideal of androgyny translates into a failure to guarantee equal opportunity to both women and men. The present evidence for this failure is the discrimination that exists against women in education, employment, and personal relations. Discrimination in education begins early in a child's formal educational experience when teachers and schoolbooks support different and less desirable roles for girls than for boys.[9] Discrimination in employment has also been well documented.[10] Women continue to earn only a fraction of what men earn for the same or comparable jobs; although women make up almost half of the paid labor force in the United States, 70 percent of them are concentrated in just twenty different job categories, only five more than in 1905.[11] Finally, discrimination in personal relations is the most entrenched of all forms of discrimination against women.[12] It primarily manifests itself in traditional family structures in which the woman is responsible for domestic work and childcare and the man's task is "to protect against the outside world and to show how to meet this world successfully."[13] In none of these areas, therefore, do women have the same prospects for success as men with similar natural talents and similar desires to succeed. Moreover, whenever women lack the desire to succeed in activities for which they have the native capabilities, we need to determine whether that lack of desire is due to previous failure to provide women with equal opportunities for acquiring the relevant desires. In such cases, affirmative action would be called for to rectify the past failure to provide equal opportunity.

Of course, contemporary welfare liberals have recognized the need to root out sexual discrimination in employment and to a lesser degree in education, but few have recognized a comparable need to root out discrimination in personal relations, particularly family life, in the name of equal opportunity.

Surprisingly, some welfare liberals have even seen the existence of the family as imposing an acceptable limit on the right to equal opportunity. Rawls, for example, claims (1971: 74):

> the principle of fair opportunity can be only imperfectly carried out, at least as long as the institution of the family exists. The extent to which natural capacities develop and reach fruition is affected by all kinds of social conditions and class attitudes. Even the willingness to make an effort, to try, and so to be deserving in the ordinary sense is itself dependent upon happy family and social circumstances. It is impossible in practice to secure equal chances of achievement and culture for those similarly endowed, and therefore we may want to adopt a principle which recognizes this fact and also mitigates the arbitrary effects of the natural lottery itself.

Thus, according to Rawls, since different families will provide different opportunities for their children, the only way to fully achieve "fair equality of opportunity" would require us to go *too far* and abolish or radically modify traditional family structures.

Yet others have argued that the full attainment of equal opportunity requires that we go even further and equalize people's native as well as their social assets.[14] For only when everyone's natural and social assets have been equalized would everyone have exactly the same chance as everyone else to attain the desirable social positions in society.

Of course, feminists have no difficulty recognizing that there are moral limits to the pursuit of equal opportunity. Accordingly, femininists could grant that other than the possibility of special cases, such as sharing a surplus organ like a second kidney, it would be too much to ask people to sacrifice their native assets to achieve equal opportunity.

Rawls, however, proposes to limit the pursuit of equal opportunity still further by accepting the inequalities generated by families in any given sector of society, provided that there is still equal opportunity between the sectors or that the existing inequality of opportunity can be justified in terms of its benefit to those in the least-advantaged position (1971: 300–301). Nevertheless, what Rawls is concerned with here is simply the inequality of opportunity that exists between individuals owing to the fact that they come from different families. He fails to consider the inequality of opportunity that exists in traditional family structures, especially between adult members, in virtue of the different roles expected of women and men. When viewed from the original position, it seems clear that this latter inequality of opportunity is sufficient to require a radical modification of traditional family structures, even if the former inequality, for the reasons Rawls suggests, does not require any such modifications.

Now feminists contend that when the right of equal opportunity endorsed by welfare liberals is correctly interpreted, the ideal of androgyny can be seen to follow in two ways. First, it would follow because the ideal requires that desirable traits be equally available to everyone. Second, it would follow because the ideal requires the same virtues of everyone, thereby equitably promoting whatever means are necessary for securing a right of equal opportunity for everyone.

Of course, it would be possible for women and men to acquire the same virtues and other desirable traits only insofar as they have the same requisite native capabilities. But in attempting to achieve the ideal of androgyny, it surely is reasonable at present for feminists to assume that the same range of native capabilities is generally found among women and men and, accordingly, to attempt to inculcate in them the same virtues and provide them with the same opportunities for acquiring other desirable traits. Insofar as women and men turn out to be unequal in their native capabilities, feminists could argue, the ideal of androgyny would not be jeopardized because it requires equal prospects only insofar as the relevant native capabilities of women and men are themselves equal.

Alison Jaggar, however, has questioned whether defenders of a Welfare Liberal Conception of Justice can consistently assume that the same range of native capabilities is generally found among women and men. (1983: 37–38). According to Jaggar, the welfare liberal's conception of human nature requires agnosticism on this point. Jaggar also challenges the adequacy of any attempt to derive the ideal of androgyny from a Welfare Liberal Conception of Justice, on the grounds that such a conception presupposes a completely ahistorical conception of human nature.(ibid.: 42–43).

Both of these criticisms seem misplaced when directed at attempts by contemporary welfare liberals to defend the ideal of androgyny. First, while it is true that welfare liberals in general deny that their view is based upon a full-fledged conception of human nature, it is surely open to them to claim that their partial account of human nature supports the assumption that the same range of native capabilities is generally found among women and men. As Jaggar notes (ibid.: 38), this was not John Stuart Mill's view, but surely contemporary welfare liberals begin with more knowledge of the native capacities of women as more opportunities open up to them than were available in Mill's time. Nor is there anything that is essential to a welfare liberal's account of human nature that demands agnosticism on this point.

Second, the Welfare Liberal Conception of Justice does not require that one endorse a completely ahistorical conception of human nature. Welfare liberals can certainly admit that human nature manifests itself in different ways in different social conditions. As Rawls has put it (1978: 55),

> everyone recognizes that the institutional form of society affects its members and determines in large part the kind of persons they want to be as well as the kind of persons they are. The social structure also limits peoples' ambitions and hopes in different ways; for they will with reason view themselves in part according to their position in it and take account of the means and opportunities they can realistically expect. So an economic regime, say, is not only an institutional scheme for satisfying existing desires and aspirations but a way of fashioning desires and aspirations in the future. More generally, the basic structure shapes the way the social system produces and reproduces over time a certain form of culture shared by persons with certain conceptions of their good.

Nor does the use of a hypothetical choice situation to model the welfare liberal's ideal of contractual fairness imply a completely ahistorical conception of justice. For the only knowledge that is discounted or abstracted from in reaching decisions in this choice situation is the knowledge that would prejudice one's choice or render unanimous agreement impossible. Thus, the knowledge of one's own particular natural and social assets would be excluded, but not the knowledge of the range of natural and social assets present in societies. Consequently, abstracting from such knowledge is perfectly compatible with recognizing that human nature is at least in part a social and historical product.

In addition, Jaggar's two criticisms seem strangely incompatible with one another. On the one hand, if welfare liberals are so agnostic with respect to human nature that they cannot even assume that women and men generally have the same range of native capabilities, it is hard to see how they can know enough about human nature to be able to endorse an ahistorical over a historical conception of human nature. On the other hand, if welfare liberals do know enough to be able to endorse an ahistorical conception of human nature, they should also know enough not to be agnostic concerning whether women and men generally have the same range of native capabilities. Fortunately, there is no similar incompatibility if we understand welfare liberals to be claiming that human nature is in part a historical and social product, and also that women and men generally have the same range of native capabilities.

Now the support for the ideal of androgyny provided by a Socialist Conception of Justice appears to be much more direct than that provided by a Welfare Liberal Conception of Justice.[15] This is because the Socialist Conception of Justice and the ideal of androgyny can be interpreted as requiring the very same equal right to self-development. What a Socialist Conception of Justice purports to add to this interpretation of the ideal of androgyny is an understanding of how the ideal is best to be realized in contemporary capitalist societies. For according to advocates of this defense of androgyny, the ideal is best achieved by socializing the means of production and satisfying people's non-basic as well as their basic needs. Thus, the general idea behind this approach to realizing the ideal of androgyny is that a cure for capitalist exploitation will also be a cure for women's oppression.

Yet many feminists have questioned whether this is the case.[16] Given that women's oppression predates capitalist oppression, why should we think that a response directed at the elimination of capitalist exploitation will also succeed in eliminating the oppression of women? Why not view women's oppression as a somewhat independent problem that can be partially remedied only by the elimination of capitalist exploitation?

Taking this criticism to heart, some feminists have argued that an adequate approach to achieving the ideal of androgyny must recognize that women's oppression is rooted not only in capitalist exploitation but also in human biology.[17] Some maintain that the biology of women, with its link to childbearing, makes them weaker and more vulnerable to exploitation by men. According to others, the biology of men makes them aggressive and dominating and leads them to oppress women. But whatever is the case, these defenders of the ideal of androgyny agree that the oppression of women that is rooted in human biology is not inevitable, because human biology itself is at least in part a social and historical product. As a consequence, these defenders of androgyny contend that the realization of the ideal will require not only the elimination of capitalist exploitation but also the transformation of human biology. As Alison Jaggar has suggested (1983: 132),

> This transformation might even include the capacities for insemination, for lactation and for gestation so that, for instance, one woman could inseminate another, so that men and nonparturitive women could lactate and so that fertilized ova could be transplanted into women's or even into

men's bodies. These developments may seem farfetched but in fact they are already on the technological horizon.

It would appear, therefore, that this approach to realizing the ideal of androgyny would lead us beyond the practical requirements of all three conceptions of justice that we have considered so far. In Chapter 9, I will argue that, contrary to appearances, this is not the case; the feminist ideal of androgyny can be practically reconciled with these other conceptions of justice. Yet before turning to the question of practical reconciliation, we need to set out the Communitarian Conception of Justice in the next chapter, noting that it too seems to go beyond the practical requirements of our other conceptions of justice.

Notes

1. Someone might object that if feminist justice is worth considering, why not racial justice? In principle I have no objection to a separate consideration of racial justice, although the main issues relevant to such a discussion have been taken up in discussions of the others conceptions of justice as a matter of course. By contrast, feminist justice raises new issues that have usually been ignored in discussions of the other conceptions of justice, and for that reason, I think, this conception of justice deserves separate consideration.

2. See, for example, Ann Ferguson (1977: 45–69); Mary Anne Warren (1982: 170); A. G. Kaplan and J. Bean, eds, *Beyond Sex-Role Stereotypes: Readings toward a Psychology of Androgyny* (Boston: Little, Brown, 1976); Andrea Dworkin (1974: Part 4).

3. On this point, see Edmund Pincoffs (1986: Chap. 5).

4. See, for example, Kathryn Pauly Morgan (1982: 256–57).

5. See, for example, Mary Daly, *Gyn-Ecology: The Meta-Ethics of Radical Feminism* (Boston: Beacon Press, 1978), p. xi.

6. Margrit Eichler, *The Double Standard* (New York, St. Martins Press, 1980), pp. 69–71; Elizabeth Lane Beardsley, (1982: 197–202); Mary Daly (1975: 20–40); and Janice Raymond (1975: 57–66).

7. For a valuable discussion and critique of these two viewpoints, see Iris Young, (1985: 173–83).

8. See, for example, Virginia Held (1984: esp. Chap. 11); Gloria Steinem (1970: 22–23); and Mary Jeanne Larrabee (1983: 18). See also National Organization for Women (NOW) Bill of Rights, and U.S. Commission on Civil Rights *Statement on the Equal Rights Amendment* (1978).

9. See, for example, Elizabeth Allgeier and Naomi McCormick (1983: Part 1).

10. See, for example Economic Agenda Working Group (1985); Jo Freeman (1984: Part 4); and *The Women's Movement: Agenda for the '80s* (an editorial research report) (Washington, D.C.: Congressional Quarterly, 1981).

11. Alison M. Jaggar and Paula Rothenberg (1984: 216).

12. See, for example, Joyce Trebilcot (1984); and Irene Diamond (1983).

13. Bruno Bettelheim, "Fathers Shouldn't Try to Be Mothers," *Parents Magazine* October 1956, pp. 40, and 126–129.

14. See Bernard Williams, "The Idea of Equality," in *Philosophy, Politics and Society,* 2nd ser. ed. Peter Ladett and W. G. Runciman (Oxford, Oxford University Press, 1969), pp. 110–31. For a literary treatment, see Kurt Vonnegut, Jr., "Harrison Bergeron," in *Welcome to the Monkey House* (New York, Dell, 1968), pp. 7–13.

15. See, for example, Ann Ferguson, (1977); and Evelyn Reed (1987: 229–36).

16. See Heidi Hartmann (1981), and other papers in *Women and Revolution,* ed. Sargent.

17. See, for example, Shulamith Firestone (1970); and Andrea Dworkin (1974: Part IV). See also Jaggar (1983: esp. Chap. 5).

6 / *Communitarian Justice*

As one might expect, many contemporary defenders of communitarian justice regard their conception of justice as rooted in Aristotelian moral theory. Like Aristotle, they endorse a fundamental contrast between human beings as they are and human beings as they could be if they realized their essential nature. Ethics is then viewed as a science that enables human beings to understand how they can make the transition from the former state to the latter. This view of ethics requires some account of potency to act and some account of the essence of human beings and the end (telos) they seek. Moreover, for human beings to make this transition from potency to act, a particular set of virtues is needed, and people who fail to acquire these virtues thereby fail to realize their true nature and reach their true end.

While many contemporary defenders of communitarian justice accept these elements of Aristotelian moral theory, many also agree with Alasdair MacIntyre that if Aristotelian moral theory is to be rationally acceptable, it must be refurbished in certain respects. Specifically, MacIntyre claims (1981) that Aristotelian moral theory must, first, reject any reliance on a metaphysical biology. Instead, MacIntyre proposes to ground Aristotelian moral theory on a conception of a practice. A practice, for MacIntyre, is "any coherent and complex form of socially established cooperative human activity through which goods internal to that form of activity are realized in the course of trying to achieve those standards of excellence which are appropriate to and partially definitive of that form of activity, with the result that human powers to achieve excellence, and human conceptions of the ends and goods involved are systematically extended (ibid.: 175). As examples of practices, MacIntyre cites arts, sciences, games, and the making and sustaining of family life.

MacIntyre then partially defines the virtues in terms of practices. A virtue such as courage, justice, or honesty is "an acquired human quality the possession and exercise of which tends to enable us to achieve those goods which are internal to practices and the lack of which prevents us from achieving any such goods (ibid.: 178). Mac-

Intyre admits, however, that the virtues that sustain practices can conflict (for example, courage can conflict with justice), and that practices so defined are not themselves above moral criticism (186–187).

Accordingly, to further ground the communitarian account, Mac-Intyre introduces the conception of a *telos* or good of a whole human life conceived as a unity (ibid.: 188–204). By means of this conception, MacIntyre proposes to morally evaluate practices and resolve conflicts between virtues. For MacIntyre, the *telos* of a whole human life is a life spent in seeking that telos; it is a quest for the good human life, and it proceeds with only partial knowledge of what is sought. Nevertheless, this quest is never undertaken in isolation, but always within some shared tradition (133–34, 167–68). Moreover, such a tradition provides additional resources for evaluating practices and for resolving conflicts while remaining open to moral criticism.

MacIntyre's characterization of the human *telos* in terms of a quest undertaken within a tradition marks a second respect in which he departs from Aristotle's view. This historical dimension to the human *telos*, which MacIntyre contends is essential for a rationally acceptable communitarian account, is absent from Aristotle's view.

A third respect in which MacIntyre's communitarian account departs from Aristotle's concerns the possibility of tragic moral conflicts. As MacIntyre points out (ibid.), Aristotle recognized only moral conflicts that are the outcome of wrongful or mistaken action. Yet Mac-Intyre, following Sophocles, wants to recognize the possibility of additional conflicts between rival moral goods that are rooted in the very nature of things. At the same time, MacIntyre wants to distinguish choice between such rival moral goods from choice between incommensurable premises (ibid.: 208). According to MacIntyre, the difference is that choice of one rival good does "nothing to diminish or derogate" the claims of the other upon the agent. The tragic chooser must simply recognize that she cannot do everything that she ought to do.[1]

By refurbishing Aristotle's view in these ways, MacIntyre hopes to avoid the radical disagreement, interminable arguments, and incommensurable premises that he claims characterize contemporary moral philosophy (1981: 241). These three features, MacIntyre claims (in chapter 7), are illustrated in the current debate between Robert Nozick and John Rawls. Thus Nozick argues for the libertarian view that principles of just acquisition and exchange set limits to the possibility of achieving certain distributive goals. According to Nozick, if the outcome of the application of the principles of just acquisition and exchange is severe inequalities in distribution, the toleration of such inequalities is the price to be paid for justice. By contrast, Rawls argues for the welfare liberal view that principles of just distribution set limits on the possibilities for acquisition and exchange. According to Rawls, if the outcome of the application of the principles of just distribution interferes with previous acquisition and exchange, the toleration of such interference is the price to be paid for justice.

For more than a decade, this Nozick-Rawls debate has engaged defenders on both sides, and certainly the debate has been characterized by radical disagreement and interminable arguments. But MacIntyre further claims that the debate proceeds from incommensurable premises. According to MacIntyre (1981: 229–31), Rawls's view is ultimately based on the principle that people's basic needs should be met, whereas Nozick's view is ultimately based on the principle that people should be able to keep what they legitimately acquire or earn and these two principles, MacIntyre contends, cannot be rationally weighed against each other and, hence, are incommensurable.

MacIntyre claims that this sad state of affairs in contemporary moral philosophy has its origin in the Enlightenment of the 17th and the 18th centuries (ibid.: Chapters 4 and 5). As MacIntyre tells the story, key philosophers of that period, such as David Hume and Immanuel Kant, attempted to provide a rational justification for morality while rejecting Aristotelian moral theory. These philosophers began with a conception of human nature as it is and attempted to derive therefrom a justification for adhering to everyday moral precepts. They attempted to show that some feature or features of human nature as it is would lead persons to endorse those everyday moral precepts. To ground morality, Hume appealed to human passions, and Kant to human reason. Yet MacIntyre argues that these attempts to ground morality not only failed but had to fail because by rejecting an Aristotelian conception of human nature as it should be and appealing only to human nature as it is, these attempts deprived themselves of what was needed to ground everyday moral precepts. According to MacIntyre, it is the failure of attempts to justify morality from the Enlightenment to the present that has led to the current predicament in contemporary moral philosophy. The only way out of this predicament, MacIntyre claims, is for contemporary moral philosophy to return to Aristotelian moral theory, the rejection of which has brought contemporary moral philosophy to its current sorry state.

While MacIntyre is more concerned to demonstrate the need to return to a Communitarian Conception of Justice based on a refurbished Aristotelian moral theory, John Finnis seeks to develop a more positive account of communitarian justice. According to Finnis (1980: 165), communitarian justice is what is required for the common good of one's communities, where the common good is a set of conditions that enables the members of communities to attain for themselves the basic goods for the sake of which they collaborate with each other in their communities. Finnis characterizes these basic goods as life, knowledge, play, aesthetic experience, friendship, religion, and practical reasonableness.[2] Any other goods we might recognize and pursue, Finnis states, will turn out to represent or be constituted by some or all of these basic goods.

In pursuing these basic goods, Finnis claims, we must adhere to requirements of practical reasonableness, the most important of which are the following: (a) no arbitrary preferences among these basic goods. (b) consequences should have limited relevance in moral decision-making. (c) Every basic good must be respected in every act. In large part, Finnis defends these requirements by attacking utilitarianism. Finnis seems to think that once utilitarianism is seen to be defective as a moral theory, the merits of his own view become apparent.

Finnis also contrasts his own account of basic human goods with Rawls's thin theory of the good. In Rawls's theory, basic human goods are generally useful means for the pursuit of whatever ends one may have. For Finnis, basic human goods are the ends for which we strive. But while this contrast does exist, there seems to be no reason why both Rawls and Finnis could not incorporate each other's account of basic human goods without affecting any substantial change in their conceptions of justice.

Where Finnis and Rawls do seem to disagree, however, is not with respect to the nature of basic human goods themselves, but rather with respect to the principles that apply to the pursuit of such goods. In particular, Finnis's requirements of practical reasonableness rule out the sacrifice of any basic good to achieve a greater total of basic goods. Thus, for Finnis, the end never justifies the means. By contrast, persons in Rawls's original position would surely sanction some such sacrifices provided there were a sufficiently large and widely distributed gain in basic human goods.

Another defender of communitarian justice who does not rule out such trade-offs of basic human goods is William A. Galston. According to Galston, the basic human goods are life, development, and happiness, and their relative priority varies with the circumstances. Yet, in general, Galston endorses the priority of life over development and happiness. Or, to put this priority somewhat differently, Galston claims (1980: Chapter 6) that only after needs have been satisfied does desert become the basis for the distribution of goods.

Galston does not balk at applying his conception of communitarian justice to distant peoples and future generations, and he recognizes that significant sacrifices are required of the members of economically developed societies if justice is to be done in these contexts.

Despite the fact that the practical requirements of Galston's conception of justice are quite similar to those that have been defended from welfare liberal and even libertarian starting points, Galston rejects any such foundation for his view. He rejects Rawls's theory because it makes justice the outcome of a choice, but he fails to see that this feature of Rawls's theory is in no way opposed to regarding justice as a natural duty that is independent of choice in everyday life. Galston also rejects Nozick's theory, because neither rights nor an ideal of liberty is an independent moral notion, but he fails to recognize that those who appeal to such notions to ground their conceptions of justice rarely claim such independence for these notions. Consequently, Galston's theoretical grounds for rejecting those conceptions of justice with which he shares the same practical recommendations are not persuasive.

Although not all the defenders of communitarian justice are explicit about their conception's practical requirements, those who are, like Finnis and Galston, would certainly agree that their ideal supports both a right to welfare and a right to affirmative action. These defenders of communitarian justice would definitely want to distribute welfare checks to those who through no fault of their own could not meet their basic needs and distribute affirmative action acceptance letters to those who are presumed to be less qualified now because they were denied equal opportunity in the past. Nevertheless, some defenders of this ideal would surely want to require more than just these rights. Finnis, for example, defends an absolute prohibition against doing evil that good may come of it, and applies this prohibition to a wide range of practices from abortion to warfare. MacIntyre thinks that a Communitarian Conception of Justice, reflecting a fuller conception of the good, will also support a much wider range of practical requirements than a Welfare Liberal Conception of Justice. So, at least initially, there appears to be serious practical conflicts between a Communitarian Conception of Justice and our other conceptions of justice.

Defenses of the Ideal

Given that a Communitarian Conception of Justice is not a widely endorsed ideal today, communitarians have frequently chosen to defend their conception by attacking other conceptions of justice and, by and large, they have focused their attacks on a Welfare Liberal Conception of Justice.

One of the best-known attacks of this sort has been put forth by Michale J. Sandel. Sandel claims that a Welfare Liberal Conception of Justice is founded upon an inadequate conception of the nature of persons, according to which none of the particular wants, interests, or ends that we happen to have at any given time constitute what we are essentially. According to this conception, we are independent of and prior to all such wants, interests, or ends. As Sandel points out, this conception of the nature of persons is similar in certain respects to Kant's doctrine of transcendental subjects of experience. Yet contemporary welfare liberals would not be particularly happy with the comparison, since they have attempted to give their conception an empirical rather than a transcendental foundation.

Sandel claims (1982: 179) that what is inadequate about this conception of the nature of persons is that

> we cannot regard ourselves as independent in this way without great cost to those loyalties and convictions whose moral force consists partly in the fact that living by them is inseparable from understanding ourselves as the particular persons we are—as members of this family or community or nation or people, as bearers of this history, as sons and daughters of that revolution, as citizens of this republic. Allegiances such as these are more than values I happen to have or aims I "espouse at any given time." They go beyond the obligations I voluntarily incur and the "natural duties" I owe to human beings as such. They allow that to some I owe more than justice requires or even permits, not by reason of agreements I have made but instead in virtue to those more or less enduring attachments and commitments which taken together partly define the person I am.

Thus, according to Sandel, the conception of the nature of persons required by a Welfare Liberal Conception of Justice is inadequate because it fails to take into account the fact that some of our wants, interests, and ends are, at least in part, constitutive of what we are essentially. Without these desires, interests, and ends, we would not be the same persons we presently happen to be.

Sandel contends that welfare liberals are led to rely upon this inadequate conception of persons for reasons that are fundamental to the conception of justice they want to defend. Specifically, welfare liberals want to maintain the priority of justice and, more generally, the priority of the right over the good. For example, according to Rawls (1971: 31), "The principles of right and so of justice put limits on which satisfactions have value; they impose restrictions on what are reasonable conceptions of one's good. We can express this by saying that in justice as fairness the concept of right is prior to that of the good."

To support these priorities, Sandel argues, welfare liberals are led to endorse this inadequate conception of the nature of persons. For example, Rawls argues (1971: 560):

> It is not our aims that primarily reveal our nature but rather the principles that we would acknowledge to govern the background conditions under

which these aims are to be found and the manner in which they are to be pursued. *For the self is prior to the ends which are affirmed by it;* even a dominant end must be chosen from among numerous possibilities. . . . We should therefore reverse the relation between the right and the good proposed by teleological doctrines and view the right as prior.

This passage shows, according to Sandel, that for welfare liberals, like Rawls, the priority of justice and the priority of the right are grounded in the priority of the self to its ends.

Furthermore, Sandel argues that welfare liberals are also led to rely upon this inadequate conception of the nature of persons because they believe that people's native assets should be regarded as common assets, on the grounds that no one deserves her or his particular set of native assets. To show that to regard native assets as common assets does not violate the Kantian injunction never to treat persons merely as means, Sandel claims that welfare liberals are required to conceive of persons as distinct from their assets, so that while their assets may be used simply as a means, they themselves would never be so used.

But, according to Sandel (1982: 79),

The notion that only *my assets* are being used as a means, not *me,* threatens to undermine the plausibility, even the coherence, of the very distinction it invokes. It suggests that . . . we can take seriously the distinction between persons only by taking metaphysically the distinction between a person and his attributes. But this has the consequence of leaving us with a subject *so* shorn of empirically-identifiable characteristics, . . . as to resemble after all a Kantian transcendent or disembodied subject.

Yet this is just the result that contemporary defenders of welfare liberal justice had hoped to avoid.

Another equally well known attack upon a Welfare Liberal Conception of Justice has been developed by Bernard Williams.[3] Williams's challenge is directed at a Welfare Liberal Conception of Justice both in its utilitarian and nonutilitarian formulations. Williams claims that both formulations require us to sacrifice our ground projects to a degree that is destructive of our personal integrity.[4] According to Williams (1981: 14),

A man who has such a ground project will be required by Utilitarianism to give up what it requires in a given case just if that conflicts with what he is required to do as an impersonal utility-maximizer when all the causally relevant considerations are in. That is a quite absurd requirement. But the Kantian, who can do rather better than that, still cannot do well enough. For impartial morality, if the conflict really does arise, must be required to win; and that cannot necessarily be a reasonable demand on the agent. There can come a point at which it is quite unreasonable for a man to give up, in the name of the impartial good ordering of the world of moral agents, something which is a condition of his having any interest in being around in that world at all.

Williams argues that what is objectionable about a Welfare Liberal Conception of Justice is the impartiality it requires. What is required is that we view the possible fulfillment of our own ground projects impartially along with the possible fulfillment of the ground projects of others. The effect of this on an agent, Williams claims (1973: 116–17), is

> to alienate him in a real sense from his actions and the source of his action in his own convictions. It is to make him into a channel between the input of everyone's objectives, including his own, and an output of optimific decision; but this is to neglect the extent to which *his* actions and *his* decisions have to be seen as the actions and decisions which flow from the projects and attitudes with which he is most closely identified. It is thus, in the most literal sense, an attack on his integrity.

Williams illustrates his objection to welfare liberalism in its utilitarian formulation by giving two hypothetical cases. In the first case George, an unemployed research chemist, can get a job in a firm specializing in research into chemical and biological warfare. If he does not take the job, his continued unemployment will cause serious hardship to his family and himself. If he does not take the job because he is opposed to chemical and biological warfare, another chemist who has no such moral qualms will take the job and carry it out with greater zeal than George.

In the second case an explorer, let us call her Janet, arrives in a South American village just as Pedro, an army officer, is about to kill a random group of twenty Indians in retaliation for protests against the local government. In honor of Janet's arrival, Pedro offers to spare nineteen of the twenty Indians if Janet will shoot one of the Indians.

Williams thinks that it is easy to determine the utilitarian resolution of these cases: George should take the job, and Janet should shoot one of the Indians. Williams rejects the utilitarian resolution of the first case, however; and while he accepts the utilitarian resolution of the second case, he thinks that arriving at that resolution should be agonizing rather than easy.

Williams's challenge to welfare liberalism, however, is not limited to its utilitarian formulation, because it is directed at welfare liberalism's requirment of impartiality—a feature that is shared by both the utilitarian and the nonutilitarian formulations of the view. Accordingly, Williams finds similar mistakes in nonutilitarian formulations of the view. Specifically, Williams cites Charles Fried's discussion of whether to save one's spouse rather than someone else from peril. Fried writes:

surely it would be absurd to insist that if a man could, at no risk or cost to himself, save one or two persons in equal peril, and one of those in peril was, say, his wife, he must treat both equally, perhaps by flipping a coin. One answer is that where the potential rescuer occupies no office such as that of captain of a ship, public health official or the like, the occurrence of the accident may itself stand as a sufficient randomizing event to meet the dictates of fairness, so he may prefer his friend, or loved one. Where the rescuer does occupy an official position, the argument that he must overlook personal ties is not unacceptable.

What is mistaken about Fried's resolution of this case, Williams contends, is Fried's concern to show that from an impartial standpoint his particular resolution is fair. For Williams, this is just one of these situations where impartiality and fairness have to give way to a person's ground projects, which, in this case, is a preference for the welfare of one's own spouse (1981: 17–18). According to Williams, the failure to appreciate the moral significance of one's ground projects is the fundamental defect of a Welfare Liberal Conception of Justice.

It would seem, therefore, that unless Sandel's and Williams's communitarian challenges to a Welfare Liberal Conception of Justice can be answered, there would be no possibility of reconciling a Communitarian Conception of Justice with our other four conceptions. In Chapter 10, I hope to show not only that there are acceptable answers to these challenges, but that the apparent conflicts between the requirements of a Communitarian Conception of Justice and our other four conceptions can be practically reconciled.

Notes

1. Notice that there is no contradiction in accepting MacIntyre's view that the tragic chooser cannot do everything that she ought to do and endorsing the "ought" implies "can" principle, provided that the former is understood to apply only to "prima facie" oughts and the latter only to "conclusive" oughts.

2. For Finnis, religion is simply the good of raising and reflecting upon the questions concerning the origin and order of the whole cosmos, however these questions are answered (1980: 89–90).

3. Bernard Williams (1973); Williams (1981, Chap. 2).

4. For Williams, a ground project is a project that is closely related to one's existence and to a significant degree gives a meaning to one's life. See 1981: 12, 14.

5. Charles Fried, *An Anatomy of Values* (Cambridge: Harvard University Press, 1970), p. 227.

PART II

Practical Reconciliation

7 / *From Liberty to Welfare and Beyond*

We have now considered all five conceptions of justice and related them to the issues of welfare and affirmative action. The Libertarian Conception appears to reject both a right to welfare and a right to affirmative action. The Socialist, Feminist, and Communitarian Conceptions appear to endorse both a right to welfare and a right to affirmative action, but seem to regard these rights as only minimal requirements. Only the Welfare Liberal Conception of Justice appears to endorse both a right to welfare and a right to affirmative action as its principal requirements.

Faced with such striking differences, some philosophers, like Alasdair MacIntyre (1981), have argued that these conceptions of justice cannot be reasonably reconciled. I contend, however, that a reconciliation is possible, at least at the practical level. Practically speaking, it does not matter whether one endorses liberty, equality, contractual fairness, androgyny, or the common good as the ultimate political ideal, because all five of these ideals, when correctly interpreted, support the same practical requirements, which, it turns out, happen to be the standardly acknowledged practical requirments of a Welfare Liberal Conception of Justice: a right to welfare and a right to affirmative action.

Spencerian Libertarians

To see that this is the case, let us begin with the ideal of liberty as defended by Spencerian Libertarians. As we have seen, Spencerian Libertarians maintain that this ideal neither justifies a right to welfare nor a right to affirmative action.

To see how Spencerian Libertarians must specify their basic right to liberty, consider a typical conflict situation between the rich and the poor. In this conflict situation, the rich, of course, have more than enough resources to satisfy their basic needs. By contrast, the poor lack the resources to meet their most basic needs, even though they have tried all the means available to them that libertarians regard as legitimate for acquiring such resources. Under such circumstances, Spencerian Libertarians usually maintain that the rich should have the liberty to use their resources to satisfy their luxury needs if they so wish. Spencerian Libertarians recognize that this liberty might well be enjoyed at the expense of the satisfaction of the most basic needs of the poor; they simply reason that liberty always has priority over other political ideals, and since they assume that the liberty of the poor is not at stake in such conflict situations, they conclude that the rich should not be required to sacrifice their liberty to the cause of meeting the basic needs of the poor.

Of course, Spencerian Libertarians allow that it would be nice of the rich to share their surplus resources with the poor, just as Milton Friedman would allow that it would be nice of you to share a found $100 with your friends, and nice of the rich-islanded Robinson Crusoe to share his resources with the poor-islanded Robinson Crusoes. Nevertheless, according to Spencerian Libertarians, such acts of charity are not required because the liberty of the poor is not thought to be at stake in such conflict situations.

In fact, however, the liberty of the poor is at stake in such conflict situations: What is at stake is the liberty of the poor not to be interfered with when taking what is necessary to satisfy their basic needs from the surplus possessions of the rich. Spencerian Libertarians would want to deny that the poor have this liberty. But how could they justify such a denial? As I specified this liberty of the poor, it is not a positive right, but a negative right of noninterference. Nor will it do for Spencerian Libertarians to appeal to a right to life or a right to property to rule out such a liberty because, on the Spencerian view, liberty is basic and all other rights are derived from a right to liberty. Clearly, what Spencerian Libertarians must do is recognize the existence of such a liberty, but then claim that it conflicts with other liberties of the rich. But when Spencerian Libertarians are brought to see that this is the case, they are genuinely surprised, perhaps even rudely awakened, for they had not previously seen the conflict between the rich and the poor as a conflict of liberties.[1]

When the conflict between the rich and the poor is viewed as a conflict of liberties, we can say either that the rich should have the liberty not to be interfered with when using their surplus resources for luxury purposes, or that the poor should have the liberty not to be interfered with when taking from the rich what they require to meet their basic needs. If we choose one liberty, we must reject the other. What needs to be determined, therefore, is which liberty is morally preferable: the liberty of the rich or the liberty of the poor.

The "Ought" Implies "Can" Principle

I submit that the liberty of the poor, the liberty not to be interfered with when taking from the surplus resources of others what is required to meet one's basic needs, is morally preferable to the liberty of the rich, the liberty not to be interfered with when using one's surplus resources for luxury purposes. To see that this is the case, we need only appeal to one of the most fundamental principles of morality, one that is common to all political perspectives, the "ought" implies "can" principle.[2] According to this principle, people are not morally required to do what they lack the power to do or what would involve so great a sacrifice that it would be unreasonable to ask them to perform such an action.[3]

For example, suppose I promised to attend a departmental meeting on Friday, but on Thursday I am involved in a serious car accident that puts me into a coma. Surely it is no longer the case that I ought to attend the meeting now that I lack the power to do so. Or suppose that on Thursday I develop a severe case of pneumonia, for which I am hospitalized. Surely I could claim that I no longer ought to attend the meeting on the grounds that the risk to my health involved in attending is a sacrifice that it would be unreasonable to ask me to bear. In this latter case, the underlying rationale is that I cannot be morally required to sacrifice my most fundamental interests so that others can satisfy their peripheral interests, unless I have freely chosen to make such a sacrifice.

It seems clear that the poor have it within their power to relinquish such an important liberty as the liberty not to be interfered with when taking from the rich what they require to meet their basic needs. Nevertheless, it would be unreasonable to ask them to make so great a sacrifice. In the extreme case, it would involve asking the poor to sit back and starve to death. Of course, the poor may have no real alternative to relinquishing this liberty. To do anything else may involve worse consequences for themselves and their loved ones and may invite a painful death. Accordingly, we may expect that the poor would acquiesce, albeit unwillingly, to a political system that denied them the right to welfare supported by such a liberty, at the same time that we recognize that such a system imposed an unreasonable sacrifice upon the poor—a sacrifice that we could not morally blame the poor for trying to evade.[4] In an analogous situation, we might expect that a woman whose life was threatened would submit to a rapist's demands, at the same time that we recognize the utter unreasonableness of those demands.

By contrast, it would not be unreasonable to ask the rich to sacrifice the liberty to meet their luxury needs so that the poor can have the liberty to meet their basic needs.[5] Of course, we might expect that the rich, for reasons of self-interest and past contribution, might be disinclined to make such a sacrifice. We might even suppose that the past contribution of the rich provides a good reason for not sacrificing their liberty to use their surplus for luxury purposes. Yet, unlike the poor, the rich could not claim to relinquish such a liberty involved so great a sacrifice that it would be unreasonable to ask them to make it; unlike the poor, the rich could be morally blameworthy for failing to make such a sacrifice.

Consequently, if we assume that, however we specify the requirements of morality cannot violate the "ought" implies "can" principle, it follows that, despite what Spencerian Libertarians claim, the basic right to liberty endorsed by them, as determined by a weighing of the relevant competing liberties according to the "ought" implies "can" principle, actually favors the liberty of the poor over the liberty of the rich.

What if Spencerian Libertarians objected to this conclusion, claiming that it would be unreasonable to ask the rich to sacrifice the liberty to meet some of their luxury needs so that the poor could have the liberty to meet their basic needs? As I have pointed out, Spencerian Libertarians don't usually see the situation as a conflict of liberties, but suppose they did. How plausible would such an objection be? Not very plausible at all, I think.

For consider: what are Spencerian Libertarians going to say about the poor? Isn't it clearly unreasonable to ask the poor to sacrifice the liberty to meet their basic needs so that the rich can have the liberty to meet their luxury needs? Isn't it clearly unreasonable to ask the poor to sit back and starve to death? If it is, then, there is no resolution of this conflict that would be reasonable to ask both the rich and the poor to accept. But that would mean that the libertarian ideal of liberty cannot be a moral ideal that resolves conflicts of interest in ways that it would be reasonable to ask everyone affected to accept. Therefore, as long as Spencerian Libertarians think of themselves as putting forth such a moral ideal, they cannot allow that it would be unreasonable *both* to ask the rich to sacrifice the liberty to meet their luxury needs in order to benefit the poor and to ask the poor to sacrifice the liberty to meet their basic needs in order to benefit the rich. But I submit that if one of these requests is to be judged reasonable, then, by any neutral assessment, it must be the request that the rich sacrifice the liberty to meet their luxury needs so that the poor can have the liberty to meet their basic needs; there is no other plausible resolution, if Spencerian Libertarians intend to be putting forth a moral ideal that reasonably resolves conflicts of interest.

But might not Spencerian Libertarians hold that putting forth a moral ideal means no more than being willing to universalize one's fundamental commitments? Surely we have no difficulty imagining the rich willing to universalize their commitments to relatively strong property rights. At the same time, we have no difficulty imagining the poor and their advocates being willing to universalize their commitments to relatively weak property rights. Consequently, if the libertarian moral ideal is interpreted in this fashion, it would not be able to provide a basis for resolving conflicts of interest between the rich and the poor in a reasonable fashion. But without such a basis for conflict resolution, how could societies flourish, as libertarians claim they would, under a minimal state?[6] For societies to flourish in this fashion, the libertarian ideal must resolve conflicts of interest in ways that it would be reasonable to ask everyone affected to accept. But as we have seen, that requirement can be satisfied only if the rich sacrifice the liberty to meet their luxury needs so that the poor can have the liberty to meet their basic needs.[7]

It should also be noted that this case for restricting the liberty of the rich depends upon the willingness of the poor to take advantage of whatever opportunities are available to them to engage in mutually beneficial work, so that failure of the poor to take advantage of such opportunities would normally cancel or at least significantly reduce the obligation of the rich to restrict their own liberty for the benefit of the poor.[8] In addition, the poor would be required to return the equivalent of any surplus possessions they have taken from the rich once they are able to do so and still satisfy their basic needs. Nor would the poor be required to keep the liberty to which they are entitled. They could give up part of it, or all of it, or risk losing it on the chance of gaining a greater share of liberties or other social goods.[9] Consequently, the case for restricting the liberty of the rich for the benefit of the poor is neither unconditional nor inalienable.

Even so, Spencerian Libertarians would have to be disconcerted about what turns out to be the practical upshot of taking a right to liberty to be basic. For Spencerian Libertarians contend that their political ideal would support a right to welfare only when constraints are "illegitimately" interpreted to include both positive and negative acts by others that prevent people from doing what they are otherwise able to do. By contrast, when constraints are interpreted to include only positive acts, Spencerian Libertarians contend, no such right to welfare can be justified.

Nevertheless, the foregoing argument demonstrates that this view is mistaken. For even when the interpretation of constraints favored by Spencerian Libertarians is employed, a moral assessment of the relevant completing liberties still requires an allocation of liberties to the poor that will be generally sufficient to provide them with the goods and resources necessary for satisfying their basic needs.

Now one might think that once the rich realize that the poor should have the liberty not to be interfered with when taking from the surplus possessions of the rich what they require to satisfy their basic needs, they should stop producing any surplus whatsoever. Yet this would be in their interest only if (a) the rich did not enjoy producing a surplus, (b) the recognition of the rightful claims of the poor would exhaust the surplus of the rich, and (c) the poor would never be in a position to be obligated to repay what they appropriated from the rich. Fortunately for the poor, all these conditions are unlikely to obtain. But suppose they did. Wouldn't the poor be justified in appropriating, or threatening to appropriate, even the nonsurplus possessions of those who can produce more in order to get them to do so? Surely this would not seem to be an unreasonable imposition on those who can produce more, because it would not seem to be unreasonable to require them to be more productive when the alternative is that the poor would, through no fault of their own, fail to meet their basic needs. And surely, it would be unreasonable to require the poor to do anything less when their basic needs are at stake.

Nevertheless, it may be the case that those who can produce more can only bring themselves to do so if they can benefit themselves to a degree that requires the denial of the basic needs of at least some of the poor. And this could be the case, even if the poor are in a position to appropriate or threaten to appropriate the nonsurplus possessions of those who can be more productive. In circumstances like these, however, there simply is no moral resolution, that is, no resolution that would be reasonable to ask all parties to accept. As we noted before, such possibilities conflict with the libertarian assumption that societies can flourish under the limited constraints of a minimal state, because, in order for this assumption to hold, the libertarian ideal must resolve conflicts of interest in ways that it would be reasonable to ask everyone affected to accept. In cases of conflict, this requries that the rich and talented sacrifice the liberty to fulfill their need for luxury so that the poor and untalented can have the liberty to meet their basic needs.

This is an important conclusion in our assessment of the libertarian ideal, because it shows that ultimately the right of the poor to appropriate what they require to meet their basic needs does not depend, as many have thought, upon the talented having sufficient self-interested incentives to produce a surplus. All that is necessary is that the talented can produce a surplus and that the poor cannot meet their basic needs in any other way.

Of course, there will be cases where the poor fail to satisfy their basic needs, not because of any direct restriction of liberty on the part of the rich but because the poor are in such dire need that they are unable even to attempt to take from the rich what they require to meet their basic needs. In such cases, the rich would not be performing any act of commission that prevents the poor from taking what they require. Yet even in such cases, the rich would normally be performing acts of commission that prevent other persons from aiding the poor by taking from the rich's own surplus possessions. And when assessed from a moral point of view, restricting the liberty of these other persons would not be morally justified for the very same reason that restricting the liberty of the poor to meet their own basic needs would not be morally justified: it would not be reasonable to ask all of those affected to accept such a restriction of liberty.

The Benefit of the Poor

Nevertheless, Spencerian Libertarians might respond that even supposing a right to welfare could be morally justified on the basis of the liberty of the poor not to be interfered with when taking from the rich in order to meet their basic needs and the liberty of third parties not be interfered with when taking from the rich to provide for the basic needs of the poor, the poor still would be better off without the enforcement of such a right.[10] For example, it might be argued that when people are not forced through taxation to support a right to welfare, they are both more productive, since they are able to keep more of what they produce, and more charitable, since they tend to give more freely to those in need when they are not forced to do so. As a result, so the argument goes, the poor would benefit more from the increased charity of a libertarian society than they would from the guaranteed minimum of a welfare state.

Yet, surely it is difficult to comprehend how the poor could be better off in a libertarian society, assuming, as seems likely, that they would experience a considerable loss of self-respect once they had to depend upon the uncertainties of charity for the satisfaction of their basic needs without the protection of a guaranteed minimum. It is also difficult to comprehend how people who are presently so opposed to a guaranteed minimum would turn out to be so charitable to the poor in a libertarian society.

Moreover, in a libertarian society, the provision of welfare would involve an impossible problem in coordination. For if the duty to provide welfare to the poor is at best supererogatory, as libertarians claim, then no one can legitimately force anyone who does not consent to provide such welfare. The will of the majority on this issue could not legitimately be imposed upon dissenters.[11] Assuming then that the provision of welfare requires coordinated action on a broad front, such coordination could not be achieved in a libertarian society because it would first require a near unanimous agreement of all its members.[12]

Nevertheless, it might still be argued that the greater productivity of the more talented people in a libertarian society would provide increased employment opportunities and increased voluntary welfare assistance which would benefit the poor more than a guaranteed minimum would in a welfare state. But this simply could not occur. For if the more talented members of a society provided sufficient employment opportunities and voluntary welfare assistance to enable the poor to meet their basic needs, then the conditions for invoking a right to a guaranteed minimum in a welfare state would not arise, since the poor are first required to take advantage of whatever employment opportunities and voluntary welfare assistance are available to them before they can legitimately invoke such a right. Consequently, when *sufficient* employment opportunities and voluntary welfare assistance obtain, there would be no practical difference in this regard between a libertarian society and a welfare state, since neither would justify invoking a right to a guaranteed minimum. Only when *insufficient* employment opportunities and voluntary welfare assistance obtain would there be a practical difference between a libertarian society and a welfare state, and then it would clearly benefit the poor to be able to invoke the right to a guaranteed minimum in a welfare state. Consequently, given the conditional nature of the right to a guaranteed minimum, and the practical possibility, and in most cases, the actuality of insufficient employment opportunities and voluntary welfare assistance obtaining, there is no reason to think that the poor would be better off without the enforcement of a right to welfare.[13]

In brief, if a right to liberty is taken to be basic, then, contrary to what Spencerian Libertarians claim, not only would a right to welfare be morally required but also such a right would clearly benefit the poor.

Lockean Libertarians

Let us now consider the view of those libertarians who take a set of rights, typically including a right to life and a right to property, as basic and then interpret liberty as being unconstrained by other persons from doing what one has a right to do. According to this view, a right to life is understood as a right not be killed unjustly, and a right to property is understood as a right to acquire goods and resources either by initial acquisition or voluntary transactions. To evaluate this view, we need to determine first what is entailed by these basic rights.

Presumably, a right to life understood as a right not to be killed unjustly would not be violated by defensive measures designed to protect one's person from life-threatening attacks.[14] Yet would this right be violated when the rich prevent the poor from taking what they require to satisfy their basic needs? Obviously, as a consequence of such preventive actions poor people sometimes do starve to death. Have the rich, then, in contributing to this result, killed the poor, or simply let them die; and, if they have killed the poor, have they done so unjustly?

Sometimes the rich, in preventing the poor from taking what they require to meet their basic needs, would not in fact be killing the poor, but only causing them to be physically or mentally debilitated. Yet since such preventive acts involve resisting the life-preserving activities of the poor, when the poor do die as a consequence of such acts, it seems clear that the rich would be killing the poor, whether intentionally or unintentionally.

Of course, Lockean Libertarians want to argue that such killing is simply a consequence of the legitimate exercise of property rights, and hence not unjust. To understand why Lockean Libertarians are mistaken in this regard, we first need to see that there are two competing interpretations of the property rights on which the Lockean view is grounded. According to the first interpretation, a right to property is *not* conditional upon whether other persons have sufficient opportunities and resources to satisfy their basic needs. This view holds that the initial acquisitions and voluntary transactions of some can leave others, through no fault of their own, dependent upon charity for the satisfaction of their most basic needs. By contrast, according to the second interpretation, initial acquisitions and voluntary transactions can confer the title of property on all goods and resources except those surplus goods and resources of the rich that, after voluntary welfare assistance is taken into account, are required to satisfy the basic needs of those poor who through no fault of their own lack the opportunities and resources to satisfy their own basic needs. As we noted in the case of the Spencerian view, there were two interpretations of the basic right to liberty on which the view is grounded: one interpretation which ignores the liberty of the poor not be interfered with when taking from the surplus possessions of the rich what they require to meet their basic needs, and the other interpretation which gives that liberty priority over the liberty of the rich not be interfered with when using their surplus for luxury purposes. Here too there are two interpretations of the right to property: the Lockean view is grounded: one interpretation which regards the right to property as *not* conditional upon the resources and opportunities available to others, and the other interpretation which regards the right to property as conditional upon the resources and opportunities available to others. And just as in the case of the Spencerian view, here we need to appeal to that fundamental principle of morality, the "ought" implies "can" principle, to decide which interpretation is morally acceptable.

It is clear that only the unconditional interpretation if property rights would generally justify the killing of the poor as a legitimate exercise of the property rights of the rich. Yet it would be unreasonable to ask the poor to accept anything other than some version of the conditional interpretation of property rights. Moreover, according to the conditional interpretation, it does not matter whether the poor would actually die or are only physically or mentally debilitated as a result of such acts of prevention. Either result would preclude property rights from arising. Of course, the poor may have no real alternative to acquiescing to a political system modeled after the unconditional interpretation of property rights, even though such a system imposes an unreasonable sacrifice upon them—a sacrifice that we could not blame them for trying to evade. At the same time, although the rich would be disinclined to do so, it would not be unreasonable to ask them to accept a political system modeled after the conditional interpretation of property rights—the interpretation favored by the poor.

Consequently, if we assume that however else we specify the requirements of morality, they cannot violate the "ought" implies "can" principle, it follows that, despite what Lockean Libertarians claim, the right to life and the right to property endorsed by them actually support a right to welfare.

Some libertarians have claimed to have found support for the unconditional interpretation of property rights in a quasi-Aristotelian ideal of human flourishing.[15] To quote Douglas Rasmussen: "just as human flourishing is the ultimate end or value of all human choices so must it also be that individual human beings exercising their own choices (and not those of others)."[16] According to these libertarians, property rights grounded in this ideal of human flourishing are unconditional even when there are circumstances in which they can be disregarded. Such circumstances are characterized as emergencies, and emergencies are defined, according to Rasmussen, as circumstances where it is impossible for the well-being of every person to be pursued and at the same time not interfere wtih the negative rights of others. Rasmussen further adds that "it makes no sense to say that the negative rights of others ought to be respected, if the terms under which negative rights are justified, viz., the pursuit of well-being, require that negative rights be ignored."[17]

But this appears to be an extremely strong condition on the applicability of negative rights in general and property rights in particular. According to this condition, respect for property rights must serve the well-being of all the relevant parties before such rights would be in force. Of course, this condition on the applicability of property rights could easily be satisfied if the notion of a person's well-being were already understood to be morally loaded, in the strongest possible sense. For example, if a person's well-being were defined in terms of respect for property rights, then clearly a person's well-being would always require respect for such rights. Even if the connection between a person's well-being and respect for property rights were not that close—as would be the case, for example, if a person's well-being were understood to involve simply having a good moral character—the requirement that property rights be respected might still not be that difficult to derive.[18]

But this is not the way that Rasmussen and other libertarians want to ground their account of property rights. Rather, they want to ground their account either in a morally neutral notion of a person's well-being or, at least, in a notion of well-being that is morally loaded in only a fairly weak sense. According to this weak sense, it does not follow from the fact that certain actions are morally good for people to do or refrain from doing that other people would be justified in forcing them to do or refrain from doing those actions. Rather, all that anyone would be justified in enforcing is what can be clearly shown to serve a person's well-being specified in a morally neutral sense.

This helps explain the attraction that some libertarians, such as Eric Mack and Tibor Machan, seem to feel for ethical egoism, because that view also justifies its requirements in terms of a morally neutral account of well-being.[19] The problem with basing a theory of rights on such an account of a person's well-being, however, is that each person will have reason to respect the rights of such a theory only to the extent that her interests are served by respecting those negative rights. If her interests are served well, she will have strong reasons to respect those rights, and if her interests are served poorly, she will have little or no reason to respect those rights.

Libertarians tend to recognize this consequence for their theory of negative rights with respect to emergency situations in which all parties affected have good reason not to respect the negative rights of others.[20] Tibor Machan, for instance, discusses the following example, drawn from Mack:

> consider the case of two men adrift on the open sea with a plank which can support only one man. Let us assume that in this case it serves the wellbeing of each man to survive, even if this survival costs the other's life. In this case, there is only one possible series of actions for each man that is sufficient for achieving his wellbeing. These actions are necessary for each of the men. In such an emergency case, rights are significantly absent. Each man ought, given the individualist principle and the assumptions in the case, to seek his own survival at the expense of the other. But neither can be said to have a right to survival. For to ascribe this right

> to either party would be to ascribe to the other party the obligation to allow the first party's survival at the expense of his own life. But the second party cannot be obligated to allow this, since we know that, given the individualist principle, he ought not to allow it.[21]

Machan agrees with Mack that in such cases negative rights do not apply, but only Mack seems to have recognized that inequalities between the rich and the poor can create analogous situations where the poor lack sufficient reason in terms of their own well-being for respecting the negative rights of the rich.[22] In such cases as well, Mack allows that rights are significantly absent.

Unfortunately, the situation is far worse for this attempt to ground a theory of negative rights on a morally neutral account of a person's well-being. For in addition to the implications of examples of the sort just discussed, it is also the case that unless a person's well-being is *best* served by respect for a particular system of negative rights, she will have good reason not to respect that system, either in whole or in part.

Nor will it do simply to point out, as Rasmussen has, that self-directedness or autonomy is constitutive of a person's well-being, whereas food, clothing, shelter, and the like are necessary conditions for a person's well-being. Indeed, both are required for a person's well-being, and the degree of self-directedness or autonomy that is allowed some people, particularly the rich with respect to their surplus possessions, will determine how the poor will do with respect to their own well-being.[23] So if a theory of negative rights is to be justified in terms of serving the well-being of all the relevant parties, the rights sanctioned by that theory must *best* serve the well-being of *all* those parties.

Needless to say, this is a very difficult condition to fulfill. In fact, it is not clear that any system of rights would best serve the well-being of all the relevant parties. One system would best serve the well-being of some, another system would best serve the well-being of others, but it just seems unlikely that any system of rights would best serve the well-being of *all* the relevant parties! And if this is the case, it has devastating consequences for the theory of negative rights these libertarians want to defend. Unconditional rights of this theory would be, for the most part, inapplicable because the condition for their applicability—that respect for them best serves the well-being of all the relevant parties—would rarely, if ever, obtain. Certainly this would be a theory of unconditional rights in name only if there ever was one.

Of course, libertarians failing to support unconditional negative rights on a neo-Aristotelian or egoistic account of human flourishing might simply choose to be egoists and thereby claim for themselves greater "liberties" than even their libertarian perspective allows. Fortunately or unfortunately, depending upon one's perspective, this choice provides no escape, because in Chapter 11 I derive the "ought" implies "can" principle which, we have seen, supports a right to welfare from an account of rationality that is acceptable to the egoist. So even egoists are committed to endorsing the same rights that, I have argued, libertarians are committed to endorsing when their view is understood as a moral ideal.

A Right to Affirmative Action

By a similar argument that weighs the conflicting liberties or rights involved, it can be shown that an ideal of liberty also supports rights to basic educational and job opportunities and, when such opportunities have been denied in the past, supports a right to affirmative action. For when people are denied basic educational and job opportunities, they are denied the liberty to use surplus resources that could be utilized to fulfill their basic needs. And when people who have suffered this kind of discrimination in the past are denied affirmative action, they are denied the liberty to use just the sort of resources that would have been available to them but for the denial of basic educational and job opportunities in the past. In both of these cases, therefore, it would be unreasonable to ask people to accept such denials of liberty.

Now it is possible that libertarians, convinced to some extent by the above arguments, might want to accept a right to welfare and a right to basic educational and job opportunities, but still want to reject a right to affirmative action for the following reasons: (a) that although serious deprivation of basic educational and job opportunities has occurred in the past, it is enough that we don't deny people such opportunities anymore; we don't need to provide affirmative action as well; (b) that although it was wrong to deprive people of basic educational and job opportunities in the past, affirmative action is also wrong in that it deprives white males of legitimate opportunities, and two wrongs don't make a right.[24]

The problem with the first reason is that it is an inconsistent stance since it affirms a right to basic educational and job opportunities but then, by ruling out a right to affirmative action, denies one form of redress that is appropriate when one has been discriminated against in the past. This is not to deny that other forms of redress, such as educational and job-training programs, are not also appropriate. In fact, when people have been rendered unqualified because of past discrimination, educational and job-training programs seem to be the most appropriate form of redress. But when people who have suffered from past discrimination are still qualified and have the capacity to become, in short order, at least as qualified as those over whom they would be preferred, affirmative action does seem to be the appropriate response to past discrimination.

The problem with the second reason attributed to libertarians is that it assumes that the most qualified white males have a right to be preferred, regardless of how they came by their qualifications. If, however, the most qualified white males have attained their qualifications by benefiting from past discrimination, surely they cannot justifiably complain if they are simply deprived of their unfair advantage. Of course, there may be some loss to society as a whole if the most qualified are not advanced; but the loss here should be minimal if those who are selected for affirmative action have the capacity to become, in short order, as qualified as those over whom they are preferred. Moreover, to seek to regress past discrimination with generalized remedial educational and job-training programs open to all would be more costly still.

Nor would it do for libertarians to endorse a right to the opportunity that is necessary for the satisfaction of one's basic needs and a corresponding right to affirmative action, and then deny that there is a right to equal opportunity and a corresponding right to affirmative action. For such a view is plausible only if we restrict the class of morally legitimate claimants to those within a given (affluent) society, for only then would a right to equal opportunity be different from the right to the opportunity necessary for the satisfaction of people's basic needs. But once it is recognized that the class of morally legitimate claimants includes distant peoples and future generations, even libertarians should grant that guaranteeing the opportunity necessary for the satisfaction of their basic needs to all morally legitimate claimants would lead to providing them all with roughly equal opportunity.

What these arguments show, therefore, is that a Libertarian Conception of Justice supports the same practical requirements as a Welfare Liberal Conception of Justice. In particular, both favor a right to welfare and a right to affirmative action when there has been a denial of equal basic educational and job opportunities in the past.

Some Further Objections

It might be objected that the rights that have been established against the libertarian are not the same as the rights endorsed by the welfare liberal. We could mark this difference by referring to the rights that have been establish against the libertarian as "negative welfare rights" and by referring to the rights endorsed by the welfare liberals as "positive welfare rights." The significance of this difference is that a person's negative welfare rights can be violated only when other people through acts of commission interfere with the exercise of those rights, whereas a person's positive welfare rights can be violated by such acts of commission as well as by acts of omission. Nonetheless, this difference will have little practical import. For once the libertarians come to recognize the legitimacy of the negative welfare rights I've defended, then in order not to be subject to the discretion of rightholders in choosing when and how to exercise these rights, libertarians will tend to favor the only morally legitimate way of preventing the exercise of such rights: they will institute adequate positive welfare rights that will then take precedence over the exercise of negative welfare rights. Accordingly, if libertarians adopt this morally legitimate way of preventing the exercise of such rights, they will end up endorsing the same sort of institutions favored by welfare liberals.

It might also be objected that while I have shown that libertarians must endorse rights to welfare and affirmative action, these rights are not as extensive as the rights to welfare and affirmative action endorsed by welfare liberals. This is true. The libertarian's ideal of liberty does not always support as high a minimum as the welfare liberal ideal of fairness. Under the Welfare Liberal Conception of Justice, the minimum for particular circumstances is determined by what individuals in a Rawlsian choice situation would favor, or alternatively by what would maximize utility. Under the Libertarian Conception of Justice, the minimum for particular circumstances is determined by what the "ought" imples "can" principle requires, and this, in effect, is determined by what is necessary to meet the basic needs of the poor, because nothing less would be reasonable to ask the poor to accept. By contrast, the Welfare Liberal Conception of Justice, restrictively applied within an affluent society, would require a much higher minimum. Nevertheless, when both ideals are applied without restriction to determine the conclusive obligations people have not only to their fellow citizens but also to distant peoples and future generations, both ideals would tend to coalesce on a basic needs minimum.

Finally, it is important to note that to achieve a practical reconciliation, I have accepted for the sake of argument the libertarian's distinction between commissions and omissions. As the libertarian employs this distinction, acts of omission are never morally blameworthy or punishable unless they are somehow grounded in acts of commission. For example, failing to fulfill the conditions of a contract is blameworthy or punishable only of one previously agreed to abide by those conditions, and neglecting to care for one's children is blameworthy or punishable only if one previously committed oneself to caring for them. Put another way, the libertarian holds that duties to perform some positive action, that is positive duties, always have their origin in acts of free choice.

Notice that this libertarian view is also much stronger than the view that negative duties have priority over positive duties, or that killing is morally worse than letting die because the latter view allows that failing to fulfill a positive duty or letting someone die can be blameworthy or punishable even when it is not grounded in an act of commission. But while I think there is some basis for the priority of negative duties over positive duties, I see no grounds for making the radical distinction endorsed by libertarians. Since the other four conceptions of justice allow that omissions that are not grounded in commissions can still be morally blameworthy or punishable, I take them to be superior to the libertarian perspective in this regard. For example, it certainly seems to me that failing to feed hungry people can be morally blameworthy or punishable even when one is neither interfering with them nor interfering with anyone who wishes to help them (possibly because in the circumstances no one wishes to help them). Yet it is difficult to convince libertarians that their view is mistaken in this regard. Fortunately, the above argument shows that we don't have to convince libertarians that their view is unsound, because it is possible to agree with them on practical requirements without having to deny that one's own perspective represents a better grasp of the relevant moral reality.

Other Attempts to Derive a Welfare Liberal Program

Needless the say, there have been other attempts to get libertarians to acknowledge a welfare liberal program. One such attempt seeks to determine the distribution of liberties and rights on the basis of what will least frustrate people's desires or what will minimize their disutility. Ernest Loevinsohn adopts this standard in arguing against the libertarian's opposition to a right to welfare. He claims (1977: 234) that when redistribution from the rich to the poor is justified, "the transfer of property brings about a decrease in the extent of the recipient's unsatisfied desires for items of property, and this decrease outweighs any increase in unsatisfied desires resulting from the transfer. So if the redistributive alternative is chosen then overall there will be less unsatisfied desire for items of property than on the non-redistributive alternative."

But it is unlikely that libertarians would endorse this standard to arbitrate conflicts between the rich and the poor. For even when the standard is limited to acts of commission, as Loevinsohn proposes, libertarians could still object to its utilitarian character. By contrast, the "ought" implies "can" principle does not regard just any elimitable dissatisfaction as a basis for welfare rights: the dissatisfaction must constitute an unreasonably severe sacrifice for at least some members of a society before the "ought" implies "can" principle would support welfare rights. Consequently, while libertarians can reject a standard of minimizing disutility as begging the question against their view, they cannot similarly reject an appeal to the "ought" implies "can" principle.

Another attempt to get libertarians to acknowldge a welfare liberal program seeks to deny the moral relevance of the commission/omission distinction on which libertarians standardly rely to support their commitment to an ideal of negative liberty over ideals of positive liberty. According to this view, any attempt to invest such a distinction with moral significance is doomed to failure, because a similar causality underlies both types of actions.[25] In particular, this view holds that we are just as much a cause of a person's death when we kill as when we let die. From which John Harris claims it follows that "in whatever sense we are morally responsible for our positive actions, in the same sense we are morally responsible for our negative actions" (Harris 1974: 211). Hence, according to this view, there is little basis for the libertarian's prohibition of acts of commission but not acts of omission when they both have the same consequences.

Nevertheless, this view fails to distinguish between the standard causal role played by acts of omission and acts of commission in the production of consequences for which people are morally responsible. For acts of omission causally contribute to the production of such consequences by failing to prevent a causal condition sufficient to produce those consequences, as in failing to save a person from drowning, while acts of commission causally contribute to the production of such consequences by creating a causal condition sufficient to produce those consequences, as in poisoning a person's food.[26] Thus, to take only the fact that both acts of omission and acts of commission contribute to such consequences to be morally relevant and to ignore the different ways in which both types of acts causally contribute to such consequences is to beg the question against libertarians and others who want to morally distinguish between these two types of acts. It seems best, therefore, to proceed as we have and base a justification for a welfare liberal program on an interpretation of constraints of liberty (and violations of rights) that involves only acts of commission for which people are morally responsible.

Still another attempt to derive a welfare liberal program from libertarian premises has been developed by Hillel Steiner.[27] Steiner's defense is directed primarily at Spencerian Libertarians and, hence, he takes a right to equal liberty as basic. Steiner contends that such a right requires an unlimited right to the fruits of one's labor once natural resources have been justly distributed. Accordingly, he focuses on what would be a just distribution of such resources. Steiner claims that previous attempts to specify a just distribution of natural resources are flawed because they preclude historically later persons from exercising the same right of initial acquisition. To avoid this result, Steiner claims, we need to view society as a joint stock company that leases its assets to persons for a limited period of time, which never exceeds a person's lifetime. On this view, each person can be seen as having an equal right that none of society's assets be disposed of without his or her consent, which is a right everyone could conceivably exercise (Steiner 1980: 259). Moreover, the effective exercise of such a right would be sufficient to ground a welfare liberal program.

An obvious merit of Steiner's defense is that it forces libertarians to explain how it is possible for everyone to exercise their rights equally. Yet because Steiner renounces any attempt to assess rights or liberties according to their value (ibid.: 245–46), all that libertarians need to do to turn aside his critique is to characterize their view as providing a right that everyone equally can exercise. This can be done by incorporating a right of acquisition within a more general right to property, which allows property to be acquired either by initial acquisition or by voluntary agreement. Then libertarians could claim that this more general disjunctive right can be possessed and exercised by all equally, despite the fact that its exercise is compatible with the poor being unable to satisfy even their most basic needs when the rich have sufficient surplus resources to satisfy most of their luxury needs.

To avoid this consequence, we need to assess the value of liberties at least to the degree that we can reject distributions of "equal liberty" whose liberties are immensely valuable to some but of little value to others. And it is obvious that one way to so assess the value of liberties is to appeal, as we have done, to the "ought" implies "can" principle. For it is only by evaluating the distribution of liberties (and rights) in some such fashion that we can support a welfare liberal program on a libertarian foundation.

Yet another attempt to derive a welfare liberal program from a libertarian foundation begins with the libertarian's endorsement of various civil and political rights, such as the rights of freedom of speech, press, assembly, due process, and equality before the law. It is then argued that because the effective exercise of these rights requries adequate social and economic resources, libertarians should be committed to guaranteeing such resources to each and every person. Allen Buchanan, for example, has defended just such provisions of resources (in Buchanan 1981) on grounds of fairness. Yet given the intimate connection between ideals of fairness and rights to welfare and affirmative action, such a defense appears to beg the question against the libertarian view.[28] A better approach would be to argue that libertarians should be committed to the provision of resources necessary to secure an effective exerise of at least those civil and political rights, such as due process and equality before the law, that relate to the imposition of significant burdens and penalties. For surely it would not be reasonable to ask people to accept the imposition of significant burdens and penalties unless they have been guaranteed an effective exercise of the rights of due process and equality before the law. But, again, this is to appeal to the "ought" implies "can" principle. Nor can it be objected that the "ought" implies "can" principle is itself a standard of fairness, since there are many impositions of burdens, which while they accord with the principle, are still unfair either because they are unequal or because they result from arbitrary procedures.

This argument, however, would not equally support the provision of resources necessary for the effective exercise of other civil and political rights, such as the rights of freedom of speech, press, and assembly. For the exercise of these rights relates not so much to the imposition of burdens and penalties in society as to the distribution of benefits. For this reason, the "ought" implies "can" principle is less likely to call for the provision of resources necessary for the effective exercise of civil and political rights of this sort. Nevertheless, effective exercise of such rights is still likely to result indirectly from the application of the principle in the case of distant peoples and future generations.

In summary, it seems clear that none of the four alternative attempts to get libertarians to endorse a welfare liberal program is preferable to the one defended in this chapter. The first attempt, by appealing to a utilitarian standard of minimizing dissatisfaction or disutility, begs the question against the libertarian view. The second attempt does the same by ignoring the possible moral relevance of the different causal roles played by acts of commission and acts of omission in the production of consequences for which people are morally responsible. The third attempt fails because it disallows any assessment of liberties according to their value. The fourth attempt, when reconstructed so as not to appear to beg the question against the libertarian view, justifies a provision of resources necessary for the effective exercise of the civil and political rights endorsed by libertarians only by appealing to some fundamental moral principle like the "ought" implies "can" principle. Hence, the approach taken in this chapter of beginning with a basic right to liberty or, alternatively, with a basic set of rights, like the right to life and the right to property, and then appealing the "ought" implies "can" principle appears to be the best way of providing a libertarian foundation for a welfare liberal program. In the next chapter, we will see how a welfare liberal program can also be given a socialist foundation.

Notes

1. See John Hospers, (1971: Chap. 7); and Tibor R. Machan (1975: 213–22).
2. Alvin Goldman, *A Theory of Human Action* (Englewood Cliffs: Prentice-Hall, 1970), pp. 208–15; William Frankena, "Obligation and Ability," in *Philosophical Analysis,* ed. Max Black (Ithaca: Cornell University Press, 1950), pp. 157–75. Judging from some recent discussions of moral dilemmas by Bernard Williams and Ruth Marcus, one might think that the "ought" implies "can" principle would be useful only for illustrating moral conflicts rather than resolving them. (See Bernard Williams, Chap. 11 and 12; Ruth Marcus, "Moral Dilemmas and Consistency," *The Journal of Philosophy* 17 [1980]: 121–26). See also Terrance C. McConnell, "Moral Dilemmas and Consistency in Ethics," *Canadian Journal of Philosophy* 8 (1978): 269–87. But this is only true if one interprets the "can" principle to exclude only "what a person lacks the power to do." If one interprets the "can" to exclude, in addition, "what would involve so great a sacrifice that it would be unreasonable to ask the person to do," then the principle can be used to resolve moral conflicts as well as state them. Nor would libertarians object to this broader interpretation of the "ought" implies "can" principle, since they do not ground their claim to liberty on the existence of irresolvable moral conflicts.

This broader interpretation of the "ought" implies "can" principle is also a natural extension of the narrower interpretation of the principle. For while the narrower interpretation excludes from the domain of obligation actions that are logically, physiologically, and psychologically impossible to perform, the broader interpretation excludes as well actions that are morally impossible because it is contrary to reason to ask people to do them. It would also be a mistake to reject this broader interpretation of the "ought" implies "can" principle on grounds of egoism, as some libertarians might want to do, because as I will explain in Chapter 11, the principle under this interpretation is derived from assumptions the egoist must accept.

3. I first appealed to this interpretation of the "ought" implies "can" principle to bring libertarians around to the practical requirements of welfare liberalism in an expanded version of an article entitled "Neo-Libertarianism," which appeared in the fall of 1979. In 1982, T. M. Scanlon in "Contractualism and Utilitarianism" appealed to much the same standard to arbitrate the debate between contractarians and utilitarians. In my judgment, however, this standard embedded in the "ought" implies "can" principle can be more effectively used in the debate with libertarians than in the debate with utilitarians, because sacrifices libertarians standardly seek to impose on the less advantaged are more outrageous and, hence, more easily shown to be contrary to reason.

4. See Sterba "Is There a Rationale for Punishment?," *The American Journal of Jurisprudence* (1984).

5. By the liberty of the rich to meet their luxury needs I continue to mean the liberty of the rich not to be interfered with when using their surplus possessions for luxury purposes. Similarly, by the liberty of the poor to meet

their basic needs I continue to mean the liberty of the poor not to be interfered with when taking what they require to meet their basic needs from the surplus possessions of the rich.

6. As further evidence, notice that those libertarians who justify a minimal state do so on the grounds that such a state would arise from reasonable disagreements concerning the application of libertarian rights. They do not justify the minimal state on the grounds that it would be needed to keep in submission large numbers of people who could not come to see the reasonableness of these rights.

7. Alan Brown (1986: 170–72, 195) has argued that the rich would gain more from their increased social relations with the poor than they would lose from failing to be able to satisfy their own luxury needs. It is obvious that if this were the case, the "ought" implies "can" principle would lead more straightforwardly to a right to welfare, because such a right would be in the interests of both the rich and the poor. But unless we add some "moral benefit" to recognizing an adequate right to welfare, as Brown clearly does not want to do (see pp. 158–59), then it is difficult to view the recognition of such a right as not requiring a net sacrifice from the rich. In addition, my argument rests upon the claim that the net sacrifice the rich would suffer from recognizing an adequate right to welfare is not significant enough to violate the "ought" implies "can" principle, whereas the sacrifice the poor would suffer in the absence of such a right is significant enough to violate that principle.

8. The employment opportunities offered to the poor must be honorable and supportive of self-respect. To do otherwise would be to offer the poor the opportunity to meet some of their basic needs at the cost of denying some of their other basic needs.

9. The poor cannot, however, give up the liberty to which their children are entitled.

10. See John Hospers, "The Libertarian Manifesto," in *Morality in Practice,* 2nd ed. James P. Sterba (Belmont, Calif.: Wadsworth, 1981), especially p. 33.

11. Sometimes advocates of libertarianism inconsistently contend that the duty to help others is supererogatory, but that a majority of a society could justifiably enforce such a duty on everyone. See Theodore Benditt, "The Demands of Justice," in *Economic Justice,* ed. Diana Meyers and Kenneth Kipnis (Totowa: Rowman & Allanheld, 1985), pp. 108–20.

12. Sometimes advocates of libertarianism focus on the coordination problems that arise in welfare states concerning the provision of welfare and ignore the far more serious coordination problems that would arise in a nightwatchman state. See Burton Leiser, "Vagrancy, Loitering and Economic Justice," in Meyers and Kipnis, eds., *Economic Justice,* pp. 149–60.

13. It is true, or course, that if the rich could retain the resources that are used in a welfare state for meeting the basic needs of the poor, they might have the option of using those resources to increase employment opportunities beyond what obtains in any given welfare state, but this particular way of increasing employment opportunities would be counterproductive with respect to meeting basic needs overall, and particularly counterproductive with respect to meeting the basic needs of those who cannot work.

14. See Sterba, "Moral Approaches to Nuclear Strategy: A Critical Evaluation," *Canadian Journal of Philosophy,* 12 (1986), Special Issue. 75–109.

15. For example, Tibor Machan (1975); Eric Mack, "Individualism, Rights and the Open Society," in *The Libertarian Alternative,* ed. Tibor Machan

(Chicago: Nelson-Hall, 1977), pp, 21–37; idem, "How to Derive Libertarian Rights," in *Reading Nozick,* ed. Jeffrey Paul (Totowa: Rowman & Littlefield, 1981), pp. 286–302; and Douglas Rasmussen, "A Groundwork for Rights: Man's Natural End," *Journal of Libertarian Studies* (1980): 65–76.

16. Douglas Rasmussen and James P. Sterba (1987: 56). In private correspondence, Tibor Machan has distinguished between emergencies that arise from natural causes and those that arise from "political tyrannies" or from other human causes. Machan suggests that only emergencies of the first sort need concern libertarians. But unless the victims of an emergency are morally responsible for their fate, then, it seems to me, others have at least a prima facie obligation not to interfere with relief efforts, even when those relief efforts happen to be utilizing their own surplus possessions.

17. Ibid., p. 68.

18. The difficulty with this approach, however, is that it may beg the question against opponents.

19. See Tibor Machan, "Recent Work on Ethical Egoism," *American Philosophical Quarterly* 16 (1979): 1–15.

20. For example, see Mack, "Individualism, Rights and the Open Society," pp. 29ff; Machan, "Human Rights: Some Points of Clarification," *Journal of Critical Analysis* 5 (1975: 30–39.

21. Mack, "Individualism, Rights and the Open Society," p. 29.

22. Mack (1977) A shorter version of this paper appeared under the same title in *Justice and Economic Distribution,* ed. John Arthur and William Shaw (Englewood Cliffs: Prentice-Hall, 1978), pp. 183–93.

23. In fact, while severe inequalities persist, there will be an inverse relationship between the amount of self-directedness or autonomy the rich are permitted to achieve and the amount of self-directedness or autonomy the poor are allowed to achieve.

24. These are stances that some libertarians have taken in conversation when I confronted them with the above arguments.

25. John Harris (1980: 58).

26. Of course, sometimes a person who performs an act of omission that contributes to the production of consequences for which the person is responsible may do so as part of a larger act of commission, which is a sufficient causal condition for the production of those consequences. And sometimes a person who performs an act of commission that contributes to the production of consequences for which the person is responsible does so as part of a larger act of omission, which simply fails to prevent those consequences. On this point see O. H. Green (1980); and Raziel Abelson, "To Do or Let Happen," *American Philosophical Quarterly* 19 (1982).

27. See the following articles by Hillel Steiner; (1974–75), (1977a), (1977b), and (1980).

28. Of course, libertarians do need to provide some account of an ideal of fairness, but a well-grounded critique of libertarianism should not begin with an ideal whose interpretation is widely contested. I made this mistake in "Neo-Libertarianism" (1978). But see its expanded version in *Justice: Alternative Political Perspectives,* ed. James P. Sterba (1979), especially pp. 185–86.

8 / Socialism with a Liberal Face

Let us now turn to the Socialist Conception of Justice. The Socialist Conception, you will recall, did endorse a right to welfare and a right to affirmative action, but it appeared to endorse these rights only as minimal requirements. In addition, socialists maintain that we are also required to meet nonbasic needs and to socialize the means of production.

Nevertheless, I contend that once we see how demanding the requirements of a Welfare Liberal Conception of Justice are, (a) the additional requirement to meet nonbasic needs will be seen to have little application, and (b) the additional requirement to socialize the means of production will be seen to be completely unnecessary.

The Requirement to Meet Nonbasic Needs

In support of the first contention, recall that in Chapter 3 I argued that a Welfare Liberal Conception of Justice requires not only that a welfare minimum be provided in our own society, but also that we take what steps we can to provide both a welfare minimum to the needy in other societies and the resources that will be required so that future generations will be able to meet their basic needs. This welfare minimum, I claimed, can be specified in terms of the satisfaction of people's basic needs. According to this standard, people are guaranteed the goods and resources necessary to meet the normal costs of satisfying their basic needs in the society in which they live. While granting that this way of specifying a social minimum introduces variation into the costs of satisfying such needs, I argued that the practice of utilizing more and more efficient means of satisfying people's basic needs in developed societies would appear to have the effect of equalizing the normal costs of meeting people's basic needs across societies. More significant still, the scope of the satisfaction of nonbasic needs would have to be drastically limited to meet the basic needs of existing as well as future generations. As a consequence, once we distribute goods and resources in accordance with a Welfare Liberal Conception of Justice so as to meet the basic needs of existing and future generations, there should be little left over for the satisfaction of nonbasic needs, as a Socialist Conception of Justice requires.

This way of reconciling a welfare liberal and a socialist conception of justice has been challenged by Michael Walzer. Walzer contends that, especially in the international arena, we lack a set of common meanings or shared values to ground the rights of distant peoples and future generations to have their basic needs satisfied. On Walzer's view, we have shared values when we are strongly motivated to act upon those values or, as he would put it, when those values are actually reflected in our choices.[1] Since there is no general tendency among people in affluent societies to recognize welfare rights for distant peoples and future generations, Walzer contends that we lack the shared values to ground such rights.

But why should the existence or justification of specific rights depend upon a general tendency among people to respect those rights? No one would deny that it is easier to get people to respect specific rights if they already have the propensity to do so. But even when people lack the propensity, they still can be brought to respect specific rights by educational or coercive means, provided they have the capacity to do so. Thus, in order to get people to respect specific rights all that is absolutely necessary is that they have the capacity to respect those rights; they need not also have the propensity to do so.

In fact, provided that people have the capacity to respect specific rights, most relevant to the justification of those rights are the reasons that can be given for or against actualizing that capacity. This is not to deny that people's propensities for respecting specific rights are not also relevant in this regard. Yet because these propensities may be ill formed or underdeveloped in various ways, they are never decisive by themselves with respect to the justification of such rights. That is why, in arguing for the justification of the welfare rights of distant peoples and future generations in Chapter 4, I implicitly assumed that people had the capacities for respecting such rights, and I simply sought to show that such rights were required by the welfare liberal ideal of contractual fairness. I argued that when judged from the perspective of the original position, the satisfaction of the basic needs of existing and future generations has precedence over the satisfaction of nonbasic needs, even when most people lacked the propensity (but not the capacity) to respect this priority. I now claim that because the welfare rights of distant peoples and future generations can be supported in this fashion, it is possible to reconcile a Welfare Liberal and a Socialist Conception of Justice.

But what about Walzer's own attempt to reconcile these two conceptions of justice? As we saw in Chapter 3, Walzer argues that welfare and security should be distributed on the basis of need and that the sphere of democratic control extends not only to cities and towns, but also to firms and factories. Yet it is clear that these arguments would have little force if they required that people already have the propensity (and not just the capacity) to act in accord with their premises. Yet if we evaluate the arguments in terms of how compelling they are from a welfare liberal perspective, they do seem to have considerable force, and they would be even more forceful still if, in order to take into account the welfare rights of distant peoples and future generations, we restricted their scope to basic needs and interests. But to do that is simply to combine Walzer's argument with my own argument for reconciling a Welfare Liberal and a Socialist Conception of Justice.

Now it should be pointed out that while my own argument for practical reconciliation does not assume that people have the propensity to respect the welfare rights of distant peoples and future generations, the absence of that propensity does create a practical problem. The problem is how to get people to respect those rights. It is a problem of incentive, and it seems to me that its solution must rely heavily upon moral incentives; people have to be strongly motivated on moral grounds to produce according to their ability so that everyone's basic needs can be met. Such a solution requires that once people realize that their most fundamental political ideals demand respect for the welfare rights of distant peoples and future generations, a sufficient number of them should be willing to take steps to acquire the appropriate propensities in this regard. If a sufficient number are willing, then it would be possible to bring others into conformity by educational or coercive means.

Of course, to some extent it may be possible to rely upon self-interested incentives to motivate the more talented. This would involve making jobs as intrinsically rewarding as possible as well as offering greater income to the more talented to get them to use their talents fully. But any inequalities of income must be kept limited if everyone's basic needs are to be met. This is because, while it is theoretically possible to have significant income differentials while respecting the welfare rights of distant peoples and future generations, this cannot be done in practice because of limited goods and resources. Hence, the only morally adequate solution to the problem of incentive is to limit income differentials, make jobs as intrinsically rewarding as possible, and then rely heavily on moral incentives to get people to produce according to their abilities so everyone's basic needs can be met.

For all practical purposes, the argument from the welfare rights of distant peoples and future generations is sufficient to show that, once the demands of a Welfare Liberal Conception of Justice are met, there would be very few goods and resources left over for the satisfaction of nonbasic needs. So this part of the argument for practical reconciliation of a Welfare Liberal and a Socialist Conception of Justice could stop here. Nevertheless, it is possible to derive additional practical implications from the welfare liberal ideal that link it even more closely with the socialist ideal of equality.

Specifically, it can be shown that if one endorses a strong welfare requirement such as

1. the welfare rights of distant peoples and future generations,

as consistent welfare liberals and libertarians (in view of the arguments of Chapter 7) must do, and also accept

2. an obligation not to bring into existence persons who would lack a reasonable opportunity to lead a good life,

then in consistency one should accept

3. an obligation to bring into existence persons who would have a reasonable opportunity to lead a good life.

And clearly (3) supports a fairly strong pro-life position with respect to abortion without assuming that the fetus is a person.

It can be argued that (3) follows from the acceptance of (1) and (2), on the grounds that any reason that has been given for accepting (2) that is consistent with (1) suggests an analogous reason for supporting (3). This view has been called the "symmetry view," since it maintains that there is a symmetry between a right not to be born and a right to be born, and even a right not to be conceived and a right to be conceived.

Obviously, if welfare liberals and libertarians are required to accept the symmetry view and thereby recognize an obligation to bring into existence persons who would have a reasonable opportunity to lead a good life, it is even less likely that they will have surplus goods and resources available for the satisfaction of nonbasic needs as socialist justice requires. But are welfare liberals and libertarians required to accept the premises and conclusion of this view?

The grounds for accepting (2), expressed in terms of a right not to be born, has been given by Joel Feinberg.

> If, before the child has been born, we know that the conditions for the fulfillment of his most basic interests have already been destroyed, and we permit him nevertheless to be born, we become a party to the violation of his rights.
>
> In such circumstances, therefore, a proxy for the fetus might plausibly claim on its behalf, a right not to be born. That right is based on his future

rather than his present interests (he has no actual present interests); but of course it is not contingent on his birth because he has it before birth, from the very moment that satisfaction of his most basic future interests is rendered impossible.[2]

Other welfare liberals, like Narveson and Parfit, similarly endorse (2). According to Narveson, "I therefore see no reason to deny that a concern for people's rights can dictate a restrictive population policy even though they are the very people who would not have existed had it been in effect."[3] Furthermore, to claim, as I did in Chapter 4, that existing persons should accept a population policy according to which the membership of future generations would never be allowed to increase beyond the ability of existing generations to make the necessary provision for the basic needs of future generations is also to endorse (2).

But could one consistently reject (2)? Such a rejection would involve endorsing the view that coming into existence is neither good nor bad for a person. According to this view, only what happens after one becomes a person can be either good or bad for a person. Thus, for example, being born healthy is neither good nor bad for a person. Moreover, on this view, one may not become a person until some time after birth, possibly as long as two years. Until that time, whether a newborn is happy or miserable is not in itself of much moral significance.[4] Until it becomes a person, the happiness or misery of a newborn has moral significance primarily in virtue of the effects it has on those who are already persons. Consequently, if existing persons would derive a net benefit from the continued existence of a miserable newborn, possibly as an experimental subject, and would, therefore, want to keep the newborn alive until it would become a person and thereby acquire a right that its miserable existence be terminated, there would be no moral objection to their doing so. Bu this is exactly the eventuality that philosophers have sought to preclude by affirming (2), and there seems to be no alternative way of guaranteeing this desired result.

Accordingly, challenges to the symmetry view have taken a different tack and have tried to show that it is possible consistently to accept (1) and (2) while rejecting (3); that is, these challenges have attempted to defend what has been called the "asymmetry view."

In an early attempt, Jan Narveson defends the asymmetry view on the grounds that there is a failure of reference in the case of the person who would have a reasonable opportunity to lead a good life.[5] Narveson argues in the following manner: If I bring into existence a person who would lack a reasonable opportunity to lead a good life, there will be a person who can reproach me that I did not prevent her from leading an unfortunate existence. But if I do not bring into existence a person who would have a reasonable opportunity to lead a good life, there will be no person who can reproach me for preventing her from leading a fortunate existence. Given this failure of reference in the case of the person who would have a reasonable opportunity to lead a good life, Narveson concludes, it would only be wrong to bring into existence a person who would lack a reasonable opportunity to lead a good life.

Unfortunately for Narveson's defense, it is possible to argue analogously: If I do not bring into existence a person who would lack a reasonable opportunity to lead a good life, there will be no person who can thank me for preventing her from leading an unfortunate existence. And if I do bring into existence a person who would have a reasonable opportunity to lead a good life, there will be a person who can thank me for not preventing her from leading a fortunate existence. Thus, whatever failure of reference there may be occurs in both cases, and hence it cannot provide a suitable defense for the asymmetry view.

Another attempt to defend the asymmetry view, also advanced by Narveson (ibid.), begins with the assumption that a person's life cannot be compared with her nonexistence unless the person already exists. This means that, if one allows a fetus to develop into a person who has a reasonable opportunity to lead a good life, one does not make that person better off than if she never existed. And it also means that if one allows a fetus to develop into a person who lacks a reasonable opportunity to lead a good life, one does not make that person worse off than if she never existed. But what then justifies a right not to be born in the latter case? According to the argument, it is simply the fact that unless the fetus is aborted, a person will come into existence who lacks a reasonable opportunity to lead a good life. But if this fact justifies a right not to be born, why, in the former case, would not the fact that unless the fetus is aborted a person will come into existence who has a reasonable opportunity to lead a good life, suffice to justify a right to be born? Clearly, no reason has been given to distinguish the cases.

Furthermore, consider the grounds for aborting a fetus that would develop into a person who lacks a reasonable opportunity to lead a good life. It is not simply that the person is sure to experience some unhappiness in her life, because in every person's life there is some unhappiness. Rather it is because the amount of expected unhappiness in this person's life would render her life not worth living. This implies that the justification for aborting in this case is based on a comparison of the value of the person's life with the value of her nonexistence. For how else can we say that the fact that a fetus would develop into a person who lacks a reasonable opportunity to lead a good life justifies our preventing the person's very existence? Consequently, this argument depends upon a denial of the very assumption with which it began, namely, that the person's life cannot be compared with her nonexistence unless that person already exists.

Still another attempt at defending the asymmetry view, proposed by Trudy Govier, maintains that there is a difference in strength between one's duty to prevent a fetus from developing into a person who lacks a reasonable opportunity to lead a good life and one's duty not to prevent a fetus from developing into a person who has a reasonable opportunity to lead a good life.[6] For example, it might be argued that the former duty is a relatively strong duty to prevent harm, whereas the latter duty is a relatively weak duty to promote well-being, and that only the relatively strong duty justifies a correlative right—in this case, a right not to be born. But even granting that our duty to prevent harm is stronger than our duty to promote well-being, in the case at issue we are dealing not just with a duty to promote well-being, but with a duty to promote *basic* well-being. And as welfare liberals (as well as libertarians who appreciate the arguments of Chapter 7) would be the first to admit, our duty to prevent basic harm and our duty to promote basic well-being are not that distinct from a moral point of view. From which it follows that, if our duty to prevent basic harm justifies a right not to be born in the one case, then our duty to promote basic well-being would justify a right to be born in the other.

Someone might object that although our duty to promote basic well-being may sometimes require that we give up our property, it never requires that we give up the use of our bodies, as would be necessary to bring a fetus to term.[7] According to this line of argument, one is no more required to bring a fetus to term than one is required to give up one's extra kidney to someone in need of a transplant. To think otherwise is to fail to recognize the difference in strength between a property right and a right to one's body.

But while welfare liberals would surely grant that there is a difference of strength between a property right and a right to one's body, they would still contend that the latter right can be overridden, at least when the following two conditions are satisfied: (a) the basic needs of others are at issue, and one's own basic needs are not at issue; and (b) most people are making their fair contribution toward meeting the basic needs that are at issue. Welfare liberals would argue that a right to one's body can be overridden in this fashion not only when it is understood as a right to one's labor, but also when it is understood as a right to use one's body, as is relevant to cases of organ transplants and bringing fetuses to term. In this regard, the welfare liberal would be willing to bite the bullet with respect to the comparison between bringing a fetus to term and providing organ transplants and hold that both can be required whenever the above two conditions have been met.[8]

Notice too that, at least with respect to bringing fetuses to term, these two conditions are interconnected, because unless most people are making their fair contribution toward meeting people's basic needs, bringing a fetus to term tends to be an unusually heavy burden that denies the woman on whom it is imposed the satisfaction of some of her basic needs. In other words, unless condition (b) is satisfied with respect to bringing fetuses to term, condition (a) is not likely to be satisfied either.

Derek Parfit's most recent attempt to defend the asymmetry view is a clear advance over previous attempts.[9] Thus, unlike Narveson's first attempt at defending asymmetry, Parfit's defense does not rest on a failure of reference in the case of the person whose life would be well worth living. And, unlike Narveson's second attempt, Parfit's defense allows that we can compare and evaluate the lives of people who do not actually exist but who would exist under certain conditions.[10] According to Parfit, we can say that to come into existence would be bad for a person whose life would not be worth living. Similarly, Parfit grants that we can say that to come into existence would be good for a person whose life would be well worth living. And unlike Govier's attempt to explain asymmetry, Parfit's defense is not grounded on the relative strength of our duty to prevent harm to others over our duty to promote the welfare of others.

What Parfit's defense of asymmetry appeals to is the following principle:[11]

1. It is wrong, if other things are equal, to do what would be either bad for or worse for the people who ever live.

Parfit calls this principle the "Narrow Principle of Beneficence" and suggests the possibility of adding to it some more stringent principle of nonmaleficence. This can be done easily, since Parfit claims (ibid.: 150) that if there is someone to whom we have failed to give some benefit, what we have done is worse for that person. We could easily interpret "worse for" in a different way, however. We might say, for example, that one of two acts would be worse for someone only if this act violates one of this person's rights. We could then defend a principle of nonmaleficence, which employs this more restrictive interpretation of "is worse for," as being more stringent than the Narrow Principle of Beneficence in just the way Parfit suggests.

At the same time, it is also possible to derive a duty of nonmaleficence and a duty of beneficence from Parfit's Narrow Principle of Beneficence alone. These duties can be characterized as follows:[12]

1a. *A Duty of Nonmaleficence:* A duty not to do *x,* other things being equal, if doing *x* is bad for or worse for people who ever live.

1b. *A Duty of Beneficence:* A duty to do *x,* other things being equal, if not doing *x* is bad for or worse for people who ever live.

Now Parfit, as we noted before, allows that coming into existence can be either good for or bad for a person. Yet when it is good for a person, it is not required, by (1b), since failing to provide that benefit is not bad for or worse for anyone who ever exists. By contrast, when coming into existence is bad for a person, imposing that burden is prohibited by (1a), since such an imposition would be bad for someone who would come to exist. For this reason, these interpretations of a duty of nonmaleficence and a duty of beneficence, if not further augmented, entail the asymmetry view. Notice too that Parfit achieves this result without assuming, as Govier's defense of the asymmetry view did, that our duty of nonmaleficence is relatively stronger than our duty of beneficence.

The basic problem with Parfit's defense of asymmetry is that it does not so much justify the view as simply restate it.[13] For why should we accept Parfit's interpretation of a duty of beneficence without also accepting the following interpretation, which together with (1) or (1a) entails the symmetry view?

1b. *A Duty of Beneficence:* A duty to do *x,* other things being equal, if doing *x* would be good for or better for people who ever live.

This interpretation, like (1b), satisfies the "Person-affecting Restriction" of explaining that part of morality concerned with human well-being entirely in terms of what is good or bad for those whom our acts affect, and so it cannot be rejected on that score.[14] Moreover, Parfit himself admits (ibid.: 149) that it is hard to accept that

2. We ought not to increase the sum of suffering

without also accepting that

3. We ought to increase the net sum of happiness.

Why then is it not likewise hard to accept Parfit's interpretation of our duty to benefit others [that is, (1) or (1b)] without also accepting a still broader interpretation of this duty [that is, (1b′)], which entails the symmetry view?

One might try to explain and justify a preference for (1b) over (1b′) by appealing to the following principle, which is basic to T.M. Scanlon's view of morality:[15]

4. For an act to be wrong there must be a complainant.

This principle clearly seems to be more general than (1a) or (1b), and if the principle did entail both of these requirements yet excludes (1b′) we could agree, I think, that it would serve to explain and justify the asymmetry view. Yet does the principle exclude (1b′)?

As it stands, the principle is subject to at least two interpretations:

4a. For an act to be wrong there must be one or more persons who can justifiably blame the agent for performing that action.

4b. For an act to be wrong there must be one or more persons who are unjustifiably harmed or not benefited by that action.

Now if we assume that the violation of the duties in (1a), (1b) and (1b′) must be wrong acts (that is, that it is not enough if they simply are not right acts), and if we assume further that wrong acts must meet (4b), then (1b′) would be excluded. But before we conclude from this that we have in (4b) the principle that justifies the asymmetry view, we should consider whether we have any reason to favor (4b), which excludes (1b′), over (4a), which does not, other than to rule out a duty to bring into existence persons whose lives would be well worth living. If this is the only grounds for choosing between these principles that could be decisive in this context, we could hardly invoke (4b) to justify our preference for the asymmetry view.[16]

In responding to this argument, Parfit has pointed out that philosophers such as T.M. Scanlon and Richard Brandt have had reasons for preferring (4b) over (4a) other than a commitment to the asymmetry view.[17] This is true. None of these philosophers, however, was concerned with the debate between the symmetry and asymmetry views. Moreover, once the terms of that debate are introduced, the reasons these philosophers have had for favoring (4b) over (4a) are no longer decisive.[18]

Consequently, all four of these attempts to defend the asymmetry view fail because the reasons that have been given for accepting (2) that are consistent with (1) suggest analogous reasons for (3). Thus each of these attempts to defend the asymmetry view has in fact generated an argument for the symmetry view in a way that seems perfectly generalizable for any similar attempt. And this support for the symmetry view obviously translates into support for a fairly strong pro-life position with respect to abortion that does not assume that the fetus is a person.

Nor will it do to reject the asymmetry view on the grounds that if the fetus is not a person, then the bearer of such a right, especially when we violate that right by performing an abortion, would seem to be a potential or possible person. For the same would hold true of the right not to be born, which is endorsed by welfare liberals such as Feinberg and libertarians such as Narveson: the bearer of such a right, especially when we respect that right by performing an abortion, would also seem to be a potential or possible person. In fact, however, neither notion necessarily entails any metaphysical commitment to possible persons who "are" whether they exist or not. For to say that a person into whom a particular fetus would develop has a right to be born is to say that there is an enforceable requirement upon certain persons the violation of which would fundamentally harm the person who would thereby come into existence. Similarly, to say that a person into whom a particular fetus would develop has a right to be born is to say that there is an enforceable requirement upon certain persons the respecting of which would fundamentally benefit the person who would thereby come into existence. So understood, neither the notion of a right to be born nor that of a right not to be born entails any metaphysical commitment to possible persons as bearers of rights.

Of course, recognizing a right to be born may require considerable personal sacrifice, and some people may want to reject any morality that requires such sacrifice. This option, however, is not open to welfare liberals who are already committed to making whatever personal sacrifice is necessary to provide for the basic needs of distant peoples and future generations. Consequently, welfare liberals cannot consistently reject a prohibition of abortion in cases involving a right to be born simply on the grounds that it would require considerable personal sacrifice.

There remains the further question of whether welfare liberals and libertarians can make a moral distinction between contraception and abortion—assuming, that is, that the fetus is not a person. In support of such a distinction, one might argue that, in cases where abortion is at issue, we can roughly identify the particular person into whom a fetus would develop and ask whether that person would be fundamentally benefited or fundamentally harmed by being brought into existence, whereas we cannot do anything comparable in cases where contraception is at issue. Yet, although this difference does exist, it does not suffice for distinguishing abortion from contraception on moral grounds. For notice that if persons do not practice contraception when conditions are known to be suitable for bringing persons into existence who would have a reasonable opportunity to lead a good life, then there will normally come into existence persons who have thereby benefited. Similarly, if persons do not practice contraception when conditions are known to be unsuitable for bringing persons into existence who would have a reasonable opportunity to lead a good life (for example, when persons who would be brought into existence would very likely have seriously debilitating and ultimately fatal genetic defects), there will normally come into existence persons who have thereby been harmed. On grounds such as these, therefore, we could certainly defend a "right not to be conceived" and a "right to be conceived" which are analogous to our previously defended "right not to be born" and "right to be born." Hence, it would follow that welfare liberals and libertarians can no more consistently support "contraception on demand" than they consistently support abortion on demand.[19]

Needless to say, considerably more sacrifice would normally be required of existing generations to fulfill a person's right to be born or right to be conceived than would be required to fulfill a person's right not to be born or right not to be conceived. For example, fulfilling a person's right to be born may ultimately require caring for the needs of a child for many years, whereas fulfilling a person's right not to be born may require only an early abortion. Therefore, because of the greater sacrifice that would normally be required to fulfill a person's right to be born, that right would often be overridden in particular circumstances by the rights of existing persons to have their own basic needs satisfied. Those existing persons whose welfare would have priority over a person's right to be born include those who would be directly involved in bringing the person into existence. They also include those distant and future persons whose welfare rights would otherwise be neglected if goods and resources were diverted by bringing additional persons into existence. This means there should be severe restrictions on any population increase in both technologically developed and underdeveloped nations, at least until it is possible to guarantee that persons in all nations will have their basic needs satisfied. As a consequence, even abortion on demand would be morally justified as a temporary measure if it were required for meeting the basic needs of distant peoples and future generations.

In addition, a right to be born or a right to be conceived requires that the burden of respecting that right be fairly distributed over all those who are capable of shouldering the burden. For only then would it be blameworthy to refuse to undertake the burden of bringing additional people into existence who would have a reasonable opportunity to lead a good life.

Moreover, it is important to notice that our obligations with respect to abortion and contraception are different in this respect from our obligations with respect to the welfare of distant peoples and future generations. For the latter obligations are not as dependent on other people's shouldering their fair burden as are our obligations with respect to abortion and contraception. This is because the failure of others to shoulder their fair burden with respect to abortion and contraception tends to place an unusually heavy burden on those who would attempt to do what is required of them, whereas the failure of others to shoulder their fair burden with respect to the welfare of distant peoples and future generations does not similarly increase the burden on those who would attempt to do what is required of them. For this reason, people can be released of their obligations with respect to abortion and contraception when others fail to shoulder their fair burden in this regard.

But suppose that at some time in the future the substantial sacrifices required to secure the welfare rights of distant peoples and future generations have been made. Suppose, in addition, that most people are shouldering their fair burden with respect to bringing people into existence who would have a reasonable opportunity to lead a good life. Under these conditions, what sort of procreative obligations would be in force?

First, there would be an obligation to forgo abortion whenever the fetus is not genetically defective and the health of the mother is not likely to be affected detrimentally. For if everyone is shouldering their fair burden during a woman's pregnancy, her other activities would not be detrimentally affected by bringing the fetus to term. And if the mother had good reasons for not wanting to raise the child, there would be a guaranteed provision for adoption into a caring home.

Second, there would be an obligation to bring into existence as many healthy children as a fair distribution of benefits and burdens between generations would support. If particular individuals did not wish to raise children, they could justify their stance only if they could establish that they are already in other ways making a fair contribution, appropriate to their abilities, toward meeting people's basic needs. And if they could not establish that they are making such a contribution, they would either be taxed additionally or be required to perform additional services that contributed to meeting people's basic needs. For only when such obligations are enforced would the priority of basic needs over nonbasic needs be firmly and fairly established.

I submit, therefore, that once we distribute resources in accordance with a Welfare Liberal Conception of Justice not only to meet the basic needs of existing and future generations but also, when appropriate, to bring into existence persons who would have a reasonable opportunity to lead a good life, there will clearly be very little left over for the satisfaction of nonbasic needs as a Socialist Conception of Justice requires.

Of course, the scope of the requirements of a Welfare Liberal Conception of Justice has not always been appreciated; yet once it is taken into account, the further requirement of a Socialist Conception of Justice to meet nonbasic needs, as well, can be seen to have little application.

The Requirement to Socialize the Means of Production

We have seen that in order to meet everyone's basic needs it would be necessary to introduce limited income differentials, make jobs more intrinsically rewarding, and rely heavily on moral incentives to encourage people to produce according to their ability. I contend, however, that it would not be necessary to go further and to socialize the means of production. Rather, it should suffice simply to distribute control over goods and resources more widely. For example, at present in the United States, 10 percent of the families own 57 percent of the total net wealth and 86 percent of total financial assets.[20] Accordingly, to meet persons' basic needs in the United States, it would surely be necessary to change that distribution. To meet persons' basic needs worldwide, it would be necessary to adopt more efficient means for meeting person's basic needs in affluent societies in general. Surely there are more efficient ways of meeting persons' basic nutritional needs than using so much grain to feed livestock at such a tremendous loss of usable protein. But since all these requirements for meeting persons' basic needs already follow from a Welfare Liberal Conception of Justice, I conclude that there is no need to adopt the Socialist Conception's additional requirement to socialize the means of production. For this additional requirement is completely unnecessary, given the demands of a Welfare Liberal Conception of Justice.

As Marx pointed out, the widespread exploitation of laborers associated with early capitalism began only when large numbers "had been robbed of all their own means of production and of all the guarantees of existence afforded by the old feudal system" by persons and economic groups who already had considerable wealth and power.[21] But the concentration of wealth and power necessary to carry out such exploitation is not likely to be found in a society that, in accordance with a Welfare Liberal Conception of Justice, provides for the basic needs of all its members as well as for the basic needs of distant peoples, future generations, and those persons who, if they were brought into existence, would have a reasonable opportunity to lead a good life. Consequently, a shift from such restricted private ownership of the means of production to socialization of those means may in fact have little practical consequence.

Approaching the issue in yet another way, it seems clear that for Marx, socializing the means of production is best construed as a means to an end. The end for Marx would be to form "an association in which the free development of each is the condition of the free development of all.''[22] But then the question arises as to why we should think that this end is best pursued by socializing the means of production rather than by widely dispersing the ownership of those means.

It might be argued that to bring about such an association would require that individuals be given control over their working conditions (or have the option of controlling those conditions), and that sooner or later this would lead to socializing the means of production. For example, Barry Clark and Herbert Gintis contend that "strengthening the system of total liberties" requires such worker control and would lead to the abolition of capitalism.[23] Yet even supposing that an appropriate degree of worker control were required to form an association in which the free development of each is the condition of the free development of all,[24] why would such worker control not be compatible with a system in which the ownership of the means of production were widely dispersed throughout the society? Under such a system, individuals *as investors* would each decide how to invest the fairly small shares of capital they own. Some would want to invest in firms in which they work so that their own productivity would contribute to a return on their investment. Others would choose not to do so, realizing that they could get a higher return from their investment if they invested their capital elsewhere. Over such investment decisions, however, individuals *as workers* would have no control. But once these decisions had been made, then the rights of individuals as workers would have to be taken into account in designing the business enterprise.

For example, suppose a group of investors decide to form a firm, Proletarians United, to produce super-widgets. Under a system of worker control, the workers whom Proletarians United employs would have to be guaranteed significant control over such features of their working conditions as job descriptions, working hours, and hiring, firing, and promotion policies. Nor would it be possible under the proposed system for Proletarians United to extract an unfair advantage from its workers by threatening to replace them with other workers. The reason is that as long as the demands for worker control are reasonable and allow a good return on the investment, workers under the proposed system normally would either be able to find other firms willing to employ them or be able to pool their own investment holdings and go into business for themselves. Thus, even granting that a Welfare Liberal Conception of Justice would require a significant degree of worker control, this requirement would still seem to be perfectly compatible with a system that permitted a certain degree of differential control of the means of production.

Of course, this is not to deny that there would be a need for some degree of democratic control of the flow of investment to ensure that individuals *as consumers* would be able to satisfy their basic needs, but again such control would be perfectly compatible with a system that permitted a certain degree of differential control of the means of production.

Furthermore, given that socialists grant that some income differentials would be necessary to motivate people to make their best contribution to society, how then could they object to similar differentials in the control of the means of production if these would also serve to motivate people to make their best contribution to society? As long as such differentials are kept within limits, as they necessarily must be if the basic needs of distant peoples, future generations and those persons who if brought into existence would have a reasonable opportunity to lead a good life are to be met, what objection could socialists have to such differentials?

Of course, socialists might contend that allowing any differentials in the control of the means of production would be unstable and would eventually lead to greater differentials over time with adverse consequences for the general welfare, but it is difficult to see why this is a serious threat. Both a system that allows some differential control of the means of production and a system that allows only uniform control could be subverted by those who occupy important positions of leadership and authority, but it is difficult to see how a system with differential control is any more likely to be subverted. In fact, a system with limited differential control may be less likely to be subverted, since it is better able to motivate people to make their best contribution to society.

In brief, I have argued that as soon as we recognize how demanding the requirements of a Welfare Liberal Conception of Justice are, the socialist's additional requirement to socialize the means of production can be seen to be completely unnecessary. Of course, it might be objected that, given the highly exploitative character of modern capitalism, it would be best to pave the way for the drastic reform or revolution that is needed by advocating the radical solution of socializing the mean of production. This may be. But then it may also be best to pave the way for the drastic reform or revolution that is needed by appealing to those frequently endorsed by rarely understood moral requirements of a Welfare Liberal Conception of Justice. At the very least, the latter approach cannot be faulted for failing to appeal to a morally adequate conception of justice.

Notes

1. Michael Walzer (1983: 5). In reaching this understanding of Walzer's view, I have profited from Norman Daniels' review of Walzer's book. See *Philosophical Review* 94 (1985): 142–48.

2. Joel Feinberg, "Is There a Right to Be Born?" in *Understanding Moral Philosophy,* ed. James Rachels, Encino: Dickenson Publishing Co. (1976), p. 354.

3. Jan Narveson, "Moral Problems of Population," *Monist* 57 (1973): 68.

4. The moral significance it would have is assumed to be the same as is possessed by animals at the same level of development.

5. Jan Narveson, "Utilitarianism and New Generations," *Mind* 26 (1967): 62–72; see also his "Moral Problems of Population."

6. Trudy Govier, "What Should We Do About Future People?," *American Philosophical Quarterly* (1979): 105–13.

7. This line of argument has been forcefully developed by Sara Ann Ketchum in response to my earlier work on the topic. See her "The Moral Status of the Bodies of Persons," *Social Theory and Practice* 13 (1984). According to this line of argument, our duty to prevent basic harm would never require that a person have an abortion, even when the person who would otherwise be brought into existence would lack a reasonable opportunity to lead a good life.

8. Under present conditions, however, it does seem possible to secure the transplants needed without requiring any greater sacrifice than death-bed donations. For example, in Great Britain the estimated 2000 people who could benefit from kidney transplants each year could easily be supplied by death-bed donations from the more than 6000 people who die in road accidents each year in that country.

9. See his "Future Generations, Further Problems," *Philosophy and Public Affairs* 11 (1982): 113–72; Sterba "A Problem for Parfit," *Philosophy and Public Affairs* 16 (1987): 188–92; and Parfit's "Reply to Sterba," *Philosophy and Public Affairs* 16 (1987): 193–94.

10. Parfit, "Future Generations, Further Problems," pp. 133–36.

11. Ibid., pp. 136–40, 150.

12. Ibid. Parfit suggests such an interpretation of a duty of beneficence on p. 150.

13. The distinction between explaining a view and simply restating it is a distinction Parfit himself makes on p. 123.

14. For Parfit's discussion of these restrictions, see pp. 149–50.

15. I owe this possibility to Parfit. I assume that this principle does not exclude the possibility of the actor and the complainant being the same person. See T. M. Scanlon, "Contractualism and Utilitarianism," in *Utilitarianism and Beyond,* ed. A. K. Sen and B. A. O. Williams (Cambridge: Cambridge University Press, 1982), p. 116.

16. Notice too that the asymmetry view requires us to endorse a quite different principle with respect to right actions. With respect to right actions, we have the following principle:

5. For an act to be right there must be an affirmant. This principle, like (2), has two analogous interpretations: 5a) for an act to be right there must be one or more persons who can justifiably approve of the agent's performing that action; 5b) for an act to be right there must be one or more persons who justifiably benefit or avoid harm by that action.

With respect to right actions, the asymmetry view requires us to endorse (5a) rather than (5b), because when people discharge their duties not to bring into existence people whose lives would be worth not living, there need not be anyone who justifiably benefits or avoids harm thereby. So the asymmetry view requires that we endorse the disanalogous principles (4b) and (5a), while the symmetry view requires that we endorse the analogous principles (4a) and

(5a). Could it then be argued that the analogous character of the principles required by the symmetry view provides us with an additional reason for favoring that view over the asymmetry view?

17. See Parfit, "Reply to Sterba," p. 194.

18. With regard to this point, Parfit writes (in correspondence), "I think I'd accept what you suggest about the views of Scanlan, Brandt, etc."

19. The only way to avoid this result is to assume that the fetus as a person at some point before birth and thereby introduce a morally relevant distinction between abortion and contraception, but this is a move liberals on the abortion question have been reluctant to make.

20. Federal Reserve Board, "Survey of Consumer Finances, 1983: A Second Report," reprinted from the *Federal Reserve Bulletin* (Washington, D.C.) December 1984, pp. 857–68. Richard Parker, *The Myth of the Middle Class* (New York, Harper & Row, 1972), p. 212.

21. Karl Marx, *Capital,* vol. 1 (New York, 1967), p. 715.

22. Marx and Engels, *Communist Manifesto,* ed. by C. P. Dutt (New York: International Publishers, 1938) p. 47.

23. Barry Clark and Herbert Gintis, "Rawlsian Justice and Economic Systems," *Philosophy and Public Affairs* 7 (1978): 312–13.

24. For considerations that favor worker control, see Harry Braveman, *Labor and Monopoly Capitalism* (New York, 1974); Carole Pateman, *Participation and Democratic Theory* (New York, Cambridge University Press, 1970); *Work in America* (Cambridge, 1973); Clark and Gintis, "Rawlsian Justice and Economic Systems," pp. 302–25.

9 / *From Fairness to Androgyny*

We have seen in Chapter 7 how a Libertarian Conception of Justice, which initially appeared to reject both a right to welfare and a right to affirmative action, when properly interpreted actually supports both of these rights. We have also seen, in Chapter 8, how once the practical implications of guaranteeing these rights to the relevant parties are taken into account, the additional requirements that a Socialist Conception of Justice might initially seem to impose turn out either to have little application (as in the case of the satisfaction of nonbasic needs) or to be completely unnecessary (as in the case of the socialization of the means of production). It would seem, therefore, that since feminists who endorse the ideal of androgyny also accept rights to welfare and affirmative action, the question that is central to the possibility of reconciling a Feminist Conception of Justice with our other conceptions is the following: Is commitment to the ideal of androgyny adequately captured by a right to welfare and affirmative action, or does commitment to this ideal go beyond these rights, as some feminists contend?

At first glance it would seem easy to establish that commitment to the ideal of androgyny is adequately captured by rights to welfare and affirmative action because, as we have seen, underlying these rights, particularly the right to affirmative action, is the right to equal opportunity endorsed by welfare liberals, and some feminists have argued that the ideal of androgyny can be derived from that right as endorsed by welfare liberals. But as we have also seen, the ideal of androgyny can also be interpreted as requiring an equal right to self-development, and so interpreted it would appear to go beyond the right to equal opportunity endorsed by welfare liberals.

Whether the ideal of androgyny does in fact exceed the requirements of a Welfare Liberal Conception of Justice depends, in part, upon how we interpret an equal right to self-development. On the one hand, if we interpret the right to require exactly the same level of self-development for each and every person, it surely could not be derived from the right to equal opportunity endorsed by welfare liberals. Interpreted in this way, an equal right to self-development would exceed the requirements of a right to equal opportunity. Yet when it is so interpreted, an equal right to self-development is also morally objectionable because it does not make the level of self-development to which people are entitled depend at all upon their own attempts to develop themselves. Under this interpretation, people would still be entitled to the same level of self-development irrespective of the extent to which they try to develop themselves. As a consequence, greater resources would have to be devoted to the self-development of those who have neglected their own self-development, which would unfairly limit the resources available for other people's self-development. On the other hand, if we interpret an equal right to self-development to require only equal prospects for equal native capabilities, it would clearly follow from the right to equal opportunity endorsed by welfare liberals. In fact, interpreted in this way, the two rights would be identical.

Still, it might be objected that if an equal right to self-development is interpreted to require only equal prospects for equal native capabilities, it would be compatible with considerable inequality of self-development. For, according to this interpretation, while people with the same native capabilities would have the same prospects, people with different native capabilities would have quite different prospects. Interpreted in this way, an equal right to self-development might seem to lead to a full-scale meritocracy, with all the excesses Michael Young has described in his book *The Rise of Meritocracy*. If this were the case, those with the more-valued native capabilities would constitute an elite class with numerous advantages over those with less-valued native capabilities. Under a Welfare Liberal Conception of Justice, however, and presumably under a Feminist Conception of Justice as well, such inequalities would not obtain because in order to meet the basic needs of all morally legitimate claimants, which include distant people and future generations, most of the opportunities that are provided would have to simply be those that are necessary for meeting people's basic needs. Since the opportunities that are necessary for meeting people's basic needs would depend upon native capabilities that are widely shared, providing people with such opportunities would make their prospects for self-development roughly equal. For this reason, there is little danger of a meritocracy arising from the right to equal opportunity, endorsed by welfare liberals and feminists.

At the same time, it should be pointed out that a right to equal opportunity interpreted to require equal prospects for equal native capabilities does not guarantee a right to welfare. Accordingly, people could possess such a right yet, because they are physically disabled, be unable to take advantage of the available resources for meeting their basic needs. Now a Welfare Liberal Conception of Justice responds to such problems by guaranteeing a right to welfare along with a right to equal opportunity. In this respect, a Feminist Conception of Justice is similar. For despite attempts to derive or identify the feminist ideal of androgyny with a right to equal opportunity or with an equal right to self-development, the ideal still transcends such rights by requiring not only that desirable traits be equally available to both women and men, but also that the same virtues be equally inculcated in both women and men.

Of course, part of the rationale for inculcating the same virtues in both women and men is to support a right to equal opportunity or an equal right to self-development. And if this support is to be fairly allocated, the virtues needed to support such rights must be equally inculcated in both women and men. Nevertheless, to hold that the virtues required to support a right to equal opportunity or an equal right to self-development must be equally inculcated in both women and men is different from claiming, as the ideal of androgyny does, that human virtues, without restriction, should be equally inculcated in both women and men. Thus, the ideal of androgyny clearly requires an inculcating of virtues beyond what is necessary to support a right to equal opportunity or an equal right to self-development. What additional virtues are required by the ideal of androgyny obviously depends upon what other rights should be recognized. In this regard, the ideal of androgyny is somewhat open-ended. Feminists who endorse the ideal would simply have to go along with the best arguments for additional rights and corresponding virtues. In particular, they would have to support a right to welfare that is necessary for meeting the basic needs of all legitimate claimants, including distant peoples and future generations, given the strong argument that can be made for such a right in terms of our other conceptions of justice.

Nevertheless, to provide all legitimate claimants with the resources necessary for meeting their basic needs, there obviously has to be a limit on the resources that will be available for each individual's self-development, and this limit will definitely have an effect upon the implementation of the ideal of androgyny. As was noted in Chapter 5, some feminists would want to pursue various possible technological transformations of human biology in order to implement their ideal. For example, they would like to make it possible for women to inseminate other women and for men to lactate and even to bring fertilized ova to term. But bringing about such possibilities would be very costly indeed.[1] Consequently, since the means selected for meeting basic needs must be provided to all legitimate claimants, including distant peoples and future generations, it is unlikely that such costly means could ever be morally justified. Rather, it seems preferable to equalize radically the opportunities that are conventionally provided to women and men and wait for such changes to ultimately have their effect on human biology as well. Of course, if any "technological fixes" for achieving androgyny should prove to be cost efficient as a means for meeting people's basic needs, then obviously there would be every reason to utilize them.

Unfortunately, the commitment of a Feminist Conception of Justice to a right of equal opportunity raises still another problem for the view. For some philosophers have contended that equal opportunity is ultimately an incoherent goal. As Lloyd Thomas has put the charge, "We have a problem for those who advocate competitive equality of opportunity: the prizes won in the competitions of the first generation will tend to defeat the requirements of equality of opportunity for the next."[2] The only way to avoid this result, Thomas claims, "is by not permitting persons to be dependent for their self-development on others at all," which obviously is a completely unacceptable solution.

But this is a problem, as Thomas points out, that exists for competitive opportunities. They are opportunities for which, even when each person does her best, there are considerably more losers than winners. With respect to such opportunities, the winners may well be able to place themselves and their children in an advantageous position with respect to subsequent competitions. But under a Welfare Liberal Conception of Justice, and presumably a Feminist Conception of Justice as well, most of the opportunities available to people are not competitive opportunities at all, but noncompetitive opportunities to acquire the resources necessary for meeting their basic needs. These are opportunities with respect to which virtually everyone who does her best can be a winner. Of course, some people who do not do their best may fail to satisfy their basic needs, and this failure may have negative consequences for their children's prospects. But under a Welfare Liberal Conception of Justice, and presumably a Feminist Conception of Justice as well, every effort is required to ensure that each generation has the same opportunities to meet their basic needs, and as long as most of the available opportunities are of the noncompetitive sort, this goal should not be difficult to achieve.

Someone might contend that if all that will be accomplished under the proposed system of equal opportunity is, for the most part, the satisfaction of people's basic needs, that would not bring about the revolutionary change in the relationship between women and men that feminists are demanding. For don't most women in technologically advanced societies already have their basic needs satisfied, despite the fact that they are not yet fully liberated?

In response, it should be emphasized that the defenders of the ideal of androgyny are concerned not just with women in technologically advanced societies. The ideal of androgyny is also applicable to women in Third World and developing societies, and in such societies it is clear that the basic needs of many women are not being met. Furthermore, it is just not the case that all the basic needs of most women in technologically advanced societies—in particular, their basic needs for self-development—are being met. This is because women are being denied an equal right to education, training, jobs, and a variety of social roles for which they have the native capabilities. In effect, women in technologically advanced societies are still being treated as second-class persons, no matter how well-fed, well-clothed, and well-housed they happen to be. This is why there must be a radical restructuring of social institutions even in technologically advanced societies if women's basic needs for self-development are to be met.

The primary focus for such radical restructuring is the family. Here two fundamental changes are required. First, all children regardless of their sex must be given the same type of upbringing consistent with their native abilities. Second, mothers and fathers must also have the same opportunities for education and employment consistent with their native capabilities. In practice, this will involve an equal sharing of the child-rearing burdens and pleasures by both parents. It will also involve a greater role for the whole society in the rearing and education of children. For only when supportive institutions such as day care are universally available will both mothers and fathers be able to satisfy their basic needs for self-development.

Yet no matter how hard a society strives to produce conditions of equal opportunity, won't some children emerge with greater advantages than others? Certainly some women and men will be more effective at child-rearing than others, and this will tend to result in some children having greater advantages than others. Nevertheless, as long as the focus is on providing all morally legitimate claimants, including distant peoples and future generations, with the noncompetitive opportunities necessary for their meeting their basic needs, and most resources are in fact devoted to this purpose, the degree of inequality attributable to the differences in upbringing should never be of much practical significance.

Someone might still object that despite its endorsement by some feminists, the ideal of androgyny could never be a common ideal for feminists given the variety of different positions feminists have endorsed. But I claim that the variety of feminist positions is due not so much to a difference in the ultimate political ideal favored by feminists, which I think is, at least implicitly, one of androgyny, as to a difference in the means favored for achieving that ideal. Thus, liberal feminists can be interpreted as claiming that the ideal of androgyny can be achieved by legal reforms within a basically capitalist society. Marxists feminists can be interpreted as claiming that the ideal requires the replacement of capitalism with socialism. Radical feminists can be interpreted as claiming that the ideal requires a drastic change of the natural order, and socialist feminists can be interpreted as claiming that the ideal requires the replacement of capitalism with socialism as well as a drastic change of the natural order.[3] In fact, the debate between these varieties of feminism parallels the debate between socialist justice and welfare liberal justice concerning whether it is necessary to socialize the means of production and to satisfy nonbasic needs along with basic needs. In the latter debate, as we have seen, once the practical implications of welfare liberal justice are recognized, the requirement to socialize the means of production is completely unnecessary, and the requirement to satisfy nonbasic needs along with basic needs has little application. Likewise, in the debate between opposing feminist views, once the practical implications of liberal feminism are recognized, the Marxist feminist requirement to replace capitalism with socialism can be seen to be completely unnecessary, and the radical feminist requirement to change human biology can be seen to have little application.

Actually, the only feminists who seem to be opposed to the ideal of androgyny, as I have interpreted it, are those who either reject so-called feminine virtues and traits in favor of so-called masculine virtues and traits, who Iris Young calls humanist feminists, or those who exalt and glorify so-called feminine virtues and traits over their masculine counterparts, who Young calls gynocentric feminists.[4] But I have argued that both of these views are extremes that need to be compromised and refashioned along the lines of the ideal of androgyny as I have interpreted it.

Of course, in a sexist society like our own, where the knowledge of virtues and desirable traits tends to be considerably distorted, much must be done to determine the exact practical implications of the ideal of androgyny. It may even be that only after we have been able significantly to overcome the sexist practices of our own society will we be able to determine precisely the practical requirements of this ideal. In a similar manner, it may be only after we have been able significantly to correct for existing injustices against distant peoples and future generations by at least providing for their nutritional requirements will we have the necessary compassion to determine precisely when people's basic needs have been satisfied. Nevertheless, at the present time, the ideal of androgyny's standard of equal virtues plus equal opportunity with respect to other desirable traits along with the ideal of contractual fairness's standard of meeting basic needs should provide ample guidance for people of good will.

In conclusion, I have argued that a Feminist Conception of Justice with its ideal of androgyny does in fact go beyond the right to equal opportunity endorsed by a Welfare Liberal Conception of Justice and the equal right to self-development endorsed by a Socialist Conception of Justice, because it is more open-ended than either of these two other conceptions of justice. But once additional arguments from libertarian, welfare liberal, and socialist perspectives are taken into account, such as arguments for a right to welfare, it seems clear that these conceptions of justice have the same practical requirements. In the next chapter, I will complete my main argument for practical reconciliation by arguing that a Communitarian Conception of Justice with its ideal of the common good can also be reconciled with the practical requirements of these other conceptions of justice.

Notes

1. See Barbara Katz Rothman, "How Science Is Redefining Parenthood," *Ms.* (August 1982): 154–58.
2. D. A. Lloyd Thomas, "Competitive Equality of Opportunity," *Mind* 86 (1977): 398.
3. For a detailed discussion and analyses of each of these feminist positions, see Alison Jaggar (1983).
4. See Iris Young (1985): 173–83.

10 / *Fairness as the Common Good*

If a Communitarian Conception of Justice is to be reconciled with our other four conceptions of justice, it is necessary to show that (a) contrary to what Alasdair MacIntyre claims, contemporary moral philosophy is not characterized by radical disagreement, interminable arguments, and incommensurable premises; (b) the particular communitarian objections to a Welfare Liberal Conception of Justice raised by Michael J. Sandel and Bernard Williams can be answered; and (c) the Communitarian Conception of Justice imposes practical requirements that are notably similar to those imposed by our other conceptions of justice. In this chapter, I will establish each of these claims in turn.

The State of Contemporary Moral Philosophy

According to MacIntyre, the only way to avoid the radical disagreement, interminable arguments, and incommensurable premises that characterize contemporary moral philosophy is to adopt a Communitarian Conception of Justice based on an Aristotelian moral theory that has been refurbished in certain respects. In particular, the theory would have to abandon any reliance on a metaphysical biology. Second, it would have to characterize the human telos in terms of a quest undertaken within a tradition. Third, it would have to allow for the possibility of tragic moral conflict.

But how would an Aristotelian moral theory that has been refurbished in these ways help us to avoid the radical disagreement, interminable arguments, and incommensurable premises that, MacIntyre claims, characterize contemporary moral philosophy? MacIntyre says little about the particular practices and tradition which, according to his theory, are to ground an account of the virtues. But without a specification of these practices and tradition and the virtues grounded upon them, how are we to avoid the radical disagreements and interminable arguments he claims characterize contemporary moral philosophy?

MacIntyre does explain how his refurbished Aristotelian moral theory avoids choice between incommensurable premises by continuing to recognize the force of the rival moral goods not chosen (1981:208). But why is that option not available as well to defenders of other contemporary views? Surely libertarians can show some regard for meeting basic needs, provided the requirements of just appropriation and exchange have been taken into account. For example, they can recognize the goal of meeting basic needs as a requirement of supererogation.[1] Likewise, welfare liberals can show some regard for previous appropriation and exchange, at least after everyone's basic needs have been met.

Yet the capacity of an ethical theory for recognizing the force of the rival moral goods not chosen does not suffice to show that the theory can avoid choice between incommensurable premises. And it no more suffices in the case of MacIntyre's refurbished Aristotelian moral theory than it does in the case of other contemporary theories, virtually all of which have this same capacity. For two theories can have this capacity even when their premises are incommensurable, because they require radically opposed priorities with respect to particular goods. For example, this would hold of Rawls's and Nozick's theories if Rawls's theory regarded the goal of meeting basic needs to be fundamentally a requirement of obligation, and if Nozick's theory regarded that goal to be fundamentally a requirement of supererogation.[2] Consequently, MacIntyre's proposed solution to avoiding choice between incommensurable premises simply will not work.

What will work, I contend, is the approach that I have adopted in this book. To show that the premises of rival political ideals are not really incommensurable and that radical disagreement and interminable arguments can be avoided, it should suffice to show that when rival political ideals are correctly interpreted, they can be shown to support the same practical requirements. In addition, in Chapter 11, I carry this argument for practical reconciliation a step further by showing that a non-question-begging conception of rationality requires that we endorse one or another of our five political ideals.

Of course, the ideal would be to be able to show that a non-question-begging conception of rationality led to just one particular political ideal and its practical requirements. Unfortunately this conception of rationality is not substantive enough to produce this result. It is only strong enough, I will argue, to show that we have to endorse one or another of our five political ideals. At that point, the argument for practical reconciliation takes over and shows that these five political ideals support the same practical requirements. In this way, I claim, it is possible to show that contemporary moral philosophy need not be characterized by radical disagreement, interminable arguments, and incommensurable premises.

Notice also that my approach in this book has been to begin with substantive values—liberty, equality, fairness, androgyny, and the common good—each of which represents a conception of human nature as it should be. This is because most contemporary moral philosophers attempt to derive specific moral requirements from such conceptions of human nature as it should be and not from conceptions of human nature as it is. I have been trying to show in this book simply that contemporary moral philosophers have been mistaken concerning what specific moral requirements follow from their conceptions of human nature as it should be. Thus neither I nor most contemporary moral philosophers have made any attempt to derive a conception of human nature as it should be from a conception of human nature as it is—the task MacIntyre mistakenly claims (1981: chaps. 5, 6, and 7) characterizes all of contemporary moral philosophy.

The Communitarian Objections of Sandel and Williams

As we have seen, Sandel argues that a Welfare Liberal Conception of Justice is objectionable because it is based upon an inadequate conception of the nature of persons. Williams also argues that a Welfare Liberal Conception of Justice is objectionable because its commitment to impartiality makes it incapable of sufficiently appreciating the moral significance of people's ground projects. These objections are basically similar, despite the different ways in which Sandel and Williams have formulated their objections to welfare liberalism. One might even imagine Sandel and Williams agreeing that the inadequate conception of the nature of persons underlying a Welfare Liberal Conception of Justice is in fact one in which the moral significance of people's ground projects are insufficiently appreciated. Nevertheless, Sandel and Williams are primarily concerned to establish quite different claims with respect to their similar objections to welfare liberalism. Sandel is primarily concerned to show that welfare liberals are actually committed to this inadequate conception of the nature of persons. Williams, by contrast, is primarily concerned to demonstrate, by means of counterexamples, what is actually wrong with this conception of the nature of persons.

At first glance, Sandel's case against welfare liberalism looks particularly strong. After all, Rawls actually does say that "the self prior to the ends which are affirmed by it," and this claim seems to express just the inadequate conception of the nature of persons that, Sandel contends, underlies a Welfare Liberal Conception of Justice. Nor is

Rawls's claim made specifically about persons in the original position. So Sandel cannot be dismissed for failing to distinguish between the characterization of persons in the original position and the characterization of persons in ordinary life, as Rawls himself seems to suggest (1985: 238–39). Nevertheless, Sandel's case against welfare liberalism presupposes that his metaphysical interpretation is the only plausible interpretation of Rawls's claim. Still, a more plausible interpretation does appear to be available. According to this interpretation, to say that persons are prior to their ends means simply that they are morally responsible for their ends, either because they can or could have changed those ends. Of course, the degree to which people can or could have changed their ends is a matter of considerable debate, but what is clear is that the degree to which people can or could have changed their ends is what determines the degree to which they are morally responsible for those ends.

Nor does this interpretation deny that certain ends may in fact be constitutive of the persons we are, so that if those ends were to change we would become different persons. Of course, the degree to which we think this happens depends upon our theory of personal identity, and most theories of personal identity do not make continuity of one's fundamental aims a requirement of personal identity. But even if we grant that a change in one's fundamental aims could constitute a change in one's personal identity, the crucial question is whether we can or could have brought about such changes (as opposed to have them just happen to us), because the degree to which we can or could have changed our ends determines the degree to which we are responsible for them.

We can see, therefore, that nothing in the above interpretation of Rawls's claim presupposes a self that is metaphysically prior to its ends. Rather the picture we are given is that of a self responsible for its ends insofar as its ends are or were revisable. Such a self may well be constituted by at least some of its ends, but it is responsible for those ends only to the degree to which they are or were revisable. So the sense in which a self is prior to its ends is simply moral: insofar as its ends are or were revisable, a self may be called upon to change them or to compensate others for their effects when they turn out to be morally objectionable. Clearly, this interpretation of Rawls's claim avoids any commitment to the inadequate conception of the nature of persons that, Sandel contends, underlies a Welfare Liberal Conception of Justice.

Sandel also contends that welfare liberals, like Rawls, are driven to endorse an inadequate conception of the nature of persons because they believe that people's native assets should be regarded as common assets. Sandel argues that the only way to show that regarding native assets as common assets does not violate the Kantian injunction never to treat persons merely as a means is for welfare liberals to conceive of persons as distinct from their assets; so while their assets may be used simply as a means, they themselves would never be so used.

To evaluate this objection to welfare liberalism, we must first get clear about the conditions under which the Kantian injunction never to treat people merely as a mean would be violated. Only then can we determine whether, as Sandel claims, welfare liberals are required to adopt an inadequate conception of the nature of persons in order to avoid violating this Kantian injunction.[3]

According to Robert Nozick, who first raised this objection to welfare liberalism, the paradigm case of being simply used is that of an exchange in which one party to the exchange does not freely accept the terms or underlying purposes of the exchange (1974: 30–32, 228–29). Nozick distinguishes between cases where the exchange is objectionable because one party judges the compensation provided by the other party to be inadequate (I'm being paid too little for my work), and cases where the exchange is objectionable because one party disapproves of the other party's purpose in carrying out the exchange (I don't want my retirement funds invested in South Africa). Unfortunately, Nozick's characterization of his paradigm case is defective, and for reasons Nozick himself should have recognized.

First, exchanges that people do not freely accept, that is, forced exchanges, do not necessarily involve simply using people. For example, Nozick allows (in chap. 5) that in the absence of free agreement a dominant protection agency would be justified in prohibiting independents from employing certain risky procedures provided that adequate compensation is paid by the agency to those independents.[4] And surely Nozick would not want to grant that this is a case of simply using someone. So there can be cases of forced exchanges that do not involve simply using people, even when the force is not being employed in response to any wrongful action.[5]

Second, even when people freely accept the terms and purposes of an exchange, this does not preclude their being simply used. People may freely accept the terms and purposes of an exchange only because they have been socially conditioned, against their most fundamental interests, to do so. Nancy Davis, who has pressed this particular objection against Nozick's account, provides the following example:

> The Victim is a lonely, shy, and insecure individual, while the Controller is a charismatic charmer. The Controller pays a lot of flattering attention to the Victim with the aim of getting her to become a live-in, all-purpose drudge: what he wants is someone who will attend to his domestic chores, fawn on him, and—since this is what she will be convinced that she wants to do—make no fuss about it. Even if the Victim is told that this is what

the Controller wants, understands that this is really all that he wants, and agrees to take on the job of all-purpose drudge, we may still think that she is being used. Though she is not ignorant of the Controller's aims and purposes, she is (given her psychological makeup) overwhelmed by his attentions. He is thus able to exercise a strong or special influence over her.[6]

This example seems to be a clear case of where a person is being used even though, in her present circumstances, she has freely agreed to be so used.

So it would seem that the defining characteristics of Nozick's paradigm case of being simply used are neither necessary nor sufficient for an adequate account of that notion. People can be used even when they have freely agreed to the terms and purposes of an exchange or relationship (as in Davis's example), and people may not be used even when they are forced to agree to the terms or purposes of an exchange or relationship (as in Nozick's own example).

What is needed, therefore, to characterize correctly the conditions under which people are being simply used is some suitably idealized standpoint that is relevantly different from the one that the party happens to be in at the moment. Not surprisingly, Rawls claims that his original position can provide us with just such a standpoint. According to Rawls (1971: 178–83), to avoid simply using people we need only treat them in accord with the requirements that would be chosen in the original position. On this view, whether exchanges, either forced or free, involve simply using people depends upon the requirements that would be chosen in the original position. For example, since a right to welfare would be chosen in the original position, to forcefully require people to help guarantee such a right would not violate the Kantian injunction not to treat people simply as a means. And because such a right would be chosen in the original position, the rich would, in fact, be violating that injunction in their dealings with the poor, even if the poor had freely agreed to inadequate wages as the only terms of their continued employment by the rich. Alternatively, to appease those who might find this use of Rawls's original position question-begging, we could adopt the idealized standpoint of the "ought" implies "can" principle and avoid simply using people by treating them in accord with the requirements it would be reasonable to ask everyone affected to accept.

Using either standard, it would turn out, given what has been established in previous chapters, that requiring people to use their native assets to help guarantee a right to welfare and a right to affirmative action would not violate the Kantian injunction not to treat people simply as a means. In view of these interpretations of the Kantian injunction, there is no need to regard the self as distinct from its assets in order to avoid violating that injunction while recognizing that people are required to regard their native assets as common assets, at least insofar as people are required to use those assets to make a fair contribution toward guaranteeing a right to welfare and a right to affirmative action. For these reasons, Sandel has failed to show that a Welfare Liberal Conception of Justice is based on an inadequate conception of the nature of persons.

Sometimes, however, Sandel objects to a Welfare Liberal Conception of Justice not so much because it is committed to an inadequate conception of the nature of persons, but because it is neutral with respect to conceptions of the good. How, Sandel asks, can agents determine what is just, independent of some conception of the good?[7] Yet despite the fact that well-known liberals, like Rawls and Dworkin, have endorsed this characterization of welfare liberalism, it is apt to be more misleading than helpful. Take Rawls's theory of justice, for example, with its commitment to equal political liberty, equal opportunity, and a maximal welfare program. With these practical requirements it is misleading, to say the least, to call Rawls's theory neutral with respect to conceptions of the good. Those who are against legally enforced welfare and equal opportunity would certainly not regard Rawls's theory as neutral in this regard. What is true of liberal theories in general is that they maintain, to use the more helpful language of the Wolfenden Report, that "there must remain a realm of private morality and immorality which is, in brief and crude terms, not the law's business."[8] But securing an area of private morality is consistent with the enforcement of an extensive public morality that constitutes a substantial, although incomplete, conception of the good, and characteristically a Welfare Liberal Conception of Justice pursues both goals. Consequently, Sandel's alternative objection to a Welfare Liberal Conception of Justice fails, as well, because this conception, like virtually every other conception of justice, is not truly neutral with respect to conceptions of the good.

Unlike Sandel, Williams is primarily concerned to expose what is objectionable about the conception of the nature of persons that he thinks underlies a Welfare Liberal Conception of Justice. According to Williams, what is objectionable about this conception of justice is its inability sufficiently to appreciate the moral significance of people's ground projects. Williams presses this objection primarily against utilitarian formulations of welfare liberalism, contending that people's ground projects are much more important to their personal integrity than utilitarianism can allow.

But while Williams's objection has some merit as a theoretical objection to the application of utilitarianism in all logically possible situations, the objection, so far developed, fails as a practical objection to the application of utilitarianism in the world in which we live. This can be seen from an examination of Williams's own counterexamples to utilitarianism: the explorer faced with a decision whether to shoot one Indian to save nineteen, and the chemist faced with the decision whether to take a job in a firm specializing in research in chemical and biological warfare. For Williams ends up endorsing the utilitarian resolution of his explorer example; his only objection is that for the utilitarian, this resolution would come too easily. R. M. Hare has pointed out (1981: 49, 130–46) that there are good utilitarian reasons why the utilitarian would not be able to resolve this case easily—reasons that Williams does not adequately take into account. With regard to Williams's example of George, the chemist, if George's relevant ground project is to limit research into chemical and biological warfare, the best way for him to pursue *that project* would be to accept the research job himself, rather than to permit someone who advocates such research to take the job. But this action would accord not with Williams's resolution of the case, but with a utilitarian resolution. Only if George's project is that of not actively (as opposed to passively) contributing to chemical and biological warfare research himself would Williams's resolution of this case be intelligible; but then the example would not be very persuasive as a practical counterexample to utilitarianism, since the pursuit of this project would actually increase rather than decrease the overall amount of such research that is done.

This is not to suggest that there are no practical counterexamples to utilitarianism, but only that such counterexamples are far more difficult to come by than is generally thought. Actually, the counterexamples likely to be most effective against utilitarianism, as Williams surmises, are those that concern whether to do evil that good may come of it. This is because the injunction not to do evil is commonly understood to have priority over the injunction to do good. By contrast, when what is at issue is simply whether to do this or that good, such as a lesser good for one's self or a greater good for others, then it is far more difficult to find practical counterexamples to utilitarianism. It is for this reason, among others, that I argued in Chapter 3 for a practical reconciliation of both utilitarian and nonutilitarian formulations of welfare liberalism with respect to rights to welfare and affirmative action.

It should also be noted that Williams's objection ultimately fails even as a theoretical objection to nonutilitarian formulations of welfare liberalism[9] Williams would argue that his objection has force against both formulations of welfare liberalism because they share the moral ideal of impartiality. But impartiality is an ideal that requires interpretation. As Williams interprets the ideal, it allows partiality only when it serves the end of impartiality, to treat relevantly similar people in a similar manner. This is the interpretation that underlies Williams's criticism of Charles Fried's rationale for preferring to save one's spouse from peril rather than someone else. Fried had argued that provided the peril was "a sufficient randomizing event," a preference for one's spouse could satisfy the dictates of fairness. Williams objects, however, that justifications of this sort, presumably because they attempt to ground partiality in terms of fairness or impartiality, provide us with "one thought too many" (Williams 1981: 18).

There is, however, another way to interpret the moral ideal of impartiality so that it is not subject to this objection. According to this interpretation, the ideal allows partiality not only when it can be justified as a means to impartiality, but also when it can be independently justified to all affected parties. When interpreted in this way, the ideal would be acceptable to all parties in Rawls's original position. Parties in the original position would recognize that there are limits to the amount of self-sacrifice that could be reasonably expected of any particular person. They would not see such limits as justified in terms of impartiality, but rather as setting the limits of justified impartiality. A similar justification for partiality can be derived, even more directly, from an application of the "ought" implies "can" principle because, in general, it would not be reasonable to require impartiality when one's fundamental needs and interests are at stake. Accordingly, it should be clear that interpreting the ideal of impartiality in this way is perfectly compatible with, if not required by, our other four conceptions of justice. Moreover, since this interpretation allows for an independent justification for partiality, it may be the view that Williams ultimately wants to defend.[10] Williams, of course, sees his view as opposed to the ideal of impartiality, and it is clearly opposed to that ideal under the first interpretation we considered, but it is not opposed to that ideal under the second. So if Williams's view is captured by this second interpretation of the ideal, as it seems to be, then at least in this respect his account of communitarian justice would be perfectly compatible with our other conceptions of justice.

The Practical Requirements of Communitarian Justice

Despite the failure of Sandel's and Williams's objections to a Welfare Liberal Conception of Justice, there still may be significant practical differences between the requirements of a Communitarian Conception of Justice and our four other conceptions of justice. In particular, as we noted before, MacIntyre has argued that a Communitarian Conception of Justice, reflecting a fuller conception of the good, would support a much wider range of practical requirements than a Welfare Liberal Conception of Justice; and Finnis has defended an absolute prohibition against doing evil that good may come of it and applied this prohibition to a wide range of practices from abortion to warfare. We need to consider, therefore, whether the practical requirements of communitarian justice do diverge from the requirements of our other conceptions of justice in these respects.

No doubt there is a clear difference in aspiration between communitarians and welfare liberals. Communitarians hope to establish a relatively complete conception of the good. By contrast, welfare liberals are doubtful whether any such conceptions can be adequately grounded. Hence, while communitarians are generally inclined to accept the practical requirements defended by welfare liberals, they contend that these requirements are incomplete, since, for example, they neither provide an account of self-regarding virtues nor an account of the requirements of supererogation.

It is obvious that the requirements of Welfare Liberal Conception of Justice, so far elaborated, represent an incomplete moral ideal. Yet this conception could, in time, be further elaborated to provide a relatively complete moral ideal, particularly given that choice in the original position can take into account all the morally relevant facts about human nature. Indeed, the only knowledge about human nature that is not taken into account in fashioning a Welfare Liberal Conception of Justice is the knowledge that would preclude unanimous agreement, and from a welfare liberal perspective that knowledge is morally suspect and should be discounted. Thus while it is true that welfare liberals have in general directed their energies at defending basic human rights, there appears to be no reason why their conception of justice could not be expanded to include a relatively complete moral ideal.[11]

At the same time, it should be noted that communitarians have done little to remedy this deficiency in welfare liberalism. For example, the conception of the good so far specified and defended by MacIntyre is actually relatively formal when compared with the conceptions developed by rival welfare liberal and libertarian theorists. In fact, communitarians, in general, have yet to provide an adequate defense of even those practical requirements they endorse in common with welfare liberals, let alone provide an adequate defense of additional practical requirements.

This latter point applies directly to Finnis's endorsement of an absolute prohibition on doing evil that good may come of it. Finnis is primarily concerned to defend this prohibition by attacking various forms of utilitarianism. But an adequate defense would have to take into account the reasons that nonutilitarian welfare liberals and others would have for rejecting this prohibition as an absolute requirement. For example, from the perspective of the original position it would not be reasonable to accept an absolute restriction on doing evil that good may come of it, because there are cases where the evil or intended harm is either (a) trivial (such as stepping on someone's foot in a crowded subway), (b) easily reparable (such as lying to a temporarily depressed friend to keep her from committing suicide) or (c) sufficiently outweighed by the consequences of the action (such as shooting one of two hundred civilian hostages to prevent, in the only way possible, the execution of all two hundred).

This does not mean, however, that persons in the original position would reject the injunction completely, but only that they would reject it as an absolute prohibition.[12] It would seem, therefore, that once the requirements of communitarian justice are sufficiently elaborated and qualified to meet various objections that can be raised against them, there should be no difficulty reconciling them with the requirements of our other conceptions of justice. At least this is the case with the account of communitarian justice that has been so far elaborated by contemporary defenders.

Notes

1. Of course, I have argued in Chapter 7 that libertarians are required to endorse much more.

2. As I argued in Chapter 7, however, the premises of Rawls's welfare liberal theory and Nozick's libertarian theory are not really incommensurable, because meeting basic needs is not fundamentally a requirement of supererogation for Nozick's libertarian theory or, for that matter, for any libertarian theory, despite the fact that many libertarians still mistakenly think that it is.

3. It has been suggested to me that Sandel's objection to welfare liberalism could be avoided simply by claiming that the Kantian injunction never to treat persons simply as a means can be overridden when it conflicts with rights to welfare and affirmative action. Possibly; but I believe the Kantian injunction expresses such a fundamental moral requirement of respect for each and every moral agent that it cannot be overridden on moral grounds.

4. This aspect of Nozick's view was also discussed in Chapter 2.

5. In Nozick's case, the independents would presumably not be acting wrongfully if they were willing adequately to compensate those affected by the use of their risky procedures.

6. Nancy Davis, "Using Persons and Common Sense," *Ethics* 94 (1984): 394.

7. Michael J. Sandel, "Morality and the Liberal Ideal," *New Republic* (May 7, 1984): 16–17.

8. Great Britain Committee on Homosexual Offenses and Prostitution, Report, CMD. No. 247 (1957).

9. What I am claiming is that Williams's objection fails to work against suitably worked-out defenses of welfare liberalism.

10. Sometimes Williams suggests that partiality is some kind of brute fact

about human relations that lies "beyond justification" (1981: 17–18). But Williams appears to mean by this only that partiality cannot always be justified on the basis of impartiality, which is just what I have allowed.

11. For example, it may be possible to use the original position to resolve conflicts between agent-relative values like providing for one's children and keeping one's promises, and the agent-neutral values of having one's children provided for and having promises kept. For a discussion of such conflicts, see Thomas Nagel, "The Limits of Objectivity," in *The Tannes Lectures on Human Values,* Vol. 1, ed. Sterling McMurrin (Cambridge, 1980), Part III; and Derek Parfit (1984: chap. 4). Of course, agreement in the original position with respect to a fuller moral ideal presupposes that there are reasonable grounds for greater agreement in society concerning a conception of the good, or at least reasonable grounds for greater agreement concerning the practical requirements of alternative conceptions of the good. But given that I have shown that there is reasonable grounds for practical reconciliation with respect to opposing political ideals, why shouldn't something similar obtain with respect to conceptions of the good?

12. For a discussion of exactly what prohibition would emerge, see Sterba, "Moral Approaches to Nuclear Strategy: A Critical Evaluation," *Canadian Journal of Philosophy,* Special Issue, 12 (1986): 75–109.

PART III

Rational Foundation

11 / *From Rationality to Morality*

I have argued that when Libertarian, Socialist, Feminist, and Communitarian Conceptions of Justice are correctly interpreted, they all can be seen to support the same practical requirements usually associated with a Welfare Liberal Conception of Justice, namely, a right to welfare and a right to affirmative action. Since most people endorse one or another of these conceptions of justice, I claim that to make people just, it should suffice to show them that all these conceptions of justice support the same practical requirements.

But what if someone were to accept my argument up to this point and then deny that she had any reason to accept any of these five conceptions of justice—no reason at all to be just. Such an individual would not be claiming that she had reason to be moral but not any reason to be just. Rather she would be rejecting not only justice but all morality as well. How could such a person be brought to accept the practical requirements of our five conceptions of justice?

Contemporary philosophers have offered three kinds of justification for morality. Some, following Plato, claim that morality is justified by self-interest.[1] Others, following Hume as he is frequently interpreted, claim that morality is justified in terms of other-regarding interests, wants, or intentions that people happen to have.[2] And still others, following Kant, claim that morality is justified in terms of the requirements of practical reason.[3] In this chapter, I argue that only the justification in terms of the requirements of practical reason can be fully adequate, and then only when it is developed in a certain way.[4] I further show that practical reason requires that we endorse at least a Libertarian Conception of Justice, the practical requirements of which we have seen in previous chapters can be reconciled with the practical requirements of our other four conceptions of justice.

I begin by showing what is defective in the other justifications. Then I consider attempts by Kurt Baier, Alan Gewirth, and Stephen Darwall to elaborate the third type of justification. Rejecting yet drawing upon their work, I present a justification based on the requirements of practical reason that demonstrates not only that the rational egoist acts contrary to reason, but also that endorsing at least a Libertarian Conception of Justice is required by reason.

Morality and Self-Interest

Those who claim that morality is justified by self-interest tend to define morality as a system of rules and virtues that take into account the interests of everyone alike.[5] Whatever differences there are among proposed definitions, they are not particularly relevant here since proponents of this justification rarely try to argue for it by defining morality in a question-begging way.[6]

Yet it is difficult to understand how a morality that takes into account the interests of everyone alike could be in the best interest of each and every person, for surely it would seem that morality so defined would require self-sacrifice from some, if not most, members of society. In particular, the rich and the powerful would seem to be required to sacrifice their interests, at least to some degree, for the sake of the poor and weak. Nevertheless, philosophers justifying morality on the grounds of self-interest deny that such sacrifice is required. They contend that conflicts between morality and self-interest are only apparent and that closer examination reveals a harmony of interests.

One way philosophers defend this view is by distinguishing between people's "true" interests and their "false" interests (or people's "true" selves and their "false" selves) and then by maintaining that the former but not the latter require people to be moral.[7] Unfortunately, this defense tends either to collapse the distinction between our first and second justifications or to collapse the distinction between our first and third justifications. For if people's true interests are taken to correspond to the other-regarding interests people happen to have, this defense would simply be maintaining, like our second justification, that morality is grounded in people's other-regarding interests, wants, or intentions. Or if people's true interests are taken to be the interests they would have if they were acting in accord with practical reason, this defense would simply be maintaining, as does our third justification, that morality is grounded in the dictates of practical reason.

A more promising defense of the first justification is that apparent conflicts between morality and self-interest have their source in our failure to understand what is in our long-term self-interest. Some philosophers, such as Robert Olson (1965: 9), claim that many violations of morality have their origin in impulsive action for which the remedy is deliberate and rational pursuit of long-term self-interest. For others, like Michael Scriven (1966: 251), apparent conflicts between morality and self-interest come from institutional obstacles that make it difficult for people to realize what is in their best self-interest. Marxists, in particular, hold that capitalism prevents both capitalists and proletarians from fully developing themselves.[8] They say that only the final stage of communist society will secure complete and harmonious self-development for all.[9] For still others, conflicts between morality and self-interest begin in people's failure to take into account an afterlife in which virtue is rewarded and vice punished.[10]

Needless to say, to ground the justification for morality on the assumption of a justice-producing afterlife is to give morality a widely contested foundation. In the end we may decide to rely on this assumption, as Henry Sidgwick did; but if we hope to rally as many as possible to the banner of morality, we should consider endorsing such an assumption only if no less-disputed alternative can be found.

By contrast, the other ways of arguing that morality is in our long-term self-interest clearly have a more general appeal. Many would frequently find it in their long-term self-interest to act morally if they only deliberated more or if their institutions were only better designed. At the same time, the world will probably always have its master criminals, and occasions will probably arise for all of us in which it is in our self-interest, to act immorally. Moreover, how could we suppose that moving from existing to ideal institutions could happen without self-sacrifice on the part of anyone?[11]

Yet even conceding that the dictates of morality and self-interest do not always coincide in the sense that "acting according to duty" (that is, doing one's moral duty but not necessarily from the motive of doing one's duty) is not always in one's best interest, one still might argue that "acting from duty" (that is, acting from the motive of doing one's moral duty but not necessarily doing one's duty) is still justified as the best way of achieving what is in one's overall self-interest.

Hoping to establish this conclusion, Peter Singer appeals to a widely recognized paradox: those who aim at their own happiness often fail to attain it, while others obtain happiness in the pursuit of other goals.[12] Singer argues that, given this paradox, to secure our own happiness we must abandon self-interest for a broader goal, the obvious candidate being the goal of morality, that is, acting from duty.

But Singer's conclusion goes beyond his premises. For although the paradox does suggest that steady attention to one's own happiness can be self-defeating, it does not follow that attending to quite different goals is the best way of securing one's happiness. All that follows is that we need to focus on activities that, experience has shown us, are closely connected with securing our own happiness, only checking from time to time whether these activities actually do make us happy. So Singer has not shown that rejecting an overall goal of furthering one's self-interest and adopting the goal of acting from duty is required for our own happiness.

Thus, most contemporary justifications for morality in terms of self-interest have either (a) confused a justification in terms of self-interest with our other two types of justification for morality; (b) failed to establish a sufficient correspondence between acting according to duty and what is in one's self-interest, without appealing to the widely disputed assumption of a justice-producing afterlife; or (c) failed to establish that acting from duty is the best way to secure one's own happiness.

Utilizing the tools of decision theory, however, David Gauthier has constructed an elaborate argument to show that acquiring a disposition to act morally can be justified in terms of self-interest or, as he would put it, that adopting a strategy of constrained maximization can be justified in terms of the maximization of individual utility (1986: chaps 5–7). This strategy of constrained maximization is said to be moral or fair in that it requires people to benefit in proportion to their relative contribution. Nevertheless, Gauthier contends (p. 158) that rational individuals fully knowledgeable about their capacities, situation, and concerns would choose to comply with such a strategy on utility-maximizing grounds. More precisely, they would "choose on utility maximizing grounds not to make further choices on those grounds."

Gauthier further contends that the disposition of a rational individual to comply with a strategy of constrained maximization is conditional upon the person's expectation that "she will benefit in comparison with the utility she could expect were no one to cooperate" (p. 169). Accordingly, when

faced with persons whom she believes to be straight-forward maximizers, a constrained maximizer does not play into their hands by basing her actions on the joint strategy she would like everyone to accept, but rather, to avoid being exploited, she behaves as a straightforward maximizer, acting on the individual strategy that maximizes her utility given the strategies she expects others to employ. A constrained maximizer makes reasonably certain that she is among like-disposed persons before she actually constraints her direct pursuit of maximum utility.

Thus, for a strategy of constrained maximization to be justified on the basis of maximizing individual utility, it must be the case that constrained maximizers can tell beforehand whether they are interacting with other constrained maximizers or with straightforward maximizers. Only in this way can they avoid being taken advantage of by straightforward maximizers. Happily, this obstacle can be overcome, Gauthier argues (p. 174), provided that constrained maximizers are present in sufficient numbers and that people's dispositions to cooperate may be ascertained by others "not with certainty but as more than mere guesswork." For example, Gauthier estimates (p. 177) that in a population evenly divided between constrained and straightforward maximizers, constrained maximizers may expect to do better than straightforward maximizers if the constrained maximizers are able to cooperate successfully in two-thirds of their encounters and to avoid being exploited by straightforward maximizers in four-fifths of their encounters.

A final condition that Gauthier maintains must be met before a strategy of constrained maximization is said to be justified on grounds of maximizing individual utility is that its adoption proceed from a noncoercive starting point (p. 200). The test for such a starting point is that, other things being equal, no one is made worse off by the actions of others than they would be if those others had never existed.[13] Thus, for example, it would not be enough for slaveholders simply to free their slaves; they must also compensate them so that they would be no worse off than they would be had the slaveholders never existed. Without such a noncoercive starting point, Gauthier contends (p. 232), it would not be rational for someone freely to adopt a strategy of constrained maximization, for "morals arise in and from the rational agreement of equals."

But does Gauthier's argument succeed in showing that morality can be justified in terms of self-interest? I think his argument clearly succeeds in showing that a limited disposition to take into account the interests of others can be justified on grounds of self-interest; or, put another way, that acting from duty, that is, from the motive of doing one's duty, can be required at least sometimes by self-interest. This is a significant result. Whether it succeeds as a justification for morality depends upon how we go further to specify our definition of morality.

For Gauthier, morality takes into account the interests of everyone alike, but it does so only within a voluntary system of mutual benefit. Thus, on Gauthier's account, attempts by slaveholders to retain their slaves or attempts by South African whites to retain their privileged status, when no other course of action would better serve their individual utility, are not immoral. Rather, they are simply beyond the pale of morality (ibid.: 227–32). On more standard accounts of morality, however, such instances of coercive exploitation constitute some of our clearest examples of immorality.

Moreover, on Gauthier's account of morality, we cannot even morally approve the actions of those who violently throw off the shackles of coercive exploitation to establish a more just society against the interest of their former slaveholders or rulers. But again, on more standard accounts of morality, such cases are among our clearest examples of justified moral action.

Some philosophers have also questioned Gauthier's strong assumption that for the requirements of morality to be justified, people must be "translucent" with respect to their disposition to cooperate. Stephen Darwall, for example, objects (1983: 196–98) that in real life such knowledge is not likely to obtain. Yet with respect to many actions whose good consequences depend on a sufficient number of other people doing likewise, such as paying one's taxes or fighting for one's country, we assume that such knowledge does obtain. This is because our obligation to perform such actions is dependent upon a sufficient number of other individuals doing likewise. In standard accounts of morality, however, we have other obligations and duties that do not depend upon other people doing likewise, such as our obligation not to torture or kill innocent people. By contrast, on Gauthier's account of morality, such obligations and duties are nonexistent.

There is also an important difference between Gauthier's account of morality and the one commonly endorsed by welfare liberals like John Rawls. On the one hand, Gauthier seems to be claiming that one's natural assets should count in determining the social goods one should receive. On the other hand Rawls, in particular, seems to be claiming that they should not count (1971: 101–2). But the real difference between Gauthier and Rawls here is simply *the degree* to which natural assets should count in determining the amount of social goods a person should receive. On the one hand, Gauthier claims that persons may use their natural assets for personal benefit subject only to the moral constraint that they not make others worse off. This point is illustrated by Gauthier when he admits that on his account of morality, "the rich man may feast on cavier and champagne while the poor woman starves at his gate," and morality not be offended (Gauthier 1986: 218). On the other hand, Rawls claims that persons may use their natural assets for personal benefit subject to the additional moral constraint that others have at least the opportunity for securing the minimal resources required for a good life. In other words, inequalities cannot be justified as long as there are ways to achieve a net transfer resources from the rich to the poor.

In addition, on Gauthier's account of morality, making people worse off is not wrong in itself (ibid.; 200–201, 208). Rather, what is wrong, and also irrational, is for people to accept conditions in which they have been made worse off as a starting point for the voluntary agreements that, on Gauthier's view, constitute morality. But when making people worse off serves to promote individual utility more than such voluntary agreements would, Gauthier has no objection to doing so. It is simply beyond the pale of morality on his account.

In sum, while Gauthier's justification for morality is successful within a limited domain, too much still falls outside of Gauthier's account of morality for it to be a fully adequate justification of morality in terms of self-interest.

Morality and Other-Regarding Interests

Our second justification for morality, the view that morality is justified in terms of people's other-regarding interests, wants, or intentions, has many prominent contemporary advocates. For example, it is common to Philippa Foot's account of morality as a system of hypothetical imperatives and to Gilbert Harman's moral relativism.

Foot thinks moral judgments are hypothetical in that their reason-giving force depends upon the interests, wants, or intentions people happen to have.[14] Thus, unless people have these other-regarding interests, wants, or intentions, Foot claims, they will have no reasons for acting morally.[15] This proclaimed relativity of the reason-giving force of moral judgments to the interests, wants and, particularly, the intentions people happen to have that Harman interprets to be a form of moral relativism (1975: 307–22). Moral judgments so grounded he calls "inner judgments." They are said to imply reasons for acting and to apply to agents who are capable of being motivated by the relevant moral considerations. Nevertheless, Harman would probably agree with Foot that "an agent may fail to be moved by a reason (for acting) even when he is aware of it, and he may be moved by something which is not a reason at all.[16]

Foot and Harman certainly do agree that there are other sorts of moral judgments that do not imply that an agent has the relevant moral reasons for acting.[17] I shall call these "outer judgments," and I shall use Harman's term "inner judgments" to refer to moral judgments that, according to Foot and Harman, do imply reasons for acting. Outer judgments allow us to say that Hitler was an evil person or that cannibals ought not to eat their captives or, more generally, that someone is wicked or immoral, even when such an agent lacks the relevant reasons for acting morally. Yet there are differences between Foot's and Harman's views. For example, Foot would probably not characterize her view as a form of moral relativism, and Harman would probably reject Foot's account of moral virtues. But here I am concerned only with their shared account of moral judgments.

The basic difficulty with Foot and Harman's shared account of moral judgments is that their distinction between what I call inner and outer judgments is irrelevant from the point of view of imputing moral responsibility. In imputing moral responsibility, it is not necessary to show that people have the relevant moral reasons for acting otherwise, since we hold people morally responsible even when they lack such reasons, provided they are morally responsible for the lack. For example, if political leaders had the capabilities and opportunities to become aware of their society's racist and sexist practices but in fact failed to do so, with the consequence that they presently lack any moral reasons to oppose such practices, we would still hold them morally responsible, because their lack of moral reasons in this regard is something for which they are morally responsible. Similarly, if people allow themselves to become so engrossed in advancing their own personal and family projects that they come to ignore the most basic needs of others even when they have a surplus of resources, and as a result, they come to lack any moral reasons to help people who are truly in need, we could still hold them morally responsible in this regard. As these examples indicate, having moral reasons to act otherwise is not necessary for imputing moral responsibility. Rather, what is necessary is that people are or were able to acquire the relevant moral reasons. And it is clear that satisfaction of this condition is compatible not only with inner but also with many outer judgments as well.[18]

This conclusion shows that Foot and Harman's justification for morality fails for a significant range of cases in which we hold people morally responsible. For in such cases the justification for those moral requirements that we hold people responsible for violating derives not from their having the relevant moral reasons, but from their having the capacity and opportunity to acquire such reasons. It follows that possession of the relevant moral reasons is *not necessary* for justifying at least some of the requirements of morality.

Nor for that matter is possession of the relevant moral reasons *sufficient* for justifying the requirements of morality. For people typically possess or have possessed not only the capabilities and opportunities necessary to acquire the other-regarding interests, wants, or intentions relevant to moral reasons for acting, but also possess (or have possessed) the capabilities and opportunities necessary to acquire the self-regarding interests, wants, or intentions relevant to self-interested reasons for acting. Accordingly, we would need to ask, given the capabilities and opportunities to develop in either direction, what sort of interests, wants, or intentions a person should develop.[19]

Usually, of course, we have both moral and self-interested reasons to get others to become other-regarding. But at best this can provide an explanation, not a justification, for why people develop in one way rather than the other.[20] What we need to ask, assuming that people can develop either way, is why they should develop (or continue to develop) their other-regarding interests, wants, or intentions rather than their self-regarding interests, wants, or intentions. Put another way, how do we show that developing into a morally good person is better than developing into a rationally self-interested person?

We may, of course, be able to provide self-interested reasons for acting according to duty, but, as we have already noted, it is implausible to think that we could always do so or that acting from duty could always be justified in terms of self-interest.[21] Why then should one person develop so as to act from or according to duty rather than to act from or according to self-interest?

The justification for morality endorsed by Foot and Harman cannot answer this question. For the possession of the relevant moral reasons for acting is neither necessary nor sufficient to justify abiding by the requirements of morality. Only the third sort of justification for morality could conceivably answer this question by showing that the requirements of morality are in fact the requirements of practical reason.

Morality and Practical Reason

I begin by considering three cases for this third sort of justification for morality: those offered by Kurt Baier, Alan Gewirth, and Stephen Darwall.

Baier's Justification for Morality

In his most recent work, Kurt Baier attempts to justify morality by providing an account of practical reason. According to his account, the key constraints are the following:

Universality: Since a fact F is a reason for someone to do A in virtue of his satisfying certain conditions D, F must be a reason to do A for anyone who satisfies D.

Empirical Substantiation: The soundness of the belief that C is the criterion that is to determine whether or not F is a reason of a certain strength for X to do A is to be determined by the way acceptance of this criterion affects the satisfactoriness of the relevant lives.

Universalizability: If F is a reason to do A for anyone who satisfies D, then F must also be capable of being a reason to do A for everyone who satisfies D.

Baier contends that only when moral reasons are taken to be supreme can these three requirements of practical reason be met, since only then would each person have the best reason grounded in the satisfactoriness of the person's own life that every person (not any person) can possible have.[22]

To evaluate Baier's defense of morality, let us consider whether the standard opponent of morality, the rational egoist, can accept or reject all three of Baier's requirements without acting contrary to reason.[23]

For a fully adequate defense of morality in terms of practical reason must show that the rational egoist acts contrary to reason. Accordingly, for Baier's defense of morality to be acceptable, we must show that the rational egoist's acceptance or rejection of Baier's requirements is not contrary to reason.

At first glance, it seems that the rational egoist would have no difficulty accepting at least the first two of Baier's three requirements. Certainly, the egoist could accept his Universality criterion. The egoist could grant, for example, that if the fact that it would make her very rich (fact F) is a reason for her to steal given that conditions are such that she could easily get away with the theft (condition D), then F must be a reason to steal for anyone who satisfies D. Baier's Empirical Substantiation criterion also seems equally acceptable. How could the egoist deny that the soundness of rational egoism depends on the effect of taking egoistic reasons to be overriding in the lives of rational egoists? Hence, at least initially, only acceptance of Universalizability seems to present a problem for the rational egoist.

Part of the problem is that Baier gives different interpretations to this proposed requirement. Sometimes he interprets the requirement to imply (a) that it must be possible for everyone always to be perfectly rational (1978b: 240). At other times, he interprets the requirement to imply, or at least to suggest, the stronger claim (b) that it must be a good thing for everyone always to be perfectly rational (1978a: 69).

Now the rational egoist would have little difficulty accepting Universalizability under interpretation (a). The rational egoist would simply argue that once the directives of rational egoism are plausibly interpreted,[24] it is surely possible for everyone always to be perfectly rational by following these directives. Yet, accepting Universalizability under interpretation (a) raises a problem for the rational egoist's initial acceptance of Empirical Substantiation. For the negative effects on the satisfactoriness of the egoist's life arising from everyone following the directives of rational egoism appear to violate it. Nonetheless, there are at least two reasons for thinking that the rational egoist can meet this requirement while accepting Universalizability under interpretation (a).

First, the effects on the satisfactoriness of the egoist's life from everyone following the directives of rational egoism may not be as disasterous as they are sometimes made out to be. For surely if we are to concede anything to the defenders of our first justification for morality, it is that a world where everyone pursues long-term self-interest under ideal institutional arrangements may not be such a bad world to live in, although it would be different, as we have argued, from a world where everyone always acted from or according to duty.

Thus, Hobbes's war of all against all may be a poor model for a state of affairs where rational egoism reigns.

Second, we must evaluate the impact on the satisfactoriness of the egoist's life when everyone follows rational egoism, together with the effects on the satisfactoriness of the egoist's life when almost everyone, save the egoist, follows morality. Obviously, for good self-interested reasons the egoist opposes the taking of self-interested reasons to be supreme by others, although she admits that such behavior is fully rational. The egoist does not want others reaping the benefits of following self-interested reasons at her expense, and she publicly endorses the following of moral reasons as strongly as anyone. The egoist observes that most people take a similar stand, and recognizes that many with the "proper upbringing" in fact come to care strongly for others and, as a result, to follow moral reasons almost instinctively. Taking all this into account, the egoist is justified in concluding that it is improbable that circumstances would arise in which everyone followed the directives of rational egoism. Given then that the egoist can be assured that others will continue to follow the directives of morality even when the egoist follows those of self-interest, the egoist can reasonably expect that the overall effect on the satisfactoriness of her life from taking self-interested reasons to be supreme would be positive, and considerably better than the overall effect from taking moral reasons to be supreme.

Of course, someone might object to the introduction of probability assessments of other people's behavior into the calculation of the overall satisfactoriness of the egoist's life.[25] But what is the ground for this objection? The egoist grants that while it is possible for everyone to follow rational egoism, it is unlikely, and accordingly the expected overall effect on the egoist's life from following rational egoism would be quite positive, and considerably better than the expected overall effect from following the directives of morality. Unlike the prisoner in the well-known Prisoner's Dilemma, the rational egoist justifiably believes that others are more likely to choose the mutually beneficial action (not confessing in the Prisoner's Dilemma). Hence, the egoist has good reason to think that the overall satisfactoriness of her life would be furthered by taking self-interested reasons to be supreme (confessing in the Prisoner's Dilemma.)[26]

Given then that the egoist can accept Baier's Universality Empirical Substantiation, and Universalizability under interpretation (a), Baier's defense of morality must ultimately rest on the claim that it is contrary to reason for the egoist to reject Universalizability under interpretation (b). That the egoist has to reject Universalizability under this interpretation seems correct. The rational egoist has to deny that it is a good thing for everyone to be perfectly rational and to take the directives of rational egoism to be supreme. But why is that rejection contrary to reason? Why is it contrary to reason to recognize that people ought to do what is in their best interest and yet not to think it is a good thing for them all to do what they ought?

Here the "oughts" found in most ordinary competitive games provide a useful analogy. Tennis players can judge that their opponents ought to put maximum spin on their serves without being committed to thinking that it is a good thing for them if their opponents serve in this way and they then counter with their best returns. If that did occur, they might lose the game. After all, not infrequently one side is victorious in a game only because the other side failed to execute its best moves.[27]

Of course, there is an important dissimilarity between these two types of "oughts." Since competitive games are governed by moral constraints when everyone does exactly what he or she ought to do, there is an accepted moral limit to what a person can lose. By contrast, when everyone takes self-interested reasons to be supreme, the only limit to what a person can lose is the point beyond which others would not benefit.[28]

But this dissimilarity does not destroy the analogy. For it is still the case that when judged from the individual player's or the egoist's point of view, it need not be a good thing for everyone to be perfectly rational. It follows, therefore, that the rational egoist cannot be convicted of acting contrary to reason for rejecting Baier's Universalizability criterion under interpretation (b), even though Baier's general strategy for constructing such a justification is surely correct.

If this third sort of justification for morality is to be successful, it will have to proceed from premises different from those Baier provides. What we are looking for is an argument supporting the requirements of morality that does not depend upon premises that beg the question against the rational egoist. Only then will we have succeeded in showing that the rational egoist acts contrary to reason.

Gewirth's Justification for Morality

Using the same general strategy as Baier, Alan Gewirth has proposed a quite different argument to justify morality (1978: chaps. 2 and 3). Gewirth's argument can be summarized as follows:

1. Every agent has to accept (a): "I must have freedom and well-being."
2. By virtue of accepting (a), every agent also has to accept (b): "I have a right to freedom and well-being."

3. Further, every agent has to accept (c): "I have a right to freedom and well-being because I am a prospective, purposive agent."

4. By virtue of accepting (c) every agent also has to accept (d): "All prospective, purposive agents have a right to freedom and well-being."

Many of Gewirth's critics have focused on the inference from (1) to (2), contending that rational agents need not endorse *moral* rights to freedom and well-being simply because they accept (a).[29] In response, Gewirth has claimed that, as he interprets the argument, rational agents in accepting (b) do not commit themselves to moral rights, but only to prudential rights. According to Gewirth, moral rights appear only in the argument in step (4) through the application of the principle of universalizability.

To many the notion of prudential rights is a strange notion, and Gewirth has attempted to elucidate the concept by pointing out that the grounds for the prudential right claim in (b) are simply the prudential purposes of the agent, not the prudential purposes or interests of other persons to whom the right claim is directed. I take this to mean that in endorsing (b), agents are not assuming that other people have any reasons in terms of their prudential or moral purposes that would lead them to respect the right claims they, the agents, are making. Notice that in this respect Gewirth's notion of prudential rights is strikingly different from the standard understanding of moral rights, because the grounds for moral rights are usually thought to include not only reasons or purposes the agent has but also reasons or purposes others have or should have as well. For example, if I say that I have a moral right based on a contractual agreement to lecture at a particular university, I imply not only that I have moral or prudential reasons for exercising this right, but also that others have moral or prudential reasons for permitting me to do so. I point this out simply to indicate the special way that Gewirth is using the notion of rights in step (2) of his argument. Once one understands how Gewirth is using the notion of rights, I see no problem with his inference from (1) to (2).

As I see it, the problematic inference in Gewirth's argument is the inference from (3) to (4). This is because, Gewirth contends, the notion of rights that an agent endorses in (4) is moral, not prudential, as it is in (2) and also in (3). According to Gewirth, it is by the process of universalizing that the prudential right claim in (3) is transformed into a moral right claim in (4). But why does Gewirth think that this inference is valid? What Gewirth says to justify the inference is the following: "Now the resulting generalization is a moral judgment, because it requires the agent to take favorable account of the interests of persons other than or in addition to himself. The agent logically must here recognize that other persons have the same rights he claims for himself because they fulfill the same justifying condition on which he has based his own right claim."[30]

Here again, a number of Gewirth's critics have not found this justification compelling, but although they have questioned this inference in Gewirth's argument, none of them, as far as I can tell, has attempted to show exactly what does follow from the application of the principle of universalizability to step (3) of the argument.[31] And it seems to me that this failure to justify an alternative inference may be what has kept Gewirth and his critics from reaching agreement concerning this important step of his argument.

To understand better what inference can be drawn from step (3), it is useful to reformulate (3) as an ought claim rather than a right claim. This gives us

3'. Every agent has to accept (c'): "I ought (prudentially and prescriptively) to have freedom and well-being simply in virtue of being a prospective, purposive agent."

Since the right in (3) is said to be prudential, the qualifier "prudentially" in (3') is self-explanatory. The other qualifier—"prescriptively"—is included simply to indicate that the ought claims to which agents are committing themselves are explicit action-guiding ought claims that require, other things being equal, an appropriate commitment to action. Now it seems to me that three possible inferences might be claimed to follow from (3') by an application of the principle of universalizability.

First, there is

4.' By virtue of accepting (c'), every agent also has to accept (d'): "All prospective, purposive agents ought (morally and prescriptively) to have freedom and well-being."

This, of course, is the inference Gewirth would want us to draw. By accepting the moral and prescriptive ought claim of (d'), agents are not only committed to acting to secure their own freedom and well-being, they are also committed to making a contribution toward securing the freedom and well-being of others. But given that the freedom and well-being of people conflict, exactly what actions would be permissible or required would have to be determined by some moral weighing of the competing interests. It is obvious that the ideals of each of our five conceptions of justice have been proposed to specify what weights should be given to the competing interests, but as I have argued in preceding chapters, when these ideals are correctly interpreted, the same practical recommendations follow. Expressed in Gewirth's terminology, what I have argued is that agents should be permitted to give a limited preference, and only a limited preference, to their own freedom and well-being over the freedom and well-being of others, and normally they should be required to make an important contribution toward securing the freedom and well-being of others.

However, the following are also possible inferences from (3'):

4''. By virtue of accepting (c'), every agent also has to accept (d''): "All perspective, purposive agents ought (prudentially and prescriptively) to have freedom and well-being."

4'''. By virtue of accepting (c'), every agent has to accept (d'''): "All prospective, purposive agents ought (prudentially but not necessarily prescriptively) to have freedom and well-being."

In his discussion of universal ethical egoism in his *Morality and Reason,* Gewirth considers the possibility of generalizations like (4'') and (4''') and rejects them both (82–89) but, as far as I can tell, without good reason.

Gewirth's reason for rejecting (4'') is that it will give rise to incompatible and self-defeating action-guiding directives. By endorsing (d''), the ought claim embedded in (4''), Gewirth thinks that agents would be committed to doing all they can to secure their own freedom and well-being and also be committed to doing all they can to secure the freedom and well-being of others. Because these two courses of action are incompatible and self-defeating, Gewirth rejects (4'') as a possible inference from (3'). Yet one need not interpret (d'') in this way. In the case of (d''), as in the case of (d'), the freedom and well-being of people conflict, and here too there is need to weigh the competing interests; but unlike in the case of (d'), the requisite weighing must be prudential, not moral, because the ought claim involved is prudential, not moral. Nonetheless, there is a way of understanding how this weighing could take place without resulting in incompatible and self-defeating action-guiding directives, for we can imagine (d'') as requiring that agents take the interests of others into account *except* when they conflict with their own interests. This interpretation of (d'') would require agents to do all they can to secure their own freedom and well-being, and when there is no conflict they would also be required to do what they can to secure the freedom and well-being of others. Of course, this would not be an acceptable moral weighing of the competing interests involved, but it would be a weighing that is prudential and prescriptive and that does not give rise to directives that are incompatible and self-defeating for agents.[32]

Gewirth's reason for rejecting (4''') is that, he claims, its use of "ought" equivocates between a use that is action-guiding or prescriptive, for example, when the agent infers from (d''') that she ought to have freedom and well-being, and a use that is not action-guiding nor prescriptive, such as when the agent infers from (d''') that others ought to have freedom and well-being.[33] Now although this use of "ought" in (d''') is differentially action-guiding in just the way Gewirth suggests, nothing seems equivocal about this usage, since it is analogous to the use of "ought" in competitive games. Thus, to adapt an example of Jesse Kalin's, if you and I are playing chess, at a certain point in the game I may judge that you ought to move your bishop and put my king in check, but this judgment is not relevantly action-guiding for me. What I in fact should do is sit quietly and hope that you do not move as you ought. If you fail to make the appropriate move and, later in the game, I judge that I ought to put your king in check, that judgment, by contrast, would be relevantly action-guiding for me.

As one might expect, Gewirth has considered the possibility that the use of "ought" in (d''') is not equivocal because it is analogous to the use of "ought" employed in competitive games. In response, he claims that the differentially action-guiding "oughts" of competive games follow conditionally from commitment to the principle that games ought to be played according to their rules and related objectives, and that our acceptance or advocacy of this principle is radically different from the acceptance or advocacy of (4''').

But is this the case? Certainly we can grant that acceptance or advocacy of the first part of the principle of games *that everyone ought to play games according to their rules* supports judgments prohibiting various forms of cheating that are uniformly action-guiding. And in this respect the "oughts" of competitive games are disanalogous to the differentially action-guiding use of "ought" in (d''').

But acceptance or advocacy of the first part of the principle of games does not explain why we make differentially action-guiding judgments such as "She ought to move her bishop and put my king in check" and I ought to move my knight and take her queen." What explains such judgments is our acceptance or advocacy of the second part of the principle of games: *that everyone ought to play games according to their related objectives.* Since the most significant of these related objectives is *to win,* and winning typically requires making one's best moves, we have the derived principle that everyone ought to make his or her best moves when playing games. And it is our acceptance or advocacy of this derived principle that explains our acceptance or advocacy of the differentially action-guiding judgments we make with respect to competitive games. And since no one thinks that this differentially action-guiding use of "ought" in competitive games is equivocal, neither should anyone think that the analoguous differen- tially action-guiding use of "ought" in (d''') is equivocal. Consequently, (4''') has not been excluded as a possible inference from step (3) of Gewirth's argument.

If I am right, three possible inferences—(4'), (4''), and (4''')—might be claimed to follow from step (3) of Gewirth's argument. All three of these possible inferences allow the agent to favor her own freedom and well-being over the freedom and well-being of others, but to varying degrees: (4') allows a limited preference in this regard, (4'') a maximal preference, and (4''') an exclusive preference. As we have seen, Gewirth favors (4'), but I have argued that his reasons for rejecting (4'') and (4''') are not sound. Moreover, in the absence of good reasons for ruling out (4'') and (4'''), it is important to see that they are the favored candidates for the appropriate inference to be drawn from (3'). This is because they both contain, in (d'') and (d'''), prudential rather than moral principles; and in the absence of good reasons to the contrary, it would seem that the appropriate generalization of the prudential claim (c') should be another prudential claim such as (d'') or (d'''), rather than a moral claim such as (d'). But if this is the case, Gewirth's central argument for the justification of morality clearly fails, because the inference from (3) to (4) has not been established.

Darwall's Justification for Morality

Using the same general strategy as Baier and Gewirth, Stephen Darwall begins his defense of morality (1983: 208–11) by appealing to the following, seemingly uncontroversial, principle:

A rational agent ought to act at *T* as there is, all things considered, reason for her to act at *t*.

Darwall then goes on to claim that there is a reason for a person to act at *t* if that person would, by a dispassionate reflection on the relevant evidence at *t,* retain or acquire that reason at *t.* For Darwall this reflection takes place either from a personal or from an impersonal standpoint (ibid.: 135–36). From a personal standpoint, such reflection gives rise to self-regarding reasons. From an impersonal standpoint, such reflection gives rise to other-regarding reasons. According to Darwall, both sorts of reasons are relevant to the rational assessment of conduct.

There are two difficulties with Darwall's specification of the class of relevant reasons. First, Darwall does not provide an argument why the rational egoist should recognize as relevant those reasons that are derived from an impersonal standpoint.[34] Second, he treats as irrelevant to the rational assessment of conduct those reasons a person could have acquired only in the past (Darwell 1983: 108). For example, on Darwall's account, the fact that people could have acquired certain reasons to oppose the racist and sexist practices in their society but now, because of their insensitivity, can no longer acquire such reasons is irrelevant to the assessment of the reasonableness of their conduct.

Nevertheless, the major difficulty with Darwall's defense of morality concerns not his interpretation of what is to count as a relevant reason, but rather his interpretation of what is to count as a rational weighing of such reasons. According to Darwall (ibid.: 208–11), since a rational weighing of such reasons applies to everyone, it must ultimately be made from an impersonal and, hence, impartial standpoint, thus resulting in reasons that are uniformly action-guiding for all rational agents. Such reasons entail that other rational agents ought not to interfere with an agent's acting as there is reason for her to act, all things considered. Unfortunately Darwall never considers why a rational weighing of the relevant reasons, even if it is to apply to everyone, could not be made from a personal standpoint, thus resulting in differentially action-guiding reasons like the "oughts" in competitive games.

This latter interpretation, of course, is the one the defender of rational egoism would endorse, and Darwall needs to argue that this interpretation would beg the question against the defender of morality. But even given such an argument, it would not thereby follow, at least not directly, that an *impartial* weighing of the relevant reasons is rationally required. One needs to argue first that some type of a compromise between conflicting self-regarding and other-regarding reasons is rationally required. Only then could one reasonably proceed to argue that the type of compromise needed should be impartial. Even then it would be surprising if the impartiality that is rationally required turned out to be, as Darwall claims (ibid.: 230–39), the same impartiality that is found in John Rawls's original position. For that would mean that moral perspectives incorporating weaker notions of impartiality, such as libertarianism, would all be contrary to reason. Yet even those who endorse the impartiality of Rawls's original position would find this result too much to hope for.

Morality as Compromise

My own justification for morality employs the same general strategy as the justifications offered by Baier, Gewirth, and Darwall. Mine primarily differs from theirs in that it draws upon and generalizes our insights about holding people morally responsible to arrive at what purports to be a non-question-begging standard of reasonable conduct that succeeds in showing that the rational egoist acts contrary to reason.

As we have already noted, the reasons a person could have acquired can be relevant when assessing a person's conduct from a moral point of view. In such assessments, people are said to be morally responsible even when they presently lack any moral reasons to act otherwise, provided that they are morally responsible for the lack. For example, if I had the capacity and opportunity to become more sensitive to my child's needs but, in fact, failed to do so, with the consequence that I presently lack the moral reasons to respond effectively to those needs, I would still be morally responsible, because my lack of moral reasons in this regard is something for which I am morally responsible.[35] What is not so generally recognized, however, is that the reasons a person could have acquired can also be relevant when assessing a person's conduct from a self-interest point of view.

Consider the following example. An acquaintance of mine bought a house on the last day it was being offered for sale, when it was too late to have the house inspected. The house was found to have such a termite infestation that it cost several thousands of dollars to correct the structural damage. Apparently, the previous owners did not know about the termites, and my acquaintance, having inspected the house on her own, did not think that she needed to have the house professionally inspected. My acquaintance now admits, I think rightly, that she acted unreasonably in purchasing the house without a professional inspection. I think it is plausible to say that her action was not unreasonable in terms of any reasons she had at the time of purchase, because at that time she didn't know or have reason to believe that the house had termites, and the opportunity to have the house inspected no longer existed. Rather, her action is best seen as unreasonable in terms of the reasons she could have had at the time of purchase if only she had arranged to have the house professionally inspected.

What these examples taken together appear to support is the following general standard:

> *A Standard for Reasonable Conduct:* Reasonable conduct accords with a rational weighing of all the relevant reasons for acting that people are or were able to acquire.[36]

According to the standard, not all the reasons people are or were able to acquire are *relevant* to an assessment of the reasonableness of their conduct. First, reasons that are evokable only from some logically possible set of opportunities are simply not relevant; the reasons must be evokable from the opportunities people actually possessed. Second, reasons that radically different people could have acquired are also not relevant. Instead, relevant reasons are those that people could have acquired without radical changes in their developing identities. Third, some reasons are not important enough to be relevant to a reasonable assessment of conduct. For example, a reason that I am able to acquire, which would lead me to promote my own interests or that of a friend just slightly more than I am presently doing, is hardly relevant to an assessment of the reasonableness of my conduct. Surely I could not be judged as unreasonable for failing to acquire such a reason. Rather relevant reasons are those that would lead one to avoid a *significant harm* to oneself (or others) or to secure a *significant benefit* to oneself (or others) at an acceptable cost to oneself (or others). Thus, the Standard for Reasonable Conduct is not concerned with the possibility of maximizing benefit or minimizing harm overall but only with the possibility of avoiding a significant harm or securing a significant benefit at an acceptable cost.[37]

It is obvious that a given individual may not actually reflect upon all the relevant reasons for deciding what to do. In fact, one could do so only if one had already acquired all the relevant reasons.[38] Nevertheless, reasonable conduct is ideally determined by a rational weighing of all the relevant reasons so that failing to accord with a rational weighing of all such reasons is to act contrary to reason.[39]

Of course, while defenders of rational egoism would certainly not deny the relevance of the self-interested reasons people are or were able to acquire to the rational assessment of conduct, they may want to deny that the moral reasons that people are or were able to acquire are similarly relevant. But what would be the basis for that denial? It could not be that rational egoists do not in fact act or choose to act upon moral reasons, for that would no more show the irrelevance of moral reasons to the rational assessment of conduct than the fact that pure altruists do not act or choose to act upon self-interested reasons would show the irrelevance of self-interested reasons to such an assessment. To argue on such grounds would simply beg the question against the opposing view, and most defenders of rational egoism have at least tried to support the view in a non-question-begging way.

In fact, most defenders of rational egoism have argued for egoism in its universal form, defending the following principle:

Every person ought to do what best serves her overall self-interest.

But defenders of rational egoism could no more support this principle by simply denying the relevance of moral reasons to a rational assessment of conduct than could defenders of pure altruism, by simply denying the relevance of self-interested reasons to a rational assessment of conduct, support their opposing principle:[40]

Every person ought to do what best serves the overall interest of others.

Consequently, defenders of rational egoism seem to have no other alternative but to grant the prima facie relevance of moral reasons to the rational assessment of conduct and then try to show that such an assessment would never rationally require us to act upon moral reasons, all things considered.[41]

Unfortunately for the defenders of rational egoism, a rational assessment of the relevant reasons does not lead to this result. Quite the contrary, such an assessment shows that we are rationally required to act upon moral reasons. To see why this is so, we will consider two kinds of cases. First, there are cases in which there is conflict between the relevant moral reasons and self-interested reasons. Second, there are cases in which there is no such conflict.

Now it seems obvious that where there is no conflict and both reasons are conclusive reasons of their kind, both reasons should be acted upon. In such contexts, we should do what is favored both by morality and by self-interest. Consider the following example. Suppose you accepted a job marketing a baby formula in underdeveloped countries, where the formula was improperly used, leading to increased infant mortality.[42] You can just as well have accepted an equally attractive and rewarding job marketing a similar formula in developed countries, where the misuse does not occur, so that a rational weighing of the relevant self-interested reasons alone would not have favored your acceptance of one of these jobs over the other.[43] At the same time, there were obviously moral reasons that condemned your acceptance of the first job—reasons that you presumably are or were able to acquire. Moreover, by assumption in this case, the moral reasons do not clash with the relevant self-interested reasons; they simply made a recommendation where the relevant self-interested reasons are silent. Consequently, a rational weighing of all the relevant reasons in this case could not but favor acting in accord with the relevant moral reasons.[44]

Yet one might object that even in cases of this sort there are frequently other reasons significantly opposed to these moral reasons—other reasons you are or were able to acquire. Such reasons would be either *malevolent* reasons seeking to bring about the suffering and death of other human beings, or *benevolent* reasons concerned to promote nonhuman welfare even at the expense of human welfare, or *aesthetic* reasons concerned to produce valuable results irrespective of the effects on human or nonhuman welfare. But assuming that such malevolent reasons are ultimately rooted in some conception of what is good for oneself or others,[45] these reasons would have already been taken into account and, by assumption, have been outweighed by the other relevant reasons in this case. And although neither benevolent reasons (concerned to promote nonhuman welfare) nor aesthetic reasons would have been taken into account, such reasons are not directly relevant to justifying morality to the rational egoist.[46] Consequently, even with the presence of these three kinds of reasons, your acceptance of the first job can still be seen to violate the standard for Reasonable Conduct.

Defenders of rational egoism can only be disconcerted with this result, since it shows that actions in accord with rational egoism are contrary to reason, at least when there are two equally good ways of pursuing one's self-interest, only one of which does not conflict with the basic requirements of morality. Notice also that in cases where there are two equally good ways of fulfilling the basic requirements of morality, only one of which does not conflict with what is in our best overall self-interest, it is not at all disconcerting for defenders of morality to admit that we are rationally required to choose the way that does not conflict with what is in our overall self-interest. Nevertheless, exposing this defect in rational egoism for cases where moral reasons and self-interested reasons do not conflict would be but a small victory for defenders of morality if it were not also possible to show that in cases where such reasons do conflict, moral reasons would have priority over self-interested reasons.

Now when one rationally assesses the relevant reasons in such conflict cases, it is best to view the conflict not as a conflict between self-interested reasons and moral reasons, but as a conflict between self-interested reasons and altruistic reasons. Viewed in this way, three solutions are possible. First, one could say that self-interested reasons always have priority over conflicting altruistic reasons. Second, one could say just the opposite: altruistic reasons always have priority over conflicting self-interested reasons. Third, one could say that some kind of a compromise is rationally required. In this compromise, sometimes self-interested reasons would have priority over altruistic reasons, and sometimes altruistic reasons would have priority over self-interested reasons.

Once the conflict is described in this manner, the third solution can be seen to be the one that is rationally required. This is because the first and second solutions give exclusive priority to one class of relevant reasons over the other, and no non-question-begging justification can be given for such an exclusive priority from the standpoint of the Standard for Reasonable Conduct. Only the third solution, by sometimes giving priority to self-interested reasons and sometimes giving priority to altruistic reasons, can provide a non-question-begging resolution from the standpoint of the Standard for Reasonable Conduct.

Consider the following example. Suppose you are in the waste disposal business and you decided to dispose of toxic wastes in a manner that was cost-efficient for you but predictably caused significant harm to future generations. Imagine that alternative waste-disposal methods are available to you that were only slightly less cost-efficient and did not cause any significant harm to future generations.[47] In this case, the Standard for Reasonable Conduct required weighing of your self-interested reasons favoring the most cost-efficient disposal of the toxic wastes against the relevant altruistic reasons favoring the avoidance of significant harm to future generations. If we suppose that the projected loss of benefit to yourself was ever so slight and the projected harm to future generations was ever so great, a nonarbitrary compromise between the relevant self-interested and altruistic reasons would have to favor the altruistic reasons. Hence, as judged by the Standard for Reasonable Conduct, your choice of method of waste disposal was contrary to the relevant reasons.

Notice that this Standard of Reasonable Conduct would not support just any compromise between the relevant self-interested and altruistic reasons. The compromise must be a nonarbitrary one, for otherwise it would beg the question with respect to the opposing egoist and altruist views. Such a compromise would have to respect the ordering of self-interested and altruistic reasons imposed by the egoist and altruist views, respectively. For example, high-ranking self-interested reasons would have to be preferred to low-ranking altruistic reasons, and high-ranking altruistic reasons would have to be preferred to low-ranking self-interested reasons.

Now it is important to see how morality can be viewed as just such a nonarbitrary compromise between self-interested and altruistic reasons. First, a certain amount of self-regard is morally required or at least morally acceptable. Where this is the case, high-ranking self-interested reasons have priority over low-ranking altruistic reasons. Second, morality obviously places limits on the extent to which people should pursue their own self-interest. Where this is the case, high-ranking altruistic reasons have priority over low-ranking self-interested reasons. In this way, morality can be seen to be a nonarbitrary compromise between self-interested and altruistic reasons, and the "moral reasons" that constitute that compromise can be seen as having an absolute priority over the self-interested or altruistic reasons that conflict with them.

Happily, this defense of morality succeeds not only against the view that rational egoism is rationally preferable to morality, but also against the view that rational egoism is only rationally on a par with morality. The "weaker view" does not claim that we all ought to be egoists. Rather, it claims that there is just as good reason for us to be egoists as to be pure altruists or anything in between. As Kai Nielson summarizes this view: "We have not been able to show that reason requires the moral point of view or that all really rational persons not be individual egoists. Reason doesn't decide here."[48] Yet since the above defense of morality shows morality to be a nonarbitrary resolution of the conflict between self-interested and altruistic reasons because the egoist and altruist views are clearly question-begging while the compromise view is not, it is not the case that there are just as good reasons for us to endorse morality as to endorse rational egoism or pure altruism. Thus, the above defense of morality succeeds against the weaker as well as the stronger interpretation of rational egoism.

Unfortunately, this approach to defending morality has been generally neglected by previous moral theorists. The reason it has been neglected is that such theorists have tended to view the basic conflict with rational egoism as a conflict between morality and self-interest. For example, according to Baier (1958: 150), "The very *raison d'être* of a morality is to yield reasons which overrule the reasons of self-interest in those cases when everyone's following self-interest would be harmful to everyone." Viewed in this light, it does not seem possible for the defender of morality to support a compromise view, for how can such a defender say that when morality and self-interest conflict, morality should sometimes be sacrificed for the sake of self-interest? But while previous theorists understood correctly that moral reasons could not be compromised in favor of self-interested reasons, they failed to recognize that this is because moral reasons are already the result of a nonarbitrary compromise between self-interested and altruistic reasons. Thus, unable to see how morality could be represented as a compromise solution, previous theorists have generally failed to recognize this approach to defending morality.

As we have seen, the basic principle of this approach to defending morality is the Standard for Reasonable Conduct, which requires that we seek a nonarbitrary compromise between conflicting self-interested and altruistic reasons—one that gives priority to the highest-ranking self-interested and altruistic reasons. I will now show that this principle requires that we endorse at least a Libertarian Conception of Justice. Then it would follow that, given the argument for practical reconciliation of the previous chapters, the requirements of practical reason would lead to the same practical demands as our five conceptions of justice, namely, a right to welfare and a right to affirmative action.

To begin, it goes without saying that for the libertarian, liberty is the ultimate political ideal; but what is less obvious, as we have seen, is that the distribution of liberty under this conception is governed by the following principle:

> *The "Ought" Implies "Can" Principle:* People are not morally required to do what they lack the power to do or what would involve so great a sacrifice that it would be unreasonable to ask them to perform such an action.

In fact, it was by appealing to this principle that I was able to show that a right to welfare and a right to affirmative action are the fundamental requirements of even a Libertarian Conception of Justice. Moreover, to say that negative liberty is the ultimate political ideal for libertarians means that what are essentially prohibited by a Libertarian Conception of Justice are commissions rather than omissions. Nevertheless, the commissions that are actually prohibited are determined by the "ought" implies "can" principle, so this principle is clearly fundamental to a Libertarian Conception of Justice. I now will show that the Standard for Reasonable Conduct would lead us to endorse this very same principle as a requirement of reason.

Consider that for each individual there is a separate ranking of that individual's relevant self-interested and altruistic reasons. We can represent these rankings from the most important to the least important as follows:

Individual A		Individual B	
Self-interested reasons	Altruistic reasons	Self-interested reasons	Altruistic reasons
1	1	1	1
2	2	2	2
3	3	3	3
•	•	•	•
•	•	•	•
•	•	•	•
N	N	N	N

Obviously any nonarbitrary compromise among such reasons will have to give priority to those reasons that rank highest in each category. Failure to give priority to the highest-ranking altruistic or self-interested reasons would, other things being equal, be contrary to reason, and as such it would be proscribed by the Standard for Reasonable Conduct. But this is essentially what the "ought" implies "can" principle also proscribes because it regards the sacrifice of highest-ranking interests as unreasonable. In this way, therefore, the Standard for Reasonable Conduct leads inevitably to the "ought" implies "can" principle. In fact, in our previous examples, the results we obtained from the application of the Standard for Reasonable Conduct implicitly appealed to that very principle. Thus, once a nonarbitrary compromise between conflicting self-interested and altruistic reasons is seen to be rationally required, the "ought" implies "can" principle emerges as the key principle for affecting such a compromise.[49]

Of course, there will always be cases in which the only way to avoid being required to do what is contrary to one's highest-ranking reasons is by requiring someone else to do what is contrary to her highest-ranking reasons. Such cases are sometimes called "lifeboat cases." But while such cases are difficult to resolve (maybe only a chance mechanism can offer a reasonable resolution), they surely do not reflect the typical conflict between the relevant self-interested and altruistic reasons that people are or were able to acquire. For typically one or the other of the conflicting reasons will rank higher on its respective scale, thus permitting a clear resolution. The resolution will in fact be clearest in just those cases where the "ought" implies "can" principle determines the appropriate distribution of liberty under a Libertarian Conception of Justice. In such cases high-ranking and mutually reinforcing self-interested and altruistic reasons favor a right to welfare and a right to affirmative action, and only low-ranking self-interested reasons favor the rejection of those rights.

Needless to say, this argument does not show that the libertarian's focus on commissions rather than omissions is also required by the Standard for Reasonable Conduct. But as we noted in Chapter 7, this aspect of the libertarian view is not well defended. In my discussion of the Libertarian Conception of Justice, I simply assumed for the sake of argument the strong omission/commission distinction endorsed by libertarians, and then focused on what distribution of liberty would be required. Consequently, it would not at all be surprising if this aspect of the libertarian view could not be shown to be a requirement of practical reason.

It is worth pointing out exactly how the justification of morality I have been defending (which we can call, for short, Morality as Compromise) avoids some of the objections I have raised to other contemporary defenses of morality. First, unlike Gauthier's justification of morality in terms of self-interest, Morality as Compromise is not limited simply to obligations based upon mutual benefit. Rather, it supports a broader range of moral requirements. Second, unlike Foot's and Harman's justifications of morality in terms of the other-regarding interests, wants, and intentions people happen to have, Morality as Compromise supports moral requirements not only when people have the relevant other-regarding interests, wants, intentions, but also when they simply possess or have possessed the capabilities and opportunities for acquiring those interests, wants, and intentions. Third, unlike Baier's, Gewirth's and Darwall's justifications of morality in terms of the requirements of practical reason, Morality as Compromise shows that to avoid arbitrariness the egoist must grant that altruistic reasons as well as self-interested reasons are relevant to the rational assessment of conduct, and also, unlike Darwall's justification, Morality as Compromise justifies on grounds that the egoist must accept a nonarbitrary resolution of conflicts between self-interested and altruistic reasons for acting. Moreover, Morality as Compromise rejects egoism not because its "oughts," like the "oughts" of competitive games, are differentially action-guiding, but because egoism fails to provide a nonarbitrary resolution of conflicts between the relevant self-interested and altruistic reasons for acting. In this way, Morality as Compromise has been designed to overcome the objections I have raised to other contemporary justifications of morality.

In sum, Morality as Compromise provides a justification for morality in terms of the requirements of practical reason that succeeds in showing not only that the rational egoist acts contrary to reason, but also that endorsing at least the basic distributive principle of the Libertarian Conception of Justice is required by reason. By combining Morality as Compromise with the practical reconciliation argument of the preceding chapters, it follows that practical reason requires that we endorse a right to welfare and a right to affirmative action. In this way, I claim, the longstanding gap between rationality and morality can be bridged at last.

Notes

1. Peter Singer (1979: chap. 10); Robert Olson (1965); Neil Cooper (1981); Michael Scriven (1966: chap. 7); D. A. Lloyd Thomas (1970: 128–39); David Gauthier (1986: esp. chaps. 5–7).

2. Philippa Foot (1978); Gilbert Harman (1975: 3–22); and Bernard Williams (1973: chap. 15). Some however, do not see this position as Humean; see W. D. Falk, "Hume on Practical Reason," *Philosophical Studies* (1975): 1–18.

3. Alan Gewirth (1978); Kurt Baier (1978c); Alan Donagan (1977); and Stephen Darwall (1983).

4. In my earlier work I argued that rational egoism is a consistent view (see Sterba 1979 and 1980b: chap. 1). I still think that this is the case, but I now think that it is possible to show that while consistent, the view is contrary to reason.

5. Thomas (1970).

6. A question-begging definition would be one that obviously presupposed the truth of some form of egoism. See, however, the discussion of Gauthier's view in this chapter.

7. Milton Fisk (1980: 139–40); Mary Gibson, "Rationality," *Philosophy and Public Affairs* (1977): 222. See also Isaiah Berlin, *Four Essays on Liberty* (New York, 1969), chap. 3.

8. Bertell Ollman, *Alienation* (New York, 1971), part III.

9. Karl Marx, *Critique of the Gotha Program,* ed. C. P. Dutt (New York, 1966). C. B. Macpherson also endorses the possibility of a harmonious development of people's interests. See his *Democratic Theory* (1973: p. 54).

10. Steven Evans, "Could Divine Rewards Provide a Reason to Be Moral?" in *Realities of Christian Learning,* ed. Harold Heie and David Wolfe. (Grand Rapids: Eedmans, 1986)

11. On this point, see Allen Buchanan, "Revolutionary Motivation and Rationality," *Philosophy and Public Affairs* (1979).

12. Singer (1979: chap. 10). But see also Scriven (1966: chap. 7); and Cooper (1981: chaps. 15 and 16).

13. Ibid., p. 204. Gauthier never considers the problem of whether the injustices of slaveholders, for example, may have resulted in particular slaves being born who would not have been born otherwise. This is relevant because if the lives of these slaves are still worth living, they would not have been made worse off than if the slaveholders had never existed, because then they would have never existed either.

14. Foot, "Morality as a System of Hypothetical Imperatives," in her *Virtues and Vices,* pp. 157–73.

15. Very few philosophers who use the expression "*X* has a reason for acting" are clear about what they mean by it. Still, I think the following conditions are common to Foot's and Harman's use of the expression as well as to Kurt Baier's and Thomas Nagel's.

X has a reason *(R)* for acting if
1. *R* is a fact which is a reason for *X* to act and
2. *X* has rationally reflected upon *R* and
3. *R* is capable of motivating *X* to act, other things being equal.
See Kurt Baier (1978c: 724–25); Thomas Nagel (1970: 110–11); E. J. Bond (1974: 333–47).

16. Foot, "A Reply to Professor Frankena," in *Virtues and Vices,* p. 179.

17. Harman, *The Nature of Morality* (New York: Oxford University Press, 1977) pp. 4–5; Foot, "Morality as a System of Hypothetical Imperatives," pp. 161–62.

18. In correspondence, Gilbert Harman says he rejects my proposed necessary condition for moral responsibility. He writes, "The thought that Hitler was so evil that he lacked such capabilities or opportunities does not seem to imply he was not morally responsible for his crimes." But I have trouble understanding what sense of moral responsibility Harman could be employing here. Clearly, an agent could be morally responsible in the sense of being strictly liable, but this sense of responsibility does not involve a judgment that the agent is evil. On the other hand, if an agent is morally responsible because she is evil, this does seem to imply at least that she possesses (or has possessed) the capabilities and opportunities to acquire reasons to act otherwise. For an interesting discussion of some similar cases where we hold people morally responsible, see Holly Smith (1983).

19. Obviously people do not have totally undeveloped capacities for acting morally or for acting self-interestedly, but usually they do have a choice of whether to continue or to undercut the development that has already taken place.

20. Foot sometimes seems to confuse explanation with justification, as when she accounts for the stringency of moral imperatives by the forcefulness of our teaching. See her (1978: 162).

21. See the discussion of the justification of morality in terms of self-interest.

22. See Baier (1978c); (1978b); (1978a); (1982); and (1986: 3–27).

23. The rational egoist is usually thought to be the opponent of morality under the assumption that the practical requirements of morality and those of self-interest conflict. But if one were to reject this assumption, the rational

egoist would still be opposed to any theoretical requirements of practical reason that place an intrinsic value on the well-being of other people.

24. See Sterba *Demands of Justice,* Chapter 1.

25. Baier (1978b: 249–50). R. M. Hare makes an analogous claim (1963: 93). John Rawls also wants to impose a similar restriction on choice in his "original position." But Rawls realizes he is importing a moral constraint (1971: 11–22).

26. The egoist's response to the occurrence of genuine Prisoner's Dilemmas would be to transform them, if possible, into choice situations favoring the practice of rational egoism.

27. When players fail to execute their best moves it may simply be due to their own lack of skill or ability, *or* they may have been tricked into not executing their best moves.

28. Defenders of our first justification for morality think this point comes fairly quickly.

29. See, for example, the articles by R. M. Hare, D. D. Raphael, Kai Nielson, and W. D. Hudson in *Gewirth's Ethical Rationalism,* ed. Edward Regis (Chicago, 1984).

30. "Reply to My Critics" in *Gewirth's Ethical Rationalism,* p. 210.

31. See, for example, the articles by R. M. Hare and Jesse Kalin.

32. As we shall see later, accepting this interpretation does require a concession from the egoist. Nevertheless, it does not lead to anything resembling a moral perspective.

33. This way of putting Gewirth's objections and my response owes much to a symposium in which Gewirth and I participated at the University of Rochester, and to subsequent conversations that continued to the door of his departing airplane.

34. See my justification for morality at the end of this chapter.

35. More precisely, to say that I am morally responsible for my lack of moral reasons in this regard is to say that at some past time (a) I had the opportunity and capacity to acquire those reasons, and (b) I also had (or could have had) overwhelming, good reasons of the relevant sort to utilize my capacity and opportunity to acquire those reasons.

36. R is a reason for action for X if rationally reflecting upon R would render (or would have rendered) X capable of motivating X to act, other things being equal. For a slightly different analysis, see Darwall, *Impartial Reason,* p. 86.

37. Utilitarians would find this interpretation of the Standard for Reasonable Conduct acceptable, because they would not regard all failures to maximize benefits overall as unreasonable. Retributivists would also find this interpretation acceptable provided their view is understood along the lines I have proposed in "Is There a Rationale for Punishment?" *The American Journal of Jurisprudence* 29 (1984). In addition, the significant harms or benefits involved may be either agent-relative or agent-neutral. See Nagel (1970).

38. I'm assuming that if one has acquired a reason for action then trivially one is or was able to acquire that reason.

39. Of course, for individuals who neither possess nor have possessed the capabilities and opportunities to acquire such reasons for acting, the question of the reasonableness of their conduct simply does not arise. Likewise, the question does not arise for those who have lost the capabilities and opportunities to acquire such reasons for acting through no fault of their own.

40. If the pure altruist is to be strictly analogous to the pure egoist, then, just as the pure egoist would not *want* others to be pure egoists, the pure

176 / HOW TO MAKE PEOPLE JUST

altruist would not *want* others to be pure altruists, since that would make it difficult for her to achieve her altruistic goals. While this sounds (is) paradoxical, the egoist is in an analogous situation.

41. This is the kind of defense of the class of relevant reasons that was lacking in Darwall's defense of morality.

42. For a discussion of the causal links involved here, see *Marketing and Promotion of Infant Formula in Developing Countries*. Hearing before the Subcommittee of International Economic Policy and Trade of the Committee on Foreign Affairs, U.S. House of Representatives, 1980. See also Maggie McComas et al., *The Dilemma of Third World Nutrition* (1983).

43. Assume that both jobs have the same beneficial effects on the interests of others.

44. I am assuming that acting contrary to reason is an important failing with respect to the requirements of reason, and that there are many ways of not acting in (perfect) accord with reason that do not constitute acting contrary to reason.

45. Otherwise, they would really fall under the classification of aesthetic reasons.

46. Of course, such reasons would have to be taken into account at some point in a complete justification for morality, but the method of integrating such reasons into a complete justification of morality would simply parallel the method already used for integrating self-interested and altruistic reasons.

47. Assume that all these methods of waste disposal have roughly the same amount of beneficial effects on the interests of others.

48. Kai Nielsen, "Why Should I Be Moral? Revisited," *American Philosophical Quarterly* 21 (1984): 90.

49. Notice that the fact the "ought" implies "can" principle is a moral principle does not show that the question has been begged against the rational egoist, since this principle was derived from the Standard for Reasonable Conduct, which clearly does not beg the question against the rational egoist.

12 / *Conclusion*

The aim of this book is to make people just. The strategy employed
was to set out five contemporary conceptions of justice and then to
show that each of these conceptions, when correctly interpreted,
supports the same practical requirements; the rights to welfare and
affirmative action usually associated with a Welfare Liberal Conception of Justice.

The first step was to show that a Welfare Liberal Conception of
Justice, with its original-position choice situation, really does support
determinate rights to welfare and affirmative action (Chapter 4). In
conflict are three views concerning what would be chosen in the
original position: a maximin view that favors principles that maximize
benefit to the least-advantaged members of a society, a utilitarian view
that favors principles that maximize average expected utility in a
society, and a compromise view that favors principles that strike a
compromise between the more-advantaged and the less-advantaged
members of a society. To resolve this conflict, I argued that the
compromise view is preferable to the maximin and utilitarian views,
under the supposition that there are sufficient resources for securing a
variety of possible minimums to all legitimate claimants. That supposition, however, can be seen to fail once the moral relevance of distant
peoples and future generations is taken into account. And without the
supposition, I argued, all three views (maximin, utilitarian, and compromise) coalesce on a lower minimum that can be specified in terms
of the satisfaction of people's basic needs. Basic needs were described
as those needs for food, shelter, medical care, protection, self-development, and companionship that must be satisfied in order not to
seriously endanger mental or physical well-being. I allowed that the
normal costs of meeting basic needs varies over time and from place
to place, but that eventually the practice of utilizing more and more
efficient means for satisfying people's basic needs will tend to equalize
the normal costs of meeting those needs across societies. Thus, in a
Welfare Liberal Conception of Justice, rights to welfare and affirmative
action are essential means for the satisfaction of people's basic needs.

Turning to the task of practical reconciliation, I argued that a Libertarian Conception of Justice, which appears to reject both a right to welfare and a right to affirmative action, can be seen to support both rights through an application of the "ought" implies "can" principle to conflicts between the rich and the poor (Chapter 7). On one interpretation, the principle supports these rights by favoring the liberty of the poor over the liberty of the rich. On another interpretation, the principle supports these rights by favoring a conditional right to property over an unconditional right to property. On either interpretation, what is crucial in the derivation of these rights is the claim that it would be unreasonable to ask the poor to deny their basic needs and to accept anything less than these rights as the condition for their willing cooperation. I also rejected recent attempts by libertarians to ground an unconditional right to property on a quasi-Aristotelian ideal of human flourishing.

Unlike a Libertarian Conception of Justice, a Socialist Conception of Justice is generally recognized to endorse rights to welfare and affirmative action, but it appears to do so only as minimal requirements. In addition, socialists maintain that we are also required to meet nonbasic needs and to socialize the means of production. However, I argued that once we see how demanding the redistributive requirements of a Welfare Liberal Conception of Justice are, primarily because of the rights of distant peoples and future generations, the additional requirement to meet nonbasic needs is seen to have little application, and the additional requirement to socialize the means of production is seen to be completely unnecessary (Chapter 8). It follows, I argued, that it will be necessary to rely heavily on moral incentives to get people to produce according to their abilities so that everyone's basic needs can be met.

As one might expect, the task of reconciling a Feminist Conception of Justice with the rights to welfare and affirmative action endorsed by welfare liberals required a critical analysis of the feminist ideal of androgyny (Chapter 5). Once objectionable interpretations of the ideal are discarded and androgyny is understood to require that the truly desirable traits in society be equally available to both men and women, or in the case of virtues, equally inculcated in both men and women, I argued that the ideal can be seen to be reconcilable with the practical requirements of a Welfare Liberal Conception of Justice (Chapter 9). More specifically, I argued that the ideal of androgyny, so understood, is common to liberal feminism, Marxist feminism, radical feminism, and socialist feminism, and that these views simply disagree concerning how best to realize the ideal. Only humanist feminists, who reject so-called feminine virtues and traits in favor of so-called masculine virtues and traits, and gynocentric feminists, who exalt and glorify so-called feminine virtues and traits over their masculine counterparts, are clearly opposed to the ideal of androgyny. But these views, I argued, are extremes that need to be compromised and refashioned along the lines of the ideal of androgyny as I have interpreted it.

In contrast to defenders of other conceptions of justice, contemporary defenders of communitarian justice have been reluctant to argue for the positive requirements of their view. As a result, the task of reconciling a Communitarian and a Welfare Liberal Conception of Justice has tended to focus on turning aside communitarian critiques of the welfare liberal view, offered most notably by Alasdair MacIntyre, Michael Sandel, and Bernard Williams (Chapter 10). Against MacIntyre, I argued that contemporary moral philosophy can avoid radical disagreement, interminable arguments, and incommensurable premises by employing the reconciliationist strategy I have used in this book. Against Sandel, I argued that Rawls's claim that the self is prior to its ends need not be interpreted as a metaphysical claim. Rather it can be interpreted to mean simply that persons are morally responsible for their ends to the degree to which they can or could have changed those ends. Against Williams, I argued that a welfare liberal ideal, especially in its nonutilitarian formulations, can allow for partiality with respect to an individual's ground projects when that partiality can be independently justified to all parties. With respect to the specific practical requirements put forward by defenders of a Communitarian Conception of Justice, I argued that once these requirements are sufficiently elaborated and qualified to meet the various objections that can be raised against them, they appear to be reconcilable with the requirements of a Welfare Liberal Conception of Justice. At least this holds true, I claimed, for the accounts of communitarian justice so far elaborated by contemporary defenders.

Given that most people endorse either a Libertarian, Socialist, Welfare Liberal, Feminist, or Communitarian Conception of Justice, I claimed that in order to make people just, it should suffice to show them that all these conceptions support the same practical requirements. Nevertheless, to make my practical reconciliationist argument even more compelling, I also argued that a rational egoist must endorse at least the moral principle basic to a Libertarian Conception of Justice (Chapter 11). I first surveyed recent attempts by Kurt Baier, Stephen Darwall, Philippa Foot, David Gauthier, Alan Gewirth, Gilbert Harman, and others to provide a justification for morality. Rejecting yet building upon these attempts, I then argued that a standard of reasonable conduct that is acceptable to a rational egoist requires (a) that in evaluating people's conduct we take into account not only the relevant reasons they have, but also the relevant reasons they could have; and (b) that in weighing these relevant reasons, we opt for a nonarbitrary compromise between self-interested and altruistic reasons that support the "ought" implies "can" principle basic to a Libertarian Conception of Justice. By combining this argument with my previous argument for practical reconciliation, I showed that practical reason requires that we endorse the rights to welfare and affirmative action usually associated with a Welfare Liberal Conception of Justice.

In developing this reconciliationist argument, I chose not to explore the historical antecedents in the works of Aristotle, Aquinas, Hobbes, Locke, Hegel, Marx, Wollstonecraft, J. S. Mill, and others of the various views I discussed. I assumed that contemporary defenders of these views already know the strengths and weaknesses of those earlier defenses, so by responding to their refurbished accounts, I have addressed the best formulations of the views they represent. Of course, there may be other conceptions of justice drawn either from the history of philosophy or from contemporary sources that cannot be subsumed under one or another of these five conceptions of justice. If faced with such a conception, I would simply opt to apply my reconciliationist strategy anew. I have no a priori argument to show that my discussion is complete. Nevertheless, given the argument from rationality to morality in Chapter 11, it is difficult to see how any morally adequate conception of justice could escape the reconciliationist argument.

In light of this argument for practical reconciliation is there any reason to prefer one of the five conceptions of justice over the others? Certainly the argument does favor a Welfare Liberal Conception of Justice by showing that alternative conceptions of justice do not lead to different practical requirements from those that are usually associated with a welfare liberal ideal. Thus, at least at the practical level, welfare liberals no longer have to face objections from advocates of the other conceptions of justice. But does the argument for practical reconciliation provide any other reason for favoring the welfare liberal ideal? Couldn't advocates of other ideals claim that, because of limited resources and the large number of legitimate claimants, their ideals and the welfare liberal ideal just happen to have the same practical requirements? Under other (hypothetical) conditions, it is clear that the practical requirements of these ideals would diverge. For example, under conditions of abundance, the libertarian ideal would require less and the socialist ideal more than the welfare liberal ideal. But suppose that a principal reason people have for favoring a libertarian ideal is that, under present conditions, it requires less sacrifice than a welfare liberal ideal; or suppose that a principal reason people have for favoring a socialist ideal is that, under present conditions, it requires more sacrifice than a welfare liberal ideal. Obviously, the argument for practical reconciliation undercuts both these reasons, and in so doing it provides additional reasons for favoring a Welfare Liberal Conception of Justice. Nevertheless, for the most part, the argument remains an argument for practical reconciliation designed simply to make people just.

But is the argument for practical reconciliation really designed to make people just, or simply to make people act in accord with the conception of justice they happen to endorse? Clearly, the argument is designed to get people who endorse one or another of the five contemporary conceptions of justice to act in accord with the practical requirements of the particular conception of justice they happen to endorse, all of which turn out to have the same practical requirements. But let us consider the possibility that people who are acting in accord with these requirements are still not acting in accord with justice, in the sense that they are not acting in accord with the most morally defensible conception of justice. For this to be the case, the most morally defensible conception of justice would have to have significantly different practical requirements from our other conceptions of justice. Is this likely?

Clearly, the most morally defensible conception of justice would have to endorse the "ought" implies "can" principle, since this principle follows from a conception of rationality that is acceptable even to a rational egoist (see Chapter 11). In virtue of endorsing the "ought" implies "can" principle, the most morally defensible conception of justice would also have to endorse a right to welfare, since the "ought" implies "can" principle secures a right to welfare within a libertarian view (see Chapter 7). Nor could the most morally defensible conception of justice endorse a right to welfare yet reject the right to equal opportunity that underlies a right to affirmative action, because once the moral relevance of distant peoples and future generations is taken into account, the same considerations that support a right to welfare support a right to equal opportunity as well (see Chapters 4 and 7). And once the most morally defensible conception of justice is seen to endorse a right to equal opportunity, it could hardly fail to endorse a right to affirmative action, which attempts to correct for failure to provide equal opportunity in the past (see Chapters 4 and 7). It would seem, therefore, that the only way that the most morally defensible conception of justice could significantly differ in its practical requirements from our other five conceptions of justice is if it were to impose some additional requirement that seemed to go beyond rights to welfare and affirmative action, such as Finnis's requirement that one never do evil that good may come of it. But once such requirements are sufficiently elaborated and qualified to meet the various objections that can be raised against them, these requirements could easily turn out, as in the case of Finnis's requirement, to be reconcilable with the requirements of our five contemporary conceptions of justice (see

Chapter 10). Of course, I have no a priori argument that the best conception of justice could not have practical requirements that are significantly different from those of our five contemporary conceptions of justice. Yet given the above considerations, it seems unlikely that this is the case.

Alasdair MacIntyre (1988:166) however, has argued that when "large-scale intellectual traditions confront one another, a central feature of the problem of deciding between their claims is characteristically that there is no neutral way of characterizing either the subject matter about which they give rival accounts or the standards by which their claims are to be evaluated." Applied to the argument of this book, it would seem that I could achieve my practical reconciliation only at the price of distorting the alternative conceptions of justice I presented. But discussions I have had with advocates of these conceptions of justice have supported a different view. When we disagreed, our disagreement tended to focus on what I claimed followed from their ideals rather than on my characterization of the ideals themselves. This is not to say that some of the features of the five conceptions of justice are not truly incommensurable. For example, the libertarian distinction between omissions and commissions and the socialist commitment to equality of result are not shared by the other conceptions of justice. At the same time, there are other features that are shared, such as a commitment to the "ought" implies "can" principle and the recognition that distant peoples as well as future generations are morally legitimate claimants, and what I have argued in this book is that these shared features suffice to support my argument for practical reconciliation.

Yet despite the capacity of the reconciliationist argument to draw together apparently divergent views and possibly bring us within striking distance of the most morally defensible conception of justice, someone might object that the reconciliationist argument is tainted with male bias. It is, after all, an argument about justice, and recent work by Carol Gilligan and others has challenged the moral adequacy of a justice perspective when contrasted with a caring perspective.[1] According to Gilligan, the two perspectives are analogous to the alternative ways we tend to organize ambiguous perceptual patterns: to first see a figure as a square and then as a diamond, depending on its relationship to the surrounding frame. More specifically, she claims (1987:23):

> From a justice perspective, the self as moral agent stands as the figure against a ground of social relationships, judging the conflicting claims of self and others against a standard of equality or equal respect (the Categorical Imperative, the Golden Rule). From a care perspective, the relationship becomes the figure, defining self and others. Within the context of relationship, the self as a moral agent perceives and responds

to the perception of need. The shift in moral perspective is manifest by a change in the moral question from "What is just?" to "How to respond?"

For example, adolescents asked to describe a moral dilemma often speak about peer or family pressure, in which case the moral question becomes how to maintain moral principles or standards and resist the influence of one's parents or friends. "I have a right to my religious opinions," one teenager explains, referring to a religious difference with his parents. Yet, he adds, "I respect their views." The same dilemma, however, is also construed by adolescents as a problem of attachment, in which case the moral question becomes: how to respond both to oneself and to one's friends or one's parents, how to maintain or strengthen connection in the face of differences in belief. "I understand their fear of my new religious ideas," one teenager explains, referring to her religious disagreement with her parents, "but they really ought to listen to me and try to understand my beliefs."

Using these perspectives as classificatory tools, Gilligan reports (ibid.: 25) that 69 percent of her sample raised considerations of both justice and care, while 67 percent focused their attention on one set of concerns (with focus defined as 75 percent or more of the considerations raised pertaining either to justice or to care). It is significant that, with one exception, all of the men who focused, focused on justice. The women divided, with roughly one-third focusing on care and one-third on justice.

The conclusion that Gilligan and others want to draw from this research is that the care perspective is an equally valid moral perspective that has been disregarded in moral theory and psychological research because of male bias. To evaluate Gilligan's conclusion, we first need to elucidate the contrast between the two perspectives. If women and men differ with regard to the perspectives on which they tend to focus, it must be possible to distinguish clearly between the two perspectives. Otherwise bias could enter into the researcher's classification of people's reasons as belonging to one or the other perspective.

Let us begin by considering the example persons who disagree with their parents over religious views. On the one hand, the individual who is said to have a justice perspective asserts, "I have a right to my religious views," and then referring to his parents adds, "I respect their views." On the other hand, the individual who is said to have a caring perspective asserts, "I understand their fears of my religious ideas," and then adds, "but they really ought to listen to me and try to understand my beliefs." How distinct are these reasons? Couldn't a person's right to her religious views go beyond a negative right of noninterference and entail that family members at least listen and try to understand one's beliefs? Likewise, couldn't understanding the fears one's parents have of one's different religious ideas be part of showing respect for their views? At one point, Gilligan characterizes (ibid.: 20) the justice perspective by the injunction "not to act unfairly toward others" and the caring perspective by the injunction "do not turn away from someone in need." But these two injunctions are inextricably linked in a Welfare Liberal Conception of Justice. In a Welfare Liberal Conception of Justice, to treat people fairly is to respond to their needs.

Sometimes Gilligan and others seem to think that a justice perspective is distinct from a caring perspective, because their understanding of a justice perspective is more restrictive than the previous characterizations would indicate. Thus, Gilligan sometimes describes the justice perspective as simply requiring a right of noninterference and a corresponding duty of others not to interfere (ibid.: 23; 1982:100, 149) Similarly, the editors of a recent collection of essays inspired by Gilligan's work contend that in a justice perspective, "People are surely entitled to noninterference; they may not be entitled to aid[2]" But this is to identify a justice perspective with a libertarian view that purports to reject rights to welfare and affirmative action. Assuming this identification, we do find a contrast between a justice perspective and a caring perspective. But not only does this characterization of a justice perspective misrepresent the libertarian view which, when correctly interpreted, endorses rather than rejects rights to welfare and affirmative action, it also fails to countenance our other conceptions of justice, which clearly go beyond a right to noninterference.

Now if it is impossible to distinguish in theory between a justice perspective and a caring perspective, it is going to be impossible for researchers to use this distinction in practice to characterize people as focusing on one or the other perspective. Of course, people will tend to use the language of rights with the frequencies Gilligan observes, but we will have to look behind this usage to see what people are claiming when they use or don't use this language. If there is no viable theoretical distinction between a justice perspective and a caring perspective, people frequently will be found to express care and concern for the needs of others by using the language of rights. It follows that the charge of male bias cannot be attributed to a work, like this one, simply because it focuses on justice. To make the charge stick, one must locate in the work an insensitivity to the needs of others, and then show that such insensitivity is more characteristic of men than women.

Finally, what does all this mean in practice? Suppose you endorse either a Libertarian, Welfare Liberal, Socialist, Feminist, or Communitarian Conception of Justice, or the conception of rationality captured by the Principle for Reasonable Conduct, and you are led by the argument of this book to endorse rights to welfare and affirmative action. What specifically should you do?

1. You should reexamine the argument of this book to make sure it really does support your endorsement of rights to welfare and affirmative action.
2. If you are still convinced the practical reconciliationist argument does support rights to welfare and affirmative action, you should become a strong advocate of the rights for all legitimate claimants nationwide, worldwide, and into the future.
3. You should try to convince others through the use of the practical reconciliationist argument that they too should be strong advocates of these rights.
4. You should push for the institutional, legal, and policy changes necessary to secure these rights for all legitimate claimants.

On (4), a few remarks may be helpful. While the U.S. Constitution guarantees its citizens many rights, it fails to guarantee them a right to equal opportunity (which underlies a right to affirmative action) and a right to welfare. That the U.S. Constitution fails to guarantee rights to equal opportunity and welfare seems clear enough. If we focus, by way of example, on educational opportunity, a majority of the Supreme Court determined, in *San Antonio School District v. Rodriguez* (1973), that there was no constitutional right to education. Likewise, in *Wyman v. James* (1971), the Supreme Court's decision presupposed that there was no constitutional right to welfare. The only right to welfare that was recognized by the Court was a right that was conditional upon the state or federal government's interest in providing welfare.

But surely, if rights to equal opportunity and welfare are fundamental requirements of five widely endorsed conceptions of justice, as my argument maintains, these rights must be guaranteed by any constitution that claims to be morally defensible. Since the U.S. Constitution does not guarantee these rights, it is a fundamentally flawed document.

Now it might be objected that this criticism of the U.S. Constitution is inappropriate because it attempts to evaluate the Constitution, which for the most part was written 200 years ago, by appealing to contemporary conceptions of justice. But this is to miss the point of my criticism of the Constitution, which is not so much directed at the Constitution as originally written as it is at the Constitution as presently amended and interpreted. For whenever a society's constitution can be seen to be morally defective in the light of its acknowledged ideals, it is incumbent upon the members of that society to amend, or at least to reinterpret, their constitution to make up for its deficiencies. If I am right that, when these five contemporary conceptions of justice are correctly interpreted, they all require a right to welfare and a right to equal opportunity, then the U.S. Constitution will remain a fundamentally flawed document until it too requires these rights.[3]

There are also numerous recommendations for legal and policy changes that would help secure rights to equal opportunity and welfare in the American bishops' 1986 pastoral letter, *Economic Justice for All: Catholic Social Teaching and the U.S. Economy*.[4] These recommendations include national eligibility standards and a national minimum benefit level for public assistance; job-training and apprenticeship programs in the private sector to be jointly administered and supported by business, labor, and government; and a reduction of military budgets and international arms sales. While the bishops' recommendations are primarily grounded on the Bible and Catholic social teaching, many of their recommendations also have a strictly philosophical or secular grounding in the practical reconciliationist argument, and for this reason I would recommend them.[5]

In brief, if the argument of this book is sound, there is much that needs to be done to make people just, and good reason to do it.

Notes

1. Carol Gilligan, *In a Different Voice* (Cambridge, Harvard University Press 1982); idem, "Moral Orientation and Moral Development," in *Women and Moral Theory,* ed. Eva Kittay and Diana Meyers (Totowa, Rowman and Littlefield 1987), pp. 19–36; Annette Baier, "What Do Women Want in a Moral Theory?" *Nous* 15 (1985): 53–63; Owen Flanagan, "Virtue, Sex and Gender: Some Philosophical Reflections on the Moral Psychology Debate," *Ethics* (1982): 499–512; and most of the articles in Kittay and Meyers, eds., *Women and Moral Theory.*

2. Eva Feder Kittay and Diana T. Meyers, eds., *Women and Moral Theory* (Totowa, N.J.: Rowman & Littlefield, 1987), p. 5.

3. For further argument, see James P. Sterba, "The U.S. Constitution: A Fundamentally Flawed Document," *Moral Theory and the U.S. Constitution,* ed. Christopher Gray (forthcoming).

4. National Conference of Catholic Bishops, "Economic Justice for All: Catholic Social Teaching and the U.S. Economy," 3rd draft, *Origins* 16 (June 5, 1986).

5. For further argument, see Sterba and Rasmussen (1987: esp. 1–44).

Bibliography

Ackerman, Bruce A. 1980. *Social Justice in the Liberal State*. New Haven: Yale University Press.

Alexander, Sidney S. 1974. "Social Evaluation Through National Choice." *Quarterly Journal of Economics* 88.

Allgeier, Elizabeth, and Naomi McCormick. 1983. *Changing Boundaries*. Washington, D.C.: Institute for Policy Studies.

Amdur, Robert. 1980. "Rawls and His Radical Critics." *Dissent* 27.

Anscombe, G. E. M. 1981. *Ethics, Religion, and Politics*. Minneapolis: University of Minnesota Press.

Arenson, Richard J. 1981. "Prospects for Community in a Market Economy. *Political Theory* 9.

Ash, William. 1977. *Morals and Politics*. London: Routledge & Kegan Paul.

Baier, Annette. 1985. "What Do Women Want in a Moral Theory." *Nous* 19.

———. 1986. "Trust and Antitrust." *Ethics* 97.

Baier, Kurt. 1958. *The Moral Point of View*. Ithaca: Cornell University Press.

———. 1978a. "Moral Reasons." In *Midwest Studies in Philosophy III*, Peter French et al., eds. Minneapolis: University of Minnesota Press.

———. 1978b. "Moral Reasons and Reasons to Be Moral." In *Values and Morals*, A. I. Goldman and J. Kim, eds. Dordrecht: Reidal Publishing Co.

———. 1978c. "The Social Source of Reason." *Proceedings and Addresses of the American Philosophical Association*. Lancaster, Pa.: Lancaster Press.

———. 1982. "The Conceptual Link Between Morality and Rationality." *Nous* 16.

———. 1986. "Justification in Ethics." In *Nomos XXVII: Justification,* J. Roland Pennock and John W. Chapman, eds. New York: New York University Press.

Barry, Brian. 1973. *The Liberal Theory of Justice*. London: Oxford University Press.

———. 1977. "Rawls on Average and Total Utility." *Philosophical Studies* 30.

Bay, Christian. 1981. *Strategies of Political Emancipation*. Notre Dame: University Notre Dame Press.

Beardsley, Elizabeth Lane. 1982. "On Curing Conceptual Confusion: Response to Mary Anne Warren." In *"Femininity," "Masculinity," and "Androgyny,"* Mary Vetterling-Braggin, ed. Totowa, N.J.: Rowman and Allenheld.

Becker, Lawrence C. 1977. *Property Rights*. London: Routledge & Kegan Paul.

Bellah, Robert, et al. 1985. *Habits of the Heart*. Berkeley: University of California Press.

Bem, Sandra Lipitz. 1981. "Gender Schema Theory: A Cognitive Account of Sex Typing." *Psychological Review* 88, no. 4.

Bishop, Sharon, and Marjorie Weinzweig, eds. 1979. *Philosophy and Women*. Belmont, Calif.: Wadsworth Publishing Co.

Bond, E.J. 1974. "Reasons, Wants and Values." *Canadian Journal of Philosophy* 4.

———. 1983. *Reason and Value*. Cambridge: Cambridge University Press.

Bowles, Samuel, and Herbert Gentis. 1976. *Schooling in Capitalist America*. New York: Basic Books.

Brandt, Richard B. 1979. *A Theory of the Good and the Right*. Oxford: Oxford University Press.

Braybrooke, David. 1987. *Meeting Needs*. Oxford: Oxford University Press.

Brock, Dan. 1982. "Utilitarianism." In *And Justice for All: New Introductory Essays in Ethics and Public Policy*, Tom Regan and Donald VanDeVeer, eds. Totowa, N.J.: Rowman & Littlefield.

Brown, Alan. 1986. *Modern Political Philosophy*. Harmondsworth: Penguin Books.

Buchanan, Allen. 1975. "Distributive Justice and Legitimate Expectations." *Canadian Journal of Philosophy* 5.

———. 1981. "Deriving Welfare Rights from Libertarian Rights." In *Income Support: Conceptual and Policy Issues*, Peter G. Brown, Conrad Johnson, and Paul Vernier, eds. Totowa, N.J.: Rowman & Littlefield.

———. 1982. *Marx and Justice: The Radical Critique of Liberalism*. Totowa, N.J.: Rowman & Allanheld.

Buchanan, James, and Gordon Tullock. 1966. *Calculus of Consent*. Ann Arbor: University of Michigan Press.

Campbell, Tom. 1983. *The Left and Right*. London: Routledge & Kegan Paul.

Cohen, G. A. 1977. "Robert Nozick and Wilt Chamberlain: How Patterns Preserve Liberty." *Erkenntnis* 11.

———. 1982. "The Structure of Proletarian Unfreedom." *Philosophy and Public Affairs* 11.

Cohen, Marshall, Thomas Nagel, and Thomas Scanlon. 1980. *Marx, Justice and History*. Princeton: Princeton University Press.

Cooper, Neil. 1981. *The Diversity of Moral Thinking*. Oxford: Oxford University Press.

Copp, David. 1974. "Justice and the Difference Principle." *Canadian Journal of Philosophy* 4.

Crocker, Lawrence. 1977. "Equality, Solidarity and Rawls's Maximin." *Philosophy and Public Affairs* 6.

Daly, Mary. 1975. "The Qualitative Leap Beyond Patriarchial Religion." *Quest* 1 (Spring).

Daly, Mary Ann. 1982. "Is Androgyny the Answer to Sexual Stereotyping?" In *"Femininity," "Masculinity," and "Androgyny,"* Mary Vetterling-Braggin, ed. Totowa, N.J.: Rowman and Allanheld.

Daniels, Norman. 1975. "Equal Liberty and Unequal Worth of Liberty." In *Reading Rawls*, Norman Daniels, ed. New York: Basic Books.

Darwall, Stephen. 1983. *Impartial Reason*. Ithaca: Cornell University Press.

DeCrow, Karen. 1975. *Sexist Justice*. New York: Vintage Books.

Diamond, Irene. 1983. *Families, Politics, and Public Policy*. New York: Longman.

DiQuatto, Arthur. 1983. "Rawls and Left Criticism." *Political Theory* 11.

Donagan, Alan. 1977. *The Theory of Morality*. Chicago: University of Chicago Press.

Doppelt, Gerald. 1981. "Rawls's System of Justice: A Critique from the Left." *Nous* 15.

Downing, Lyle, and Robert Thigpen. 1984. "After Telos: The Implications of MacIntyre's Attempt to Restore the Concept in *After Virtue.*"*Social Theory and Practice* 10.

Dworkin, Andrea. 1974. *Women Hating.* New York: E. P. Dutton.

Dworkin, Ronald. 1973. "The Original Position." *University of Chicago Law Review* 40.

———. 1981. "What Is Equality? Parts I and II." *Philosophy and Public Affairs* 10.

———. 1985. *A Matter of Principle.* Cambridge: Harvard University Press.

Eichler, Margaret. 1980. *The Double Standard.* London: Croom Helm.

Eisenstein, Zillah. 1984. *Feminism and Sexual Equality.* New York: Monthly Review Press.

Elshtain, Jean Bethke. 1981. "Against Androgyny." *Telos 47.*

English, Jane. 1977. "Justice Between Generations." *Philosophical Studies* 30.

Ewin, R. E. 1981. *Co-Operation and Human Values.* New York: St. Martin's Press.

Ferguson, Ann. 1977. "Androgyny as an Ideal for Human Development." In *Feminism and Philosophy,* Mary Vetterling-Braggin, Frederick Elliston, and Jan English, eds. Totowa, N.J.: Rowman and Allanheld. Repr. 1985.

Finnis, John. 1980. *Natural Law and Natural Rights.* Oxford: Clarendon Press.

———. 1983. *Fundamentals of Ethics.* Washington, D.C.: Georgetown University Press.

Firestone, Shulamith. 1970. *The Dialectic of Sex.* New York: William Morrow.

Fisk, Milton. 1975. "History and Reason in Rawls's Moral Theory." In *Reading Rawls,* Norman Daniels, ed. New York: Basic Books.

———. 1980. *Ethics and Society.* New York: New York University Press.

Flanagan, Owen. 1982. "Virtue, Sex and Gender: Some Philosophical Reflections on the Moral Psychology Debate." *Ethics* 93.

Foot, Phillippa. 1978. *Virtues and Vices.* Los Angeles: University of California Press.

Fowler, Mark. 1980. "Self Ownership, Mutual Aid, and Mutual Respect: Some Counterexamples to Nozick's Libertarianism." *Social Theory and Practice* 9.

Frankena, William. 1983. "MacIntyre and Modern Morality." *Ethics* 94.

Friedman, Milton. 1962. *Capitalism and Freedom.* Chicago: University of Chicago Press.

Freeman, Jo. *Woman: A Feminist Perspective.* Palo Alto, Calif.: Mayfield Publishing Co.

Fried, Charles. 1978. *Right and Wrong.* Cambridge: Harvard University Press.

———. 1982. "Is Liberty Possible." In *The Tanner Lectures on Human Values* Vol. III, Sterling McMurrin, ed. Salt Lake City: University of Utah Press.

Frye, Marilyn. 1983. *The Politics of Reality.* New York: The Crossing Press.

Fuchs, Alan. 1982. "Justice as Fairness." In *The Limits of Utilitarianism,* Harland Miller and William Williams, eds. Minneapolis: University of Minnesota Press.

Fullinwider, Robert K. 1976. "Hare on Rawls: A Worry About Possible Persons." *Philosophical Studies* 29.

Galston, William A. 1980. *Justice and the Human Good.* Chicago: University of Chicago Press.

Gardener, Michael R. 1975. "Rawls on the Maximum Rule and Distributive Justice." *Philosophical Studies* 28.

Gauthier, David. 1970. *Morality and Rational Self-Interest*. Englewood Cliffs, N.J.: Prentice Hall.

———. 1974. "Justice and Natural Endowment." *Social Theory and Practice* 7.

———. 1982. "On the Refutation of Utilitarians." In *The Limits of Utilitarianism*, Harlan Miller and Williams Williams, eds. Minneapolis: University of Minnesota Press.

———. 1986. *Morals by Agreement*. Oxford: Oxford University Press.

Geach, Peter. 1977. *The Virtues*. Cambridge: Cambridge University Press.

Gelpi, Barbara. 1974. "The Politics of Androgyny." *Women's Studies* 2, no. 2.

Gewirth, Alan. 1978. *Reasons and Morality*. Chicago: University of Chicago Press.

Gilligan, Carol. 1982. *In a Different Voice: Psychological Theory and Women's Development*. Cambridge: Harvard University Press.

———. 1987. "Moral Orientation and Moral Development." In *Women and Moral Theory*, Eva F. Kittay and Diana T. Meyers, eds. Totowa, N.J.: Rowman & Littlefield.

Goldman, Holly Smith. 1980. "Rawls and Utilitarianism." In *John Rawls's Theory of Social Justice*, H. Gene Blocker and Elizabeth H. Smith, eds. Athens: Ohio University Press.

Gould, Carol C. 1978. *Marx's Social Ontology*. Cambridge: MIT Press.

Gould, Carol C., and Marx W. Wartofsky, eds. *Women and Philosophy: Toward a Theory of Liberation*. New York: G. P. Putnam's Sons.

Gray, John. 1980. "On Negative and Positive Liberty." *Political Studies* 29.

Grcic, Joseph M. 1980. "Rawls and Socialism." *Philosophy and Social Criticism* 7.

Green, O. H. 1980. "Killing and Letting Die." *American Philosophical Quarterly* 17.

Green, Philip. 1981. *The Pursuit of Inequality*. New York: Pantheon Books.

Grice, Russell. 1967. *Reason and Value*. Cambridge: Cambridge University Press.

Gutman, Amy. 1980. *Liberal Equality*. Cambridge: Cambridge University Press.

Haksar, Vinit. 1979. *Equality, Liberty, and Perfection*. Oxford: Clarendon Press.

Hare, R. M. 1963. *Freedom and Reason*. Oxford: Oxford University Press.

———. 1977a. "Justice and Equality." *Etyka* (Warsaw) 15.

———. 1977b. "Rawls's Theory of Justice—I and II." *Philosophical Quarterly* 27.

———. 1981. *Moral Thinking*. Oxford: Oxford University Press.

Harman, Gilbert. 1975. "Moral Relationism Defended." *Philosophical Review* 56.

———. 1977. *The Nature of Morality*. Oxford: Oxford University Press.

———. 1983. "Human Flourishing, Ethics, and Liberty." *Philosophy and Public Affairs* 12.

Harrington, Michael. 1972. *Socialism*. New York: Bantam Books.

Harris, John. 1974. "The Marxist Conception of Violence." *Philosophy and Public Affairs* 3.

———. 1980. *Violence and Responsibility*. London: Routledge & Kegan Paul.

Harsanyi, John C. 1975. "Can the Maximum Principle Serve as a Basis for Morality?" *American Political Science Review* 69.

———. 1976. *Essays on Ethics, Social Behavior, and Scientific Explanation.* Dordrecht, Holland: Reidel Publishing Co.

Hart, H. L. A. 1973. "Rawls on Liberty and Its Priority." *University of Chicago Law Review* 40.

Hartmann, Heidi. 1981. "The Unhappy Marriage of Marxism and Feminism." In *Women and Revolution*, Linda Sargent, ed. Boston: South End Press.

Hauerwas, Stanley, and Alasdair MacIntyre. 1983. *Revisions.* Notre Dame: University of Notre Dame Press.

Hayek, F. A. 1960. *The Constitution of Liberty.* Chicago: University of Chicago Press.

Held, Virginia. 1984. *Rights and Goods.* New York: Free Press.

Hodson, John. 1977. "Nozick, Libertarianism, and Rights." *Arizona Law Review* 8.

Holbrow, Les. 1975. "Desert, Equality, and Injustice." *Philosophy* 50.

Holmes, Robert. 1977. "Nozick on Anarchism." *Political Theory* 5. Reprinted 1984 in *Reading Nozick: Essays on Anarchy, State, and Utopia*, Jeffrey Paul, ed. Totowa, N.J.: Rowman & Littlefield.

Hospers, John. 1971. *Libertarianism.* Los Angeles: Nash Publishing Co.

Hudson, Stephen D. 1981. "Taking Virtue Seriously." *Australasian Journal of Philosophy* 59.

Jaggar, Alison M. 1983. *Feminist Politics and Human Nature.* Totowa, N.J.: Rowman & Allanheld.

Jaggar, Alison M., and Paula Rothenburg Struhl. 1984. *Feminist Frameworks*, 2nd ed. New York: McGraw-Hill.

Kavka, Gregory S. 1975. "Rawls on Average and Total Utility." *Philosophical Studies* 28.

Kaye, David. 1980. "Playing Games with Justice: Rawls and the Maximum Rule." *Social Theory and Practice* 10.

Kearl, J. R. 1977. "Do Entitlements Imply that Taxation is Theft?" *Philosophy and Public Affairs* 7.

Koedt, Anne, Ellen Levin, and Anita Rapone, eds. 1973. *Radical Feminism.* New York: Times Books.

Kontos, Alkis, ed. 1979. *Powers, Possessions, and Freedom.* Toronto: University of Toronto Press.

Kronman, Anthony. 1981. "Talent Pooling." In *Nomos XXII: Human Rights*, J. Roland Pennock and John W. Chapman, eds. New York: New York University Press.

Kuflik, Arthur. 1982. "Process and End State in the Theory of Economic Justice." *Social Theory and Practice* 11.

Larrabee, Mary Jeanne. 1983. "Feminism and Parental Roles: Possibilities for Change." *Journal of Social Philosophy* 14.

Leiss, William. 1976. *The Limits to Satisfaction.* Toronto: University of Toronto Press.

Lessnoff, M. H. 1974. "Barry on Rawls's Priority of Liberty." *Philosophy and Public Affairs* 3.

———. 1978. "Justice, Social Contract, and Universal Prescriptivism." *Philosophical Quarterly* 28.

Levine, Andrew. 1981. *Liberal Democracy: A Critique of Its Theory.* New York: Columbia University Press.

Lieberman, Jethro K. 1977. "The Relativity of Injury." *Philosophy and Public Affairs* 6.

Lindblom, Charles M. 1977. *Politics and Markets*. New York: Basic Books.

Loevinsohn, Ernest. 1977. "Liberty and the Redistribution of Property." *Philosophy and Public Affairs* 6.

Lowden, Robert B. 1984. "On Some Vices of Virtue Ethics." *American Philosophical Quarterly* 21.

Lucas, J. R. 1980. *On Justice*. Oxford: Oxford University Press.

Lukes, Steven. 1980. "Socialism and Equality." In *Justice: Alternative Political Perspectives,* James P. Sterba, ed. Belmont, Calif.: Wadsworth Publishing Co.

Machan, Tibor. 1975. *Human Rights and Human Liberties*. Chicago: Nelson-Hall.

MacIntyre, Alasdair. 1981. *After Virtue*. Notre Dame: University of Notre Dame Press.

————. 1988. *Whose Justice? Which Rationality?* Notre Dame: University of Notre Dame Press.

Mack, Eric. 1977. "Liberty and Justice." In *Justice and Economic Distribution,* John Arthur and William Shaw, eds. Englewood Cliffs, N.J.: Prentice-Hall.

————. 1978. "Nozick's Anarchism." In *Nomos XIX: Anarchism Nomos,* J. Roland Pennock and John W. Chapman, eds. New York: New York University Press.

————. 1981. "Nozick on Unproductivity: The Unintended Consequences." In *Reading Nozick:* Essays on Anarchy, State, and Utopia, Jeffrey Paul, ed. Totowa, N.J.: Rowman and Littlefield.

————. 1983. "Distributive Justice and the Tensions of Lockeanism." *Social Philosophy and Policy* 3.

Mackensie, Hollaig. 1978. "A Note on Rawls's Decision-Theoretic Argument for the Difference Principle." *Theory and Decision* 8.

Macpherson, C. B. 1973a. "Rawls's Models of Man and Society." *Philosophy of the Social Sciences* 3.

————. 1973b. *Democratic Theory*. Oxford: Clarendon Press.

————. 1977. *The Life and Times of Liberal Democracy*. Oxford: Oxford University Press.

————. 1978. *Property*. Toronto: University of Toronto Press.

————. 1985. *The Rise and Fall of Economic Justice and Other Essays*. London: Oxford University Press.

Martin, Rex. 1985. *Rawls and Rights*. Lawrence: University Press of Kansas.

McBride, William. 1972. "Social Theory Sub Specie Aeternitatis." *The Yale Law Journal* 81.

McConnell, Terrance C. 1981. "Moral Blackmail." *Ethics* 92.

McInerny, Ralph. 1982. *Ethica Thomistica*. Washington, D.C.: Catholic University of America Press.

Miller, David. 1976. *Social Justice*. Oxford: Clarendon Press.

————. 1983. "Constraints on Freedom." *Ethics* 94.

Miller, Fred D., Jr. 1982. "The Natural Rights to Private Property." In *The Libertarian Reader,* Tibor R. Machan, ed. Totowa, N.J.: Rowman & Allanheld.

Miller, Richard W. 1974. "Rawls and Marxism." *Philosophy and Public Affairs* 3.

————. 1975. "Rawls, Risk, and Utilitarianism." *Philosophical Studies* 28.

Morgan, Kathryn Pauly. 1982. "Androgyny: A Conceptual Critique." *Social Theory and Practice* 8.

Mueller, Dennis C., Robert Tottison, and Thomas Willette. 1974. "The Utilitarian Contract: A Generalization of Rawls's Theory of Justice." *Theory and Decision* 21.

Murphy, Jeffrie. 1980. "Blackmail: A Preliminary Inquiry." *The Monist* 64.

Musgrave, R. A. 1974. "Maximin, Uncertainty, and the Leisure Trade-Off." *Quarterly Journal of Economics* 88.

Nagel, Thomas. 1970. *The Possibility of Altruism*. Oxford: Oxford University Press.

Narveson, Jan. 1982. "Rawls and Utilitarianism." In *The Limits of Utilitarianism*, Harlan Miller and William Williams, ed. Minneapolis: University of Minnesota Press.

Nell, Edward, and Onora O'Neill. 1980. "Justice Under Socialism." In *Justice: Alternative Political Perspectives*, James P. Sterba, ed. Belmont, Calif.: Wadworth Publishing Co.

Nelson, William. 1980. "The Very Idea of Pure Procedural Justice." *Ethics* 91.

Nielson, Kai. 1984. "Why Should I Be Moral? Revisited." *American Philosophical Quarterly* 21.

———. 1985. *Equality and Liberty*. Totowa, N.J.: Rowman & Littlefield.

Nielson, Kai, and Steven C. Pattin. 1981. *Marx and Morality*. Guelph, Ontario: Canadian Association in Publishing in Philosophy.

Nozick, Robert. 1974. *Anarchy, State, and Utopia*. New York: Basic Books.

Oldenquist, Andrew. 1986. *The Non-Suicidal Society*. Bloomington: Indiana University Press.

Olson, Robert. 1965. *The Morality of Self-Interest*. New York: Harcourt Brace & World.

O'Neill, Onora. 1981. "Nozick's Entitlements." In *Reading Nozick: Essays on Anarchy, State, and Utopia*, Jeffrey Paul, ed. Totowa, N.J.: Rowman & Littlefield.

Okin, Susan Moller. 1986. "Justice and Gender." *Philosophy and Public Affairs* 15.

Parfit, Derek. 1984. *Reasons and Persons*. Oxford: Oxford University Press.

Paul, Jeffrey. 1980. "The Withering of Nozick's Minimal State." *Philosophical Research Archive*. Reprinted 1981 in *Reading Nozick*, Jeffrey Paul, ed. Totowa, N.J.: Rowman & Littlefield.

Pielke, Robert G. 1982. "Are Androgyny and Sexuality Compatible?" In *"Femininity," "Masculinity," and "Androgyny,"* Mary Vetterling-Braggin, ed. Totowa, N.J.: Rowman and Allenheld.

Pincoffs, Edmund. 1986. *Quandaries and Virtues*. Lawrence: University of Kansas Press.

Postema, Gerald J. 1980. "Nozick on Liberty, Compensation, and the Individual's Right to Punish." *Social Theory and Practice* 7.

Rabinowitz, Joshua T. 1977. "Emergent Problems and Optimal Solutions." *Arizona Law Review* 8.

Rawls, John. 1971. *A Theory of Justice*. Cambridge: Harvard University Press.

———. 1974a. "Some Reasons for the Maximim Criterion." *American Economic Review* 64.

———. 1974b. "Reply to Alexander and Musgrave." *Quarterly Journal of Economics* 88.

———. 1975a. "A Kantian Conception of Equality." *Cambridge Review*.

————. 1975b. "Fairness to Goodness." *Philosophical Review* 60.

————. 1978. "The Basic Structure as Subject." In *Values and Morals,* A. I. Goldman and J. Kim, eds. Dordrecht, Holland: Reidel Publishing Co.

————. 1980. "Kantian Constructivism in Moral Theory." *The Journal of Philosophy* 76.

————. 1982a. "The Basic Liberties and Their Priority." In *The Tanner Lectures on Human Values,* Sterling McMurrin, ed. Salt Lake City: University of Utah Press.

————. 1982b. "Social Unity and Primary Goods." In *Utilitarianism and Beyond,* Amartya Sen and Bernard Williams, eds. Cambridge: Cambridge University Press.

————. 1985. "Justice as Fairness: Political not Metaphysical." *Philosophy and Public Affairs* 14.

————. 1987. "The Idea of an Overlapping Consensus." *Oxford Journal of Legal Studies* 7.

Raymond, Janice. 1975. "The Illusion of Androgyny." *Quest* 2.

Reed, Evelyn. 1987. "Women: Caste, Class, or Oppressed Sex?" In *Morality in Practice,* James P. Sterba, ed. Belmont, Calif.: Wadsworth.

Reiman, Jeffrey H. 1981. "The Fallacy of Libertarian Capitalism." *Ethics* 92.

————. 1984. "The Labor Theory of the Difference Principle." *Philosophy and Public Affairs* 13.

Rescher, Nicholas. 1975. *Unselfishness.* Pittsburgh: University of Pittsburgh Press.

Richards, David A. 1971. *A Theory of Reasons for Action.* Oxford: Oxford University Press.

Rothbard, Murray. 1977. "Robert Nozick and the Immaculate Conception of the State." *The Journal of Libertarian Studies* 1.

————. 1978. *For A New Liberty.* New York: Collier Books.

————. 1982. *The Ethics of Liberty.* Atlantic Highlands, N.J.: Humanities Press.

Rothman, Barbara Katz. 1982. "How Science Is Redefining Parenthood." *Ms.* (August).

Sandel, Michael J. 1982. *Liberalism and the Limits of Justice.* Cambridge: Cambridge University Press.

Sartorius, Rolf E. 1975. *Individual Conduct and Social Norms.* Belmont, Calif.: Dickinson Publishing Co.

Sayward, Charles, and Wayne Wasserman. 1981. "Has Nozick Justified the State?" *Pacific Philosophical Quarterly* 62.

Scanlon, Thomas. 1981. "Nozick on Rights, Liberty, and Property." In *Reading Nozick: Essays on Anarchy, State, and Utopia,* Jeffrey Paul, ed. Totowa, N.J.: Rowman & Littlefield.

Schaefer, David Lewis. 1979. *Justice or Tyranny.* New York: Kennikat Press.

Scheewind, J. B. 1982a. "Moral Crisis and the History of Ethics." In *Midwest Studies in Philosophy,* Peter French et al., eds. Minneapolis: University of Minnesota Press: 525–39.

————. 1982b. "Virtue, Narrative, and Community." *The Journal of Philosophy* 79.

Scheffler, Samuel. 1976. "Natural Rights, Equality, and the Minimal State." In *Reading Nozick,* Jeffrey Paul, ed. Totowa, N.J.: Rowman & Littlefield.

Schick, Frederic. 1984. *Having Reasons.* Princeton: Princeton University Press.

Schweichkart, David. 1978. "Should Rawls Be a Socialist?" *Social Theory and Practice* 4.

———. 1980. *Capitalism or Worker Control?* New York: Praeger Publishers.

Scriven, Michael. 1966. *Primary Philosophy.* New York: McGraw-Hill.

Sher, George. 1979. "Effort, Ability, and Personal Desert." *Philosophy and Public Affairs* 8.

Shue, Henry. 1980. *Basic Rights.* Princeton: Princeton University Press.

Singer, Marcus G. 1961. *Generalization in Ethics.* New York: Athenenum.

———. 1976. "The Methods of Justice: Reflections on Rawls." *Journal of Value Inquiry* 10.

———. 1977. "Justice, Theory, and a Theory of Justice." *Philosophy of Science* 44.

Singer, Peter. 1979. *Practical Ethics.* New York: Oxford University Press.

Smart, J. C. 1978. "Utilitarianism and Justice." *Journal of Chinese Philosophy* 5.

Smart, J. C., and Bernard Williams. 1973. *Utilitarianism: For and Against.* Cambridge: Cambridge University Press.

Smith, Holly. 1983. "Culpable Ignorance." *Philosophical Review* 64.

Steinem, Gloria. 1970. "What It Would Be Like if Women Win." *Time:* August 31.

Steiner, Hillel. 1974–75. "Individual Liberty." *Proceedings of the Aristotelian Society* 75.

———. 1977a. "The Structure of a Set of Compossible Rights." *Journal of Philosophy* 74.

———. 1977b. "The Natural Right to the Means of Production." *Philosophical Quarterly.*

———. 1980. "Slavery, Socialism and Private Property." *Nomos XXII: Property.* J. Roland Pennock and John W. Chapman, eds. New York: New York University Press.

Sterba, James P. 1974. "Justice as Desert." *Social Theory and Practice* 1.

———. 1976. "Prescriptivism and Fairness." *Philosophical Studies* 29.

———. 1978a. 'Neo-Libertarianism." *American Philosophical Quarterly* 15.

———. 1978b. "In Defense of Rawls Against Arrow and Nozick." *Philosophia* 7.

———. 1979. "Ethical Egoism and Beyond." *Canadian Journal of Philosophy* 9.

———. 1980. "Neo-Libertarianism" (rev. version). In *Justice: Alternative Political Perspectives,* James P. Sterba, ed. Belmont, Calif.: Wadsworth Publishing Co.

———. 1980a. "Abortion, Distant Peoples, and Future Generations." *The Journal of Philosophy* 57.

———. 1980b. *The Demands of Justice.* Notre Dame: University of Notre Dame Press.

———. 1981a. "A Rawlsian Solution to Arrow's Paradox." *Pacific Philosophical Quarterly* 62.

———. 1981b. "The Welfare Rights of Distant Peoples and Future Generations: Moral Side-Constraints on Social Policy." *Social Theory and Practice* 7.

———. 1982a. "A Marxist Dilemma for Social Contract Theory." *American Philosophical Quarterly* 19.

———. 1982b. "How Best to Critique Utilitarianism." In *Praxis and Reason: Studies in the Philosophy of Nicholas Rescher,* Robert Almerder, ed. Washington, D.C.: University Press of America.

196 / *Bibliography*

———. 1985. "National Defense vs. Social Welfare." In *Social Conflict,* R. G. Frey, ed. Bowling Green: Bowling Green University Press.

———. 1986. "Recent Work on Alternative Conceptions of Justice." *American Philosophical Quarterly* 23.

———. 1987. "Justifying Morality: The Right and the Wrong Ways." *Synthese (Kurt Baier festschrift),* Vol. 72.

Sterba, James P., and Douglas Rasmussen. 1987. *The Catholic Bishops and the Economy: A Debate.* London: Transaction Books.

Stretton, Hugh. 1976. *Capitalism, Socialism, and the Environment.* Cambridge: Cambridge University Press.

Thomas, D. A. Lloyd. 1970. "Why Should I Be Moral?" *Philosophy:* 128–39.

Trebilcot, Joyce. 1977. "Two Forms of Androgynism." Repr. in *Feminism and Philosophy,* Mary Vetterling-Braggin, Frederick Elliston, and Jane English, eds. Totowa, N.J.: Rowman & Allanheld.

———. ed. 1984. *Mothering: Essays in Feminist Theory.* Totowa, N.J.: Rowman & Allanheld.

U.S. Commission on Civil Rights. 1978. *Statement on the Equal Rights Amendment.* Washington, D.C.: Government Printing Office.

Von Magnus, Eric. 1982. "Risk, State, and Nozick." In *Midwest Studies in Philosophy.* Peter French et al., eds. Minneapolis: University of Minnesota Press.

Wachbroit, Robert. 1983. "A Genelogy of Virtues." *Yale Law Journal* 92.

Wallace, James. 1978. *Virtues and Vices.* Ithaca: Cornell University Press.

Walzer, Michael. 1983. *Spheres of Justice.* New York: Basic Books.

Warren, Mary Anne. 1982. "Is Androgyny the Answer to Sexual Stereotyping?" In *"Femininity," "Masculinity" and "Androgyny,"* Mary Vetterling-Braggin, ed. Totowa, N.J.: Littlefield, Adams.

Williams, Bernard. 1973. "A Critique of Utilitarianism." In *Utilitarianism: For and Against,* Bernard Williams and J. J. G. Smart, eds. Cambridge: Cambridge University Press.

———. 1973. *Problem of the Self.* Cambridge: Cambridge University Press.

———. 1981. *Moral Luck.* Cambridge: Cambridge University Press.

Wolfe, Alan. 1977. *The Limits of Legitimacy.* New York: Free Press.

Wolgast, Elizabeth. 1980. *Equality and the Rights of Women.* Ithaca: Cornell University Press.

Women's Economic Agenda Working Group. 1985. *Toward Economic Justice for Women.* Washington, D.C.: Institute for Policy Studies.

Wong, David. 1984. *Moral Relativity.* Berkeley: University of California Press.

Yanal, Robert J. 1979. "Notes on the Foundations of Nozick's Theory of Rights." *The Personalist* 60.

Young, Iris. 1985. "Humanism, Gynocentrism, and Feminist Politics." *Women's Studies International Forum* 8, no. 3.

Index